Strategy

Also by Terry Hill

Small Business: Production/Operations Management
Production/Operations Management: Text and Cases

MANUFACTURING STRATEGY

The Strategic Management of the Manufacturing Function

Second Edition

Terry Hill
London Business School

First edition 1985
Reprinted 1987 (twice), 1989, 1990, 1991, 1992
Second edition 1993

Published by
THE MACMILLAN PRESS LTD
Houndmills, Basingstoke, Hampshire RG21 2XS
and London
Companies and representatives
throughout the world

ISBN 0–333–57647–0 hardcover
ISBN 0–333–57648–9 paperback

A catalogue record for this book is available
from the British Library

Printed in Hong Kong

To PM, AJ and JB

Contents

List of Figures

List of Tables

List of Abbreviations

ABC   activity-based costing
AMT   advanced manufacturing technology
CAD   computer-aided design
CECIMO   Comité Européen de Coopération des Industries de la
           Machine-outil
CNC   computer numerical control
FG   finished goods
FMS(s)   flexible manufacturing system(s)
GDP   gross domestic product
JIT   just-in-time
LEV(s)   low-emission vehicles
MPC   manufacturing, planning and control
MPS   master production schedule
MRP   material requirements planning
NC   numerical control
OE   original equipment
OECD   Organisation for Economic Cooperation and
           Development
OEM   Original equipment manufacturer
OPT   optimised production technology
PIMS   profit impact of market strategies

PWP	plant-within-a-plant
RAM	random access memory
R&D	Research and Development
ROI	return on investment
TI	Texas Instruments
UK	United Kingdom
ULEV(s)	ultra-low-emission vehicle(s)
US	United States (adjective)
USA	United States of America (noun)
WIP	work-in-progress

Preface

Currently in many industrial companies, strategic developments are predominantly based on corporate marketing decisions. Since, typically, manufacturing managers come late into these discussions, it proves difficult for them successfully to influence the outcomes. All too often it results in the formulation of strategies which manufacturing is unable to successfully support.

This is not to say that this happens because of intent or through lack of trying. The problem is that if the basic link between manufacturing process/infrastructure investments and developments (i.e. manufacturing strategy) and the market is not made, then, by definition, the overall business will suffer.

The main reasons why this happens are addressed in the book. Significant among them is that the attention of manufacturing managers focuses primarily upon the day-to-day part of their task. It concerns operational details and is output-orientated, while in strategic terms their role is seen as being reactive.

The purpose of this book is to attempt to raise manufacturing managers' sights. It is intended to help them analyse and discuss strategic issues and think in a strategic way. Currently, the area of manufacturing strategy is short of concepts, ideas and language. The book's prime aim is to address this deficit. It helps provide insights and evaluates manufacturing's corporate contribution through strategic perspectives rather than just through operational performance. It not only helps manufacturing managers to provide appropriate corporate-level inputs, but also enables other executives to recognise and appreciate the strategic perspectives which eminate from manufacturing and which need to be given due consideration within the corporate debate.

The manufacturing perspective forms the basis on which the book is written, but the approach places these issues within the rightful context of corporate strategy. The book therefore emphasises the essential requirement to link marketing and manufacturing perspectives in order to determine the best strategies for the business as a whole.

Thus the book is written as an attempt to:

1. Close the gap between manufacturing and marketing in terms of corporate strategy formulation.
2. Offer an analytical approach to the development of manufacturing strategy rather than advocate a set of prescriptive solutions. As each business and each part of each business is different, strategy resolution through prescription does not work. The book argues strongly against such approaches. Instead it offers a methodology for developing a manufacturing strategy based on and linked to a firm's markets.
3. Provide a set of principles and concepts which are pragmatic in nature and designed to be applied to relevant facets within a business.

Outlined in the book is a basic approach to developing a manufacturing strategy which has been used successfully in many companies. It provides a logical, practical and effective way for manufacturing to interface with marketing in formulating corporate strategy. And the link is the market.

The book comprises eight chapters. The first sets the scene by drawing important international comparisons at national, corporate and plant level. The figures embody a growing awareness of the fact that those countries which clearly emphasise the importance of manufacturing's contribution to business success have constantly outperformed others, some of which have a sound industrial tradition.

The core of the book is in the centre six chapters. The headings highlight some key developments within manufacturing strategy. Together they form the substance of the developments in language and concepts as well as the framework to be used in its formulation.

Chapter 2 explains the approach to be adopted and details what needs to be completed at each step with illustrations to help with the explanations. Chapter 3 highlights the idea of order-winners and qualifiers and provides examples to illustrate the key dimensions on which companies compete.

Chapter 4 deals exclusively with the choice of manufacturing process, the basis for that choice and the business trade-offs which follow. Chapter 5 deals with the concept of focus as a practical and successful approach to handling difference. Many companies are finding that in markets which are increasingly different, supporting these differences with a single set of manufacturing processes and working to one set of rules, procedures and performance measures is no longer serving them well. Chapter 6 is concerned with examining make or buy decisions and the process positioning implications which follow. Chapter 7 addresses the key aspects of infrastructure, thus recognising the critical nature of these facets of a business and the need for them to have strategic alignment.

The final chapter concerns the area of accounting and finance. The key link between the time dimensions of manufacturing and its translation into money which is the corporate base on which corporate decisions are made is duly recognised. It is not intended to be a comprehensive statement of the art but represents some key management views of serious shortcomings and essential developments which need to be made within the function. The professional accountant may find the approach provocative; it is intended, however, to be more constructive than that. The issues raised aim to challenge current practice and ideas as a way of structured improvement.

Finally, I trust you will find the book helpful. Manufacturing is a complex area but its essential business orientation makes it a key function in a firm's overall success and a key dimension which needs to be understood by all executives within a firm. It is vital that manufacturing takes its full part in strategic formulation if industrial companies are to prosper in the face of world competition. The aim of this book is to contribute to this essential task.

TERRY HILL

International Comparisons

1

The 1980s symbolised a new stark reality – the impact of industrial competition. In most industrial nations, the cut and thrust and the struggle for giant companies to survive had become, by then, an integral part of each industry's way of life. To close down a plant, once an anathema to business, had now become an acceptable course of action to follow based upon necessity or as an integral part of some comprehensive corporate strategic decision. The economic world of the 1980s was very different to that of the 1960s and 1970s. The 1990s are continuing the trend but increasing the pace.

For the most part, however, production decision-making in manufacturing industry has not changed to meet these new challenges. In most Western companies, manufacturing management still takes a subordinate role in strategic terms to the marketing and finance functions. It continues to concern itself primarily with short-term issues. The argument of this book is that a strategic approach to manufacturing management is essential if companies are going to be able to survive, let alone hold their own or grow by competing effectively in domestic and world markets.

This chapter provides some national and corporate comparisons. It shows how some nations with strong industrial traditions have come to be outperformed, and attempts to set the scene by illustrating the extent of the changes which have taken place and comparing different approaches to the management of manufacturing. The final section turns its attention to the area of manufacturing strategy, not only to link this chapter to the remainder of the book but also to start to highlight the increasing awareness of manufacturing as a strategic force at both national and corporate level.

1.1   Manufacturing Output

Trends in a nation's performance within its wealth-creating sectors reflect on its overall prosperity. As manufacturing is for most countries the most significant activity in this regard, then reviewing this sector provides an insight into a country's general well-being.

Comparative figures on manufacturing output in the 1970s and 1980s reveal the mixed fortunes of major industrial nations. Some countries of manufacturing repute have lost ground particularly in the 1970s, whilst others (for example, Japan, the USA and Germany) have maintained sound growth throughout – see Table 1.1.

TABLE 1.1
Comparative manufacturing output, 1978–90 (1975 = 100)

Country	1978	1981	1984	1987	1989	1990
Australia	104	114	107	113	116	113
Belgium	112	113	117	123	119	127
Denmark	116	120	137	145	129	130
France	114	109	107	112	108	109
Germany	113	116	117	125	118	124
Italy	116	127	124	132	115	114
Japan	123	142	160	169	142	148
Netherlands	108	116	120	128	120	125
Spain	120[1]	111	113	124	119	119
UK	103	90	94	103	123	122
USA	126	129	141	150	136	137

Note: [1] Figures for 1977

Source: OECD, *Indicators of Industrial Activity*, 1979 and 1991

However, of equal concern to these nations is how well they fared within the increasingly competitive markets they serve. Table 1.2 looks at the trends in percentage share gained by selected countries of the export sales of manufactured goods from main manufacturing countries. It shows the changes in share from 1969 to 1981 and from 1981 to 1991, as well as over the whole period. The performances within the different countries are noticeably different, particularly at the extremes. On the whole, though, it reinforces the main message in Table 1.1. Japan again demonstrated its improvement in the manufacturing sector showing by far the largest improvement in the period reviewed. It also illustrates Germany's strong export position which has remained fairly constant throughout. Whereas the decline in the UK and USA (the countries which preceded Japan as the world's number one manufacturing nation) are very marked. And, in between, the steady improvement by a number of West European countries sets an important benchmark.

To complete this initial review, the export–import trade ratios of manufacturing countries are given in Table 1.3 to provide an insight into relative trading performances of main manufacturing nations.

For the UK and particularly the USA the overall manufacturing position is worrying. The UK has been a net importer of manufactured goods since the early 1980s and this adverse trend continues; whereas for the USA, this negative position happened in the late 1960s and by 1987 the export–import ratio had fallen dramatically to 0.55, a figure reflected in the overall North American picture.* Most West European countries, however, secured a positive ratio, but some, like France and Denmark are just in the red. Again, over the twenty-five-year period reviewed, Japan has achieved a significantly favourable ratio with exports close on three times its imports of manufactured goods.

The decline in the UK's competitive position in the world industrial markets is there for all to see – loss of market-share abroad, increased imports at home. UK industry has performed badly for a long time, whatever measure is used. A more in-depth review of her trading performance shows that from 1973, imports

---

* In 1987 Canada's export-import ratio stood at 0.95.

TABLE 1.2
Main manufacturing countries' exports of manufactured goods – selected countries only

Year	Belgium/Luxembourg	France	Germany	Italy	Japan	Netherlands	UK	USA
				Percentage share				
1969	6.2	8.2	19.1	7.3	11.2	4.4	11.2	19.2
1975	5.8	10.2	20.3	7.4	13.6	4.9	9.1	17.7
1981	4.9	9.2	18.4	7.7	17.9	4.1	8.5	18.6
1985	4.6	8.5	18.6	7.8	19.7	4.1	7.8	16.8
1986	5.0	8.8	20.7	8.2	19.4	4.5	7.6	14.2
1987	5.2	9.0	21.4	8.4	18.0	4.6	8.1	14.0
1988	5.2	9.0	19.5	8.2	18.3	4.5	8.4	15.3
1989	5.3	8.8	20.4	8.4	17.5	4.3	8.2	16.1
1990	5.4	9.7	20.5	8.6	15.8	4.8	8.6	15.8
1991[1]	5.0	9.5	19.9	8.4	16.8	4.7	8.6	16.9
+ (−) % change								
1969–1981	(21)	12	(4)	5	60	(7)	(24)	(3)
1981–1991	2	3	8	9	(6)	15	1	(9)
1969–1991[2]	(19)	16	4	15	54	7	(23)	(12)

Note: [1] 1991 figures are based on the first three quarters of the year
[2] Discrepancies are due to rounding

Source: Central Statistical Office, *Monthly Review of External Trade Statistics*, no 14 (Nov. 1976); no 96 (Dec. 1983); and no 193 (Feb. 1992)

TABLE 1.3

Export–import ratio – selected sectors (1982–7) and total manufacturing (1972, 1982 and 1987)

Country	Aerospace		Electrical/ electronic		Office machinery and computers		Drugs		Total manufacturing		
	1982	1987	1982	1987	1982	1987	1982	1987	1972	1982	1987
Belgium	0.78	0.58	0.95	0.97	0.57	0.63	1.21	1.23	–	1.08	1.07
Denmark	0.32	0.30	0.87	0.86	0.29	0.32	1.92	2.14	–	0.97	0.96
France	1.72	1.62	0.99	0.93	0.58	0.71	3.76	1.80	1.10	1.02	0.95
Germany	0.95	0.86	1.54	1.37	1.00	0.87	1.78	1.73	1.53	1.48	1.48
Italy	1.28	1.19	1.11	0.82	0.90	0.70	1.11	0.78	1.31	1.33	1.15
Japan	0.16	0.11	9.34	8.96	3.18	6.53	0.24	0.29	2.82	2.99	2.73
Netherlands	0.78	0.82	1.00	0.81	0.71	0.67	1.25	1.07	–	1.21	1.06
Spain	0.53	0.70	0.44	0.35	0.42	0.38	0.68	0.90	–	1.14	0.81
UK	1.69	1.73	0.86	0.71	0.69	0.83	2.51	2.01	1.09	0.94	0.83
USA	3.20	2.89	0.82	0.45	2.63	1.04	2.40	1.23	0.84	0.91	0.55
North America	4.15	3.44	0.75	0.41	2.58	0.93	2.07	1.09	–	0.95	0.52
EC	1.37	1.20	1.18	0.92	0.50	0.47	2.61	2.13	–	1.41	1.24

– = not available

Source: OECD Main Science and Technology Indicators 1974, 1984 and 1991(2)

took an increasing market share for manufacturing goods overall whilst making significant and very worrying inroads into certain sectors as shown in Table 1.4

Against this background of decline it is interesting to note that successive UK Governments have tended to act on the some-times painful premise that exposure to overseas competition is a necessary ingredient for the development of a strong, domestic manufacturing base. What is, however, of deep concern is that

TABLE 1.4
Ratio of UK imports to home demand for all manufacturing and selected sectors

Manufacturing sector	Imports–home-demand ratio							1989 (1973 = 100)
	1973	1980	1985	1986	1987	1988	1989[1]	
Motor vehicles and their parts	23	39	50	51	48	50	51	222
Paper, printing and publishing	19	19	21	21	22	21	22	116
Engineering mechanical	26	29	36	37	38	39	40	154
electrical and electronic	27	31	47	47	49	50	52	193
instruments	46	52	57	56	58	58	60	130
Chemicals and man-made fibres	22	29	41	41	43	42	42	191
Food, drink and tobacco	19	16	18	18	18	18	18	93
Textile industry	21	34	44	45	47	48	48	229
Clothing and footwear	18	29	35	36	39	39	40	222
Total manufacturing industry	21	26	34	34	35	36	37	176

Note: [1] Six months ended June 1989

Source: Central Statistical Office, *Annual Abstract of Statistics, Import Penetration Ratio for Products of Manufacturing Industry*, no 121 (1985) Table 12.1, and no 127 (1991) Table 12.2

manufacturing industry's response to that exposure has been woefully slow. Many firms have tended to complain about 'unfair' external competition and have kept their corporate eyes on domestic rather than overseas competitors. The result is that they have adopted inadequate, reactive strategies because the consequences for manufacturing have not been appreciated. Typically, they have filled capacity by chasing orders, increasing variety and reducing batch sizes, leaving overseas competitors with substantial advantages in the higher-volume segments of their markets. One outcome has been the loss of high-volume markets such as motorcycles, automobiles, trucks and shipbuilding, whereas, for the nations which are prospering, these same sectors have often formed the bedrock on which their wealth base has been built.

Many business have failed to recognise, until too late in the day, that the sellers' markets of the 1950s and 1960s have long since passed. They typically became entangled in the period of transition during the 1970s and in the decade which followed. Current responses require new strategies which must aim to gain and maintain some specific and significant advantages against the most, not least powerful of competitors.

Whereas the UK and USA in particular were being buffeted by this new competitive surge, that was not so for some countries which seemed to have moved from strength to strength. Of deeper concern still for the UK and some other nations with long manufacturing traditions, however, are the facts underlying these trends, especially that of comparative productivity.

1.2 Productivity: National Comparisons

The prosperity of nations is recognised as being dependent on their comparative productivity. In the past two decades of increasing competition, this has been brought sharply into focus. Although not a precise measure in the definitive sense of the word, it affords a way of assessing trends both for the performance of individual countries and their relative positions in appropriate world rankings.

Thus, there are two important dimensions of a productivity slowdown for any nation. The first is the rate of the slowdown itself, whilst the second is the cumulative effect of the slowdown on the comparative level of productivity between a country and its competitors.

Where the growth rate lags substantially behind that of other industrialised countries and does so for a protracted period, then a decline in living standards will follow and companies will find themselves at a serious competitive disadvantage. If it goes un-checked, this in turn will lead to a position where recovery is more difficult to achieve, and breaking free from the downward spiral, a major task.

Productivity measures the relationship between outputs (in the form of goods and services produced) and inputs (in the form of labour, capital, material and other resources). Although in prac-tice productivity is not so simple to measure because of the global nature of the figures involved, it does provide an overall review of improvement and one which lends itself to trend analysis. Two types of productivity measurement are commonly used: labour productivity and total-factor or multi-factor productivity. Labour productivity measures output in terms of hours worked or paid for. Total-factor or multi-factor productivity not only includes the labour input but also all or some of the plant, equipment, energy and materials. However, when there is a change in a single-factor productivity ratio, it is important not to attribute the change solely to that one input. Owing to the interrelated nature of the total inputs involved, the change may well be influenced by any or all of the many variables which could contribute to the change. For example, production methods, capital investment, process tech-nology, labour force, managerial performance, capacity utilisa-tion, material input/usage rates, capacity scale and product mix are all potential contributors to productivity improvements. Further-more, the relative importance of these will vary from nation to nation, industrial sector to industrial sector, company to company, plant to plant and one time period to the next.

Although it may be difficult to get a consensus on the quanti-tative dimensions of productivity measurement, the qualitative conclusions on the differing levels and trends within nations are clearly shown in Table 1.5. It signals the steady, often significant, growth of some nations throughout the period, a fact reflected in the earlier data on performance.

TABLE 1.5
Trends in output per hour in manufacturing – selected countries (1950–90)

Country	1950	1960	1970	1980	1985	1986	1987	1988	1989	1990
				Year (1977 = 100)						
Belgium	N/A	33	60	119	159	165	159	166	167	N/A
Denmark	28	37	66	119	118	119	121	115	117	119
France	23	37	70	111	133	136	141	143	148	150
Germany	19	40	71	109	129	131	132	128	133	137
Italy	20	35	73	117	152	153	159	161	164	168
Japan	9	23	65	123	161	164	171	164	168	173
Netherlands	20	32	64	114	145	145	142	147	150	153
UK	46	56	80	102	135	139	148	151	157	158
USA	51	62	81	101	124	129	132	137	138	141

Notes: N/A = not available

Source: US Department of Labor, Bureau of Labor Statistics, June 1988, and
   Monthly Labour Review, December 1991

1.3   Productivity: Plant-Level Comparison

In the 1990s, Europe is set to be the region in which competition will heighten in many key markets. The strong 'domestic' companies will be joined by the big battalions from Japan, the USA and the Far East. Setting aside the arguments concerning trade practices, a key factor in who will gain ground and market share is comparative productivity.

The car industry, a core-sector in many European countries given the combined size of its assembly-activity and supply-chain requirements, is one example of the fierce fighting which will take place. European car-makers such as Fiat, General Motors, Peugeot-Citroen and Volkswagen are hard-pressed to maintain sales levels even though European car registration rose by 0.4 per cent in 1991 to a record 13.5 million. However, with the production capacity available to the top ten car-makers exceeding market forecast, companies used to dominating the home European market, will be forced to slim down in search of higher efficiency to

TABLE 1.6
Estimates of Car Productivity (1991)

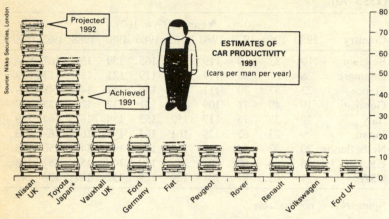

Source: K. Eason, 'Japan makes inroads', *The Times*, 12 February 1992, p. 24 (with permission – © Times Newspapers Ltd 1992)

compete against new rivals and fresh benchmarks. Table 1.6 illustrates the marked difference and the task which lies ahead. The gap for some is enormous. Others such as Vauxhall (UK) have made up significant ground since the mid-1980s. But with the more open markets of the European Community in place, productivity will be one key factor in the comparative success of companies and hence nations.

1.4   Why Has This Happened?

The reasons why this has happened are many and varied. Some are unsubstantiated opinions, others are supported by fact. Some will be more relevant to some nations, sectors and companies, and others, less. However, learning from past failures is a step towards determining how to build a more successful competitive future.

1.4.1   *Failure to recognise the size of the competitive challenge*

There has been a failure, conscious or otherwise, of industry and society at large to recognise the size of the competitive challenge, the impact it was having and would have on our very way of life, and to recognise the need to change.

One illustration of UK industry's lack of awareness is provided in a selection from the corporate responses to the 1976 Select Committee of Science and Technology (Japan Subcommittee) seeking evidence on several aspects of Japanese industry.[1] The Subcommittee wrote in September 1977 to many leading British manufacturing companies and related associations seeking their views on a number of perspectives within Japanese industry. There follows a précis of some of the points raised in the replies received, with the name of the organisation, and particular aspect(s) to be addressed.

Ford Motor Company's comments on the success with which Japanese industry has handled its process and product development:

> **I am not sure that we have anything useful to contribute on this issue so far as the motor industry is concerned because all the processes and products used by the Japanese motor industry are known to us and their success depends on achieving economies of scale based on a large home market, on a different attitude adopted by labour in their industry and also on their apparent success in containing inflation more effectively than we have been able to do in this country.**
>
> **In short, as far as the motor industry is concerned the general superiority of the Japanese seems to me to be in the area of attitudes and economies rather than technology.[2]**

The reply also mentions that the Japanese 'are very competitive in their strategic thinking and their marketing plans, but . . . there is nothing they do in these areas either that is not known and practised by some of us at least in the motor industry in the West'.

Yet, less than three years later, the Ford Motor Company was holding seminars within all its major suppliers to detail the critical nature of the Japanese challenge and examining the stark comparisons of performance, amongst others, which were provided earlier in the chapter. Based on the improving percentage of the Japanese free-world vehicle-production (10 to 26 per cent from 1966 to 1979) and the decline in the European percentage (38 to 34 per cent) in the same period, Ford concentrated much of its discussion on the manufacturing perspective as the foundation for this challenge. As the Ford Report admitted, the extent and nature of the superiority was not appreciated until Ford went to see for themselves.

However, Ford was not the only company which failed to appreciate the extent of the challenge as the Report shows. Rank Organisation and the Motor Industry Research Association are further examples of organisations misunderstanding the nature of the competitive trends in the manufacturing sector. (see note 2). Others, however, had a clear view of what lay ahead. The Electrical Research Association recognised that Japanese industry's success was due to its 'total commitment to manufacturing high quality, reliable goods on a very large scale, [with] as much effort being committed to the production process and technology as the products themselves'. Similarly, EMI recognised that

- Japanese manufacturers study competitors' products, technologies and market needs in much greater depth than their European counterparts.
- Advanced developments are embodied in the products and in the manufacturing processes. This gives the commercial products a technological lead and a cost advantage – two significant factors in establishing a significant market position.

Some companies even recognised the gravity of the problem and the speed of response which must be made. For instance, BOC Ltd identified 'certain technical aspects of small-batch manufacturing in which considerable practical experience has been obtained in Japan and for which no equivalent knowledge exists in the UK'. Linked machining centres which had been in operation for five years in Japan were not known to exist in the UK or even being contemplated by any British machine-tool manufacturer. In summary, BOC's reply concludes that 'the action we in Britain take in the next two years can be critical in ensuring a continuing viable manufacturing industry in this field, and especially the machine tool aspect'. As Table 1.7 shows, BOC's predictions were fulfilled with the emerging nations representing a new, competitive threat.

TABLE 1.7
**Production of machine tools without parts and accessories –
selected countries**

Country	Machine tool production Swiss frs (millions)			1990 (1985 = 100)
	1985	1988	1990	
Belgium	229	303	395	172
Denmark	102	92	118	116
France	1225	1157	1621	132
Germany	7755	9614	12110	156
Italy	2729	4086	5137	188
Japan	13038	12706	15206	117
Korea	439	924	1186	270
Netherlands	92	97	194	211
Spain	617	1027	1410	229
Taiwan	676	1125	1307	193
US	6465	3861	4688	73
UK	1780	2035	2077	117

Source: CECIMO, *Statistical Overview of the Machine Tool Industry within CECIMO's Countries, 1985–1990* (1991)

1.4.2 *Failure to appreciate the impact of increasing manufacturing capacity*

World manufacturing capacity up to the mid-1960s was, by and large, less than demand and in this period companies could sell all they could make. With the rebuilding of some industrial nations and the emergence of others, output in both traditional and new industrial nations began to outstrip total demand. The most significant and consistent outcome has been the impact on competition. A scenario of over-capacity has contributed to the competitive nature of markets. The results have added to the dynamic nature of current markets both in terms of the form that competition takes and the timescales of change experienced.

TABLE 1.8
Gross domestic expenditure on R&D as a percentage of gross domestc product (GDP)

Country	1981	1985	1989	1990	1991
Belgium	1.53[a]	1.68	1.64[b]	N/A	N/A
Canada	1.23	1.44	1.35	1.37	1.40
Denmark	1.10	1.25	1.53	N/A	N/A
France	2.01	2.25	2.34	2.42	N/A
Germany	2.45	2.71	2.88	2.81	N/A
Italy	1.01	1.12	1.25	1.36	1.35
Japan	2.32	2.77	2.98	N/A	N/A
Netherlands	1.99	2.09	2.17	N/A	N/A
Spain	0.40	0.55	0.75	0.86	N/A
UK	2.42	2.31	2.25	N/A	N/A
USA	2.45	2.93	2.82	2.79	2.75

Notes: [a] Figure is for 1983
       [b] Figure is for 1988
       N/A = Not available

Source: OECD, *Management Science and Technology Indicators*, 1981–89 and 1991(2)

1.4.3 *Willingness to invest in research and development* (R&D)

The pressure to market more and better products has heightened in recent years because of increasing competition and shorter product life-cycles. One significant factor to help achieve that is the relative size and trend in research and development investments. Table 1.8 reflects the clear commitment of major manufacturing nations to continue to increase the size of their national spend. The USA and UK, although investing at a level higher than most of the major industrial countries, were the only countries to reduce the percentage of gross domestic product spent on R&D. By 1989, Japan headed the list for the first time.

Furthermore, government R&D expenditure on industrial productivity and technology reflects another set of priorities within the overall trend. Table 1.9 shows the upward trends in some West

TABLE 1.9
Technology balance of payments – coverage ratio

Country	1984	1985	1986	1987	1988	1989	1990
Belgium	0.83	0.87	0.86	0.71	0.70	0.77	0.75
Denmark	0.90	1.14	–	–	–	–	–
France	0.90	0.84	0.83	0.78	0.80	–	–
Germany	0.52	0.51	0.83	0.82	0.84	0.84	–
Italy	0.29	0.26	0.31	0.38	0.54	0.50	0.58
Japan	0.99	0.80	0.86	0.76	0.79	1.00	–
Netherlands	0.51	0.36	0.60	0.55	0.54	0.44	–
Spain	0.25	0.25	0.24	0.18	0.13	0.18	0.18
UK	1.05	1.13	0.95	0.92	0.92	–	–
USA	5.52	6.73	6.83	6.65	5.29	5.26	5.78

Note: Figure > 1 show receipts greater than payments

Source: OECD, *Management Science and Technology Indicators*, 1991(2)

European countries with the exception of the UK. Besides the marked difference in resource allocation, these figures also provide a clear signal of the perceived importance of this research and development support for the industrial sector as recognised by the governments of different nations.

The final perspective on issues of R&D expenditure is provided by Table 1.9. Many countries with the committed R&D levels of spending shown in Table 1.8 top this up by importing technology at a rate higher than that at which they sell.

1.4.4 *Top management's lack of manufacturing experience*

Top management's lack of experience in manufacturing has further ramifications for a business. Considering the fact that manufacturing accounts for some 70–80 per cent of assets, expenditure and people, then it is imperative that senior executives fully appreciate the arguments and counter-arguments in manufacturing so as to ensure that the accompanying wide range of perspectives is taken into account when making important manufacturing decisions. Once large investments have been made then rarely does a company invest a second time to correct the mistake. This lack of experience is certainly not so in Japan and West Germany where a full and perceptive insight into manufacturing is seen as a prerequisite for top management.

However, the consequences of this knowledge gap do not stop here. As Wickham Skinner observes:

> **to many executives, manufacturing and the production function is a necessary nuisance – it soaks up capital in facilities and inventories, it resists changes in products and schedules, its quality is never as good as it should be and its people are unsophisticated, tedious, detail-orientated and unexciting. This makes for an unreceptive climate for major innovations in factory technology and contributes to the blind spot syndrome.[3]**

And this brings with it many important consequences. One is that senior executives do not perceive the strategic potential of manufacturing. Typically it is seen in its traditional productivity-efficiency mode with the added need to respond to the strategic overtures of marketing and finance. The result is that manufacturing concentrates its effort and attention on the short-term whilst adopting its classic, reactive posture towards the long-term strategic issues of the business.

1.4.5   *The production manager's obsession with short-term performance issues*

The emphasis within the production manager's role has, in turn, been directed towards short-term issues and tasks. The overriding pressures to meet day-to-day targets and the highly quantifiable nature of the role have reinforced the tendency of manufacturing executives to concern themselves with this feature to the exclusion of the important long-term. The skills of production managers are high on short-term tasks such as scheduling, maintaining efficiency levels, controls, delivery, quality and resolving labour problems. Skinner rightly believes that:

> **most factories were not managed very differently in the 1970s than in the 1940s and 1950s. Manufacturing management was**

dominated by engineering and a technical point of view. This may have been adequate when *production* management issues centred largely on efficiency and productivity and the answers came from industrial engineering and process engineering. But the problems of operations managers in the 1970s had moved far beyond mere physical efficiency.[4]

This trend has continued in line with the fast changing nature of markets. By the 1990s the production job has changed from one which concerns maintaining steady-state manufacturing by sound day-to-day husbandry to one which is multidimensional. It is now increasingly concerned with managing greater complexity in product range, product mix, volume changes, process flexibility, inventory, cost and financial controls and employee awareness because of the more intensive level of domestic and international competition.

This is the nature of the new task. No longer are the key issues solely confined to operational control and fine-tuning the system. The need is for broad, business-orientated manufacturing managers but companies have produced too few of them. The use of specialists as the way to control our businesses has increasingly led to a reduction in the breadth of a line manager's responsibilities which has narrowed the experience base. Furthermore, many manufacturing managers have been outgunned by specialist argument and found themselves unable to cope with the variety of demands placed upon them. The response by many has been to revert increasingly to their strengths. This has, therefore, reinforced their short-term role and their inherently reactive stance to corporate strategic resolution.

Manufacturing executives do not, on the whole, explain the important, conceptual aspects of manufacturing to others in the organisation. Seldom do they evaluate and expose the implications for manufacturing of corporate decisions, so that alternatives can be considered and more soundly based, corporate decisions agreed. Part of the reason for this is that there is a lack of developed language to help to provide a way of explaining the corporate production issues involved. Lacking, therefore, in strategic dimension, manufacturing has often been forced into piecemeal change achieving what it can as and when it has been able. The result has been a series of intermittent responses lacking corporate coordination.

1.5   Manufacturing Strategy

What has happened in the past decade and a half is that countries such as Japan, Germany and Italy, as well as emerging industrial nations such as Korea and Taiwan have gained the competitive upper hand, and this advantage has been achieved through manufacturing. The Japanese, in particular, have gone for existing markets and provided better goods with few, if any, inherent benefits derived from material and energy resources. The early examples serve to illustrate this.

One of the keys to this achievement through manufacturing has been the integration of these functional perspectives at the level of corporate strategy debate, and it is appropriate now to explain what this embodies and how it differs from the conventional approaches to the management of production. In broad terms, there are two important roles which manufacturing can offer as part of the strategic strengths of a company.

The first is to provide manufacturing processes which will give the business a distinct advantage in the market-place. In this way, manufacturing will offer to provide a marketing edge through distinct, unique technology developments in its process and manufacturing operations which competitors are unable to match. This role is quite rare, but examples include Pilkington's float glass process.

The second way is to provide coordinated manufacturing support for the essential ways in which products win orders in the market-place at a level which is better than its competitors are able to do. In this way, manufacturing develops a set of policies in both its process choice and infrastructure design (for example, controls, procedures, systems and structures) which are consistent with the existing way(s) that products win orders whilst being able to reflect future developments in line with changing business needs. Most companies share access to the same processes and thus technology is not inherently different. Similarly, the systems, structures and other elements of infrastructure are equally universal. What is different is the degree to which manufacturing matches process and infrastructure to those criteria which win orders. In this way, manufacturing constitutes a coordinated response consistent with the business needs and which will embrace all those aspects of a company for which manufacturing is responsible.

To do this effectively manufacturing needs to be involved

throughout the whole of the corporate strategy debate to explain, in business terms, the implications of corporate marketing proposals and, as a result, be able to influence strategy decisions for the good of the business as a whole. Too often in the past, manufacturing has been too late in this procedure. Corporate executives have tended to assume that competitive strategies are more to do with, and often in fact are one and the same as, marketing initiatives. Implicit, if not explicit, in this view are two important assumptions. The first is that manufacturing's role is to respond to these changes rather than to make inputs into them. The second is that manufacturing has the capability to respond flexibly and positively to these changing demands. The result has been an inability to influence decisions which has led to a posture which appears to be forever complaining about the unrealistic demands placed upon production.

The need for a manufacturing strategy to be developed and shared by the business is not only to do with the critical nature of manufacturing within corporate strategy but also a realisation that many of the decisions are structural in nature. This means that they are hard to change. Unless the issues and consequences are fully appreciated by the business, then it can be locked into a number of manufacturing decisions which will take years to change. These can range from process investments on the one hand, through to human-resource management practices and controls on the other. Decisions not in line with the needs of the business can contribute significantly to a lack of corporate success. To change them is costly and time-consuming. But even more significantly, they will come too late. The development of a corporate policy consisting of a coordinated set of main function inputs will mean that the business would be able to go in one consistent, coherent direction based on a well-argued, well-understood and well-formed strategy. This is achieved, in part, by moving away from argument, disagreement, misunderstanding and short-term, parochial moves based on interfunctional perspectives, to the resolution of these differences at the corporate level. Currently, marketing-led strategies leave the aftermath to be resolved by manufacturing, who without adequate appropriate guidance or discussion and agreement at the corporate level, resolve the issues as best they can largely from their unilateral view of what is best for the business as a whole.

In the majority of cases, manufacturing is simply not geared to the business's corporate objectives. The result is a manufacturing system, good in itself, but not designed to meet company needs. Manufacturing left in the wake of corporate decisions is often at best a neutral force, and even sometimes inadvertently pulls in the opposite direction. Seen as being concerned solely with efficiency, the question of production's strategic contribution is seldom part of the corporate consciousness.

What does all this mean for production managers? One clear consequence is the need to change from a reactive to a proactive stance. The long-term inflexible nature of manufacturing means that the key issues, and there are many of them, involved in process choice and infrastructure development need to be reflected in business decisions with the business being made aware of the implications for manufacturing of proposed corporate changes. When this is achieved, the strategy decisions which are then taken reflect what is best for the business as a whole. So manufacturing management's attention must increasingly be towards strategy. This does not mean that operations are unimportant. But the balance and direction of management activity needs to reflect the relative impact on business performance of strategy and operations whilst recognising that both need to be done well. Top management have, by and large, perceived corporate improvements as coming mainly through broad decisions concerning new markets, takeovers and the like. However, the building blocks of corporate success are to be found in creating effective, successful businesses where manufacturing supports the market requirement within a well-chosen, well-argued and well-understood corporate strategy.

1.6   Conclusion

The emphasis in successfully managed manufacturing functions is increasingly towards issues of strategy. And there is evidence of a growing and consistent awareness of this fact. For example, in the early 1980s the Advisory Council for Applied Research and Development's booklet, *New Opportunities in Manufacturing: the Management of Technology* specifically recommended for industry that 'companies in manufacturing should review the balance of

TABLE 1.10
Manufacturing Futures Survey, **1990: responses to the questions asking for 'the most important improvements in the next two years'**

Country/Region	Rating for the answer 'linking manufacturing strategy to business strategy'
Europe	1
Japan	5
USA	1

Note: A rating of 1 indicates the highest priority

their senior management and ensure that the role of a suitably qualified board member includes responsibility for manufacturing strategy'.[5] When surveys on manufacturing in Europe, Japan and North America posed questions under the heading on which were the 'most important improvement programmes in the next two years', the 1990 survey showed a high ratio across the board (see Table 1.10).[6]

It is important to stress that top management needs to pay a great deal more than lip-service to the task of ensuring that manufacturing's input into the strategic debate is comprehensive and that the agreed corporate decisions fully reflect the complex issues involved. Much determination will need to be exercised to ensure that the more superficial approaches to incorporating the wide-ranging aspects of manufacturing into corporate decisions are avoided. The rewards for this are substantial.

The implications for manufacturing executives are that they must begin to think and act in a more strategic manner. In an environment traditionally geared to meeting output targets, the pressure on manufacturing has been to manage reactively, and to be operationally efficient rather than strategically effective. It has been more concerned with doing things right (efficiency), than doing the right things (effectiveness). This has over the years created the view that this comprises the appropriate manufacturing task and contribution. Furthermore, it has given rise to the related assumption that any other posture would imply negative attitudes, with manufacturing appearing to be putting obstacles in the way of achieving key corporate objectives. At times this puts manufacturing in the vicious circle of corporate demands on manufacturing, manufacturing's best response, a recriminating corporate appraisal of that response, new corporate demands for improved manufacturing performance and so on. The purpose of this book is to help to avoid the all-too-common corporate approach to manufacturing by providing a set of concepts and approaches which together create a platform from which manufacturing can make a positive, strategic contribution to developing powerful competitive strategies. But, manufacturing executives must first accept that they need to manage their own activities strategically, and this is almost as much a change in management attitude as it is an analytical process.

The purpose of thinking and managing strategically is not just to improve operational performance or to defend market share. It is to gain competitive advantage and it implies an attempt to mobilise manufacturing capability to help to gain this competitive edge. Kenichi Ohmae, a leading Japanese consultant with McKinsey,[7] suggests that when managers are striving to achieve or maintain a position of relative superiority over competitors the management mind works very differently from the way it does when the objective is to make operational improvements against often arbitrarily set, internal objectives.

This chapter has highlighted the tendency for manufacturing to place more emphasis on operational efficiency than on competitive advantage. The danger for the business is that manufacturing gets so used to absorbing and responding to demands that reacting becomes the norm. Each crisis is viewed as a 'temporary situation' which often militates against recognising the need to fundamentally review strategies. By the time that this need becomes obvious the business is often at a serious competitive disadvantage.

The aims of this book are to reverse the reactive response and short-term perspectives held by manufacturing and to turn the role into one which seeks to manage manufacturing strategically by setting out the managerial and corporate issues which need to be addressed to establish competitive advantage.

There is much evidence that in many of the traditional manufacturing nations the capability exists to turn domestic manufacturing around and to challenge and beat overseas competition in both home and world markets. There are already examples of that turnaround in competitive performance, but the key ingredients include tough, professional management, combining strategic analysis of key issues with that intuitive, creative flair, for so long directed primarily towards solving operational problems.

It is imperative that manufacturing managers take the initiative. For some organisations or functions within a business, the *status quo* even suits them. In those same organisations, manufacturing is played off against a forever-changing set of objectives and targets, and it hurts. If manufacturing waits for other corporate initiatives they will not come soon enough. The lack of empathy and understanding by top management towards manufacturing often means that when difficulties arise, the preferred course of action is to get rid of the problem by selling-off the business or buying-in from outside. The causes of the problem are seldom addressed. Companies should realise that there are no long-term profits to be made in easy manufacturing tasks – anyone can provide these. It is in the difficult areas where profits are to be made. Furthermore, selling off inherent infrastructure can lead to an inability to compete effectively in future markets. The critical task facing manufacturing managers is to explain the essential nature of manufacturing in business terms and this must embrace both process technology and infrastructure development.

Notes and References

1. Reported in K. Eason's article, 'Japan Makes Inroads', *The Times*, 12 February 1992, p. 24.
2. Second Report from the Select Committee on Science and Technology, 1977/78, 'Innovation, Research and Development in Japanese Science-based Industry', vols 1 and 2 (HMSO, August 1978). These corporate responses provided as appendices to the Minutes of Evidence taken before the Select Committee on Science and Technology (Japan Subcommittee) are as follows:

Page(s)	Appendix	Company	Date
109	1	Ford Motor Company	Oct. 1977
111–112	3	Rank Organisation	Oct. 1977
179	31	Motor Industry Research Association	Oct. 1977
180	32	Electrical Research Association	Nov. 1977
131	17	EMI Group	Nov. 1977
100	2	BOC	Sept. 1977

3. W. Skinner, 'Operations Technology: Blind Spot in Strategic Management', Harvard Business School Working Paper 83–85 (1983) p. 11.
4. W. Skinner, 'Operations Technology', p. 6. These views are also confirmed by the author in his book entitled *Production/Operations Management* (Englewood Cliffs, New Jersey: Prentice-Hall, 1991) pp. 186 and 187.
5. Advisory Council for Applied Research and Development, *New Opportunities in Manufacturing: the Management of Technology* (London: HMSO Cabinet Office, October 1983) p. 48.
6. Manufacturing Futures Survey (1990), INSEAD, Fontainebleau, France.
7. Kenichi Ohmae, *The Mind of the Strategist* (New York: McGraw-Hill, 1982) pp. 36–7.

Manufacturing Implications of Corporate Marketing Decisions

Companies invest in processes and infrastructure in order to make products and sell them at a profit. Consequently, the degree to which manufacturing is aligned to the product needs in the market-place will make a significant contribution to the overall success of a business. The size and fundamental nature of the manufacturing contribution is such, however, that the wrong fit will lead to the business being well wide of the mark. Many executives are still unaware 'that what appear to be routine manufacturing decisions frequently come to limit the corporation's strategic options, binding it with facilities, equipment, personnel and basic controls and policies to a non-competitive posture which may take years to turn around'.[1]

The reason for this is that companies having invested inappropriately in process and infrastructure, cannot afford to reinvest to put things right. The financial implications, systems development, training requirements and the time it would take to make the changes would leave it, at best, seriously disadvantaged. To avoid this companies need to be aware of how well manufacturing can support the market-place, and to be conscious of the investments and time dimensions to change current positions into future proposals.

2.1 Strategic Dominance: Perspectives Over Time

In broad terms, changes in the balance of world demand and capacity have brought with them a change in the fortunes of different functions. Up to the mid-1960s, many industries enjoyed a market situation in which world demand was greater than available capacity, a situation which favoured manufacturing's position in terms of strategic influence. This, together with post-war growth, helped to create the dominance of the manufacturing function in many corporations. As the demand/capacity balance began to even out, and selling into existing and new markets became more difficult, the power base of corporate influence began to swing away from manufacturing and heralded the rise of marketing. By the mid-1970s the impact of recessions and energy crises had, in turn, opened the door to the influence of accounting and finance. These varying fortunes, however, rarely seemed to be based upon what was best for the total good of the business, but more on which functional perspective appeared to provide the key which opened the door to corporate success or salvation. As a result, those functions which were out in the cold were themselves left without due corporate influence.

The consequence has been that many companies have failed to align effectively all parts of their business to agreed and achievable corporate objectives. Functional strategies are typically formulated independently of one another and are not cross-related. This failure to debate strategy has been a major factor in creating a situation in which the essential perspectives and contributions of key functions are not incorporated into corporate-strategy decisions.

However, in times of increasing world competition, an over-capacity in many sectors of manufacturing industry, an increasing scarcity of key resources and decreasing product life cycles there is an overriding logic for businesses to incorporate all the key functional perspectives when determining policy decisions. Why then does this not happen? In many organisations, manufacturing adopts or is required to take a reactive stance in corporate deliberations. Yet how can the function which controls such a large slice of the assets, expenditure and people, thus under-pinning the very welfare of a company, be left out?

2.2 Reasons for Manufacturing's Reactive Role in Corporate Strategy

The fact that manufacturing executives have an exacting and critical corporate role to play is undisputed. Why then do they adopt their current role and why does this situation exist and not appear to be improving?

2.2.1 *The production manager's view of himself*

One of the major contributions to this situation appears to be that production managers also see themselves holding a reactive corporate brief. They too define their role as being one which requires them to react as well as possible to all that is asked of the production system. They see their role as:

- the exercise of skill and experience in effectively coping with the exacting and varying demands placed on manufacturing;
- to reconcile the trade-offs inherent in these demands as best they can.

Thus, rarely do they adequately contribute to the making of corporate decisions which result in a demand on manufacturing.

They do not explain the different sets of manufacturing implications created by alternative policy decisions and changes in direction. They fail, by default, to contribute at the corporate level and hence to help the company arrive at decisions which embrace all the important business perspectives.

2.2.2 *The company's view of the production manager's role*

Production management's perceived role of reacting to the demands placed upon it and a prime concern for the short term which this implies, is reinforced by the corporate view of manufacturing's contribution and hence the qualities which incumbents should possess. Many companies typically promote operators to foremen, foremen to managers and managers to directors with scant regard for the change in emphasis which needs to take place and with little help to make this transition a success. One major UK company, recognising the important corporate contribution to be made by its manufacturing executives undertook a series of tailor-made courses in manufacturing strategy. The first of these was for sixteen factory managers who, during the course, reflected that as a group their aggregate company service exceeded 300 years, yet the collective training they had received to help them prepare for their manufacturing executive roles was less than 30 days.

The outcome is that the short-term, 'looking after the store' role is reinforced through corporate expectations. Thus, the perceived contribution of manufacturing executives tends to be confined to the day-to-day, and the reactive role in strategic decision becomes a reality.

2.2.3 *Production managers are too late in the corporate debate*

Production managers are often not involved in corporate policy decisions until these decisions have started to take shape. This position having been partly created by the last two points will, once established, tend to become standard practice. The result is that production executives have less opportunity to contribute to decisions on strategy alternatives and, as a consequence, always appear to be complaining about the unrealistic demands made of them and the problems which invariably ensue.

2.2.4 *The 'can't say no' syndrome*

The 'can't say no' syndrome is still the hallmark of the production culture. But this helps no one. Manufacturing executives tend to respond to corporate needs and difficulties without evaluating the consequences or alternatives which need to be considered and then explaining these to others. Rarely is it a 'yes' or 'no' decision. The need to be able to say 'no' from a total business perspective and with sound corporate-related arguments is an important part of any senior executive's role, and manufacturing is no exception. At this time, production managers accept the current and future demands placed upon the systems and capacities they control and then go away to resolve them. In this way they decide between corporate alternatives but only from a narrow functional perspective of what appears best for the business. It is essential that this changes. Resolving corporate-related issues in a unilateral way is not the most effective method to resolve the complex alternatives on hand. This resolution needs corporate debate to ensure that the relevant factors and options are taken into account so that an appropriate corporate decision can be concluded.

For strategic decisions need to encompass the sets of important trade-offs which are embodied in alternatives which have their roots in the process and infrastructure investments associated with manufacturing and which are reflected in the high proportion of assets and expenditure under their control.

2.2.5 *Lack of language*

On the whole, production managers do not have a history of explaining their function clearly and effectively to others in the organisation. This is particularly the case in terms of the manufacturing-strategy issues which need to be considered and the production consequences which will arise from the corporate decisions under discussion. On the other hand, marketing and financial executives have explained their function well. They can talk about policy alternatives in a straightforward and intelligible manner.[2]

The reason for this difference cannot, however, be wholly placed at the production manager's door. The knowledge base, concepts and language have not been developed in the same way. Consequently, shared perspectives within manufacturing, let alone between functions, are not held, which adds fuel to the lack of interfunctional understanding.

To illustrate this last point, just review the number of books and articles written and postgraduate and post-experience courses provided in the area of manufacturing strategy compared with the other major functions of marketing and accounting/finance and to those disciplines such as operational research and organisational behaviour, which purport to relate to business. Similarly, a check on the faculty mix within major business schools clearly reveals the disproportionate allocation of resources between these various areas and an understanding of why these critical developments in manufacturing have not been forthcoming.

2.2.6 *Functional goals and measures*

In many organisations, the managers of different functions are measured in terms of their departmental efficiency (an operational

FIGURE 2.1
The dichotomy of business views illustrated by the different figures included on typical customer-order paperwork

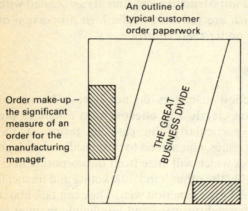

An outline of typical customer order paperwork

Order make-up – the significant measure of an order for the manufacturing manager

THE GREAT BUSINESS DIVIDE

Order value – the significant measure of an order for accountants and salesmen

perspective) and not in terms of overall effectiveness (a business perspective). Furthermore, their career prospects are governed by their performance within the functional value system. As a consequence, this leads to managers making trade-offs which are sub-optimal for the business as a whole.

Figure 2.1 illustrates this dichotomy. A typical accountant or salesman when receiving a customer order will look at one figure as being significant – the total value of the order placed. For them, sales value is the important measure of business relevance.

In the same situation, manufacturing managers will look at the order make-up. For them, the business relevance of an order is not its value but its volume, product mix and delivery promise. It is this aspect which determines the ease with which an order can be made in terms of the process configurations already laid down. It is this which will reflect manufacturing's ability to meet the cost base of the product(s) involved and hence the profit margin which will result.

Where marketing is measured by the level of sales turnover

achieved, each £1 of sales in their value system will carry the same
weight as any other £1 of sales. Hence, all sales are deemed equal.
In reality, however, this is not the case. Orders are not of the same
value to a business. The higher the degree of fit between the
anticipated volumes and product mix and the actual sales, then the
more the target levels will normally be met. Product costs based
upon one level of volumes and process configurations based upon
a given product mix are rarely, if ever, realigned with incremental
volume and mix changes. Even the costing base which underpins
initial forecasts is rarely, if ever, adjusted each time the market
picture changes. A great business divide, therefore, separates the
two realities of the market-place and manufacturing. The simplistic measure of total sales value disguises those product characteristics so essential to manufacturing's ability to sustain cost and
profit margin structures in a business.

2.2.7 *Functional support for manufacturing is weak*

Building on the last point, many companies exercise control of
their business through establishing specialist functions with,
originally, the prime role and *raison d'être* of supporting the needs
of the line and, in particular, manufacturing. However, in most
firms the clarity of this perspective is now at best blurred, and at
worst distorted. Typically, the performance of these specialist
departments is measured in terms of their own functionally
derived goals and perspectives rather than line management and
hence business requirements. Getting adequate and timely
resources committed to the manufacturing needs of a business is
difficult.

Competing in different value systems, being measured against
different performance criteria and gaining prominence and promotion through different departmental opinions of what constitutes
importance within their contribution has gradually fragmented the
business. It has created a situation where shared perspectives and
overlapping views are left to individual accomplishment and en-
deavour rather than in response to clear corporate direction (these
issues are covered in more detail in Chapter 7).

2.2.8   *Tenure*

A growing tendency since the mid-60s has been to reduce the length of tenure for job incumbents, which militates against a manager's responsibility to provide for the necessary level of continuity. The short-term perspectives which result not only affect functional continuity but also discourage longer-term corporate perspectives from being pursued and implemented. The result is an inclination to maintain the *status quo* and to meet functional goals above all else. In times of change, neither of these promotes the corporate goodwill. Instead it leads a manager into taking decisions which are unduly weighted towards the standpoint of how they will affect him politically in the future rather than how they will affect the business's competitive position.

2.2.9   *Top management's view of strategy*

The authors of business plans and corporate marketing reviews look outward from the business. Top executives associate themselves with these activities, seeing them as legitimate corporate strategy issues. They concentrate their attention on the external environment in which the business operates.

Manufacturing plans are built in line with the stated business needs and are based upon the internal dimensions of the processes involved, and top executives are less likely to associate themselves with these activities. Typically they request a manufacturing strategy statement from the production executive without becoming involved in its structure and development. They assume that it is not an inherent part of their role, which increases the difficulties in establishing a corporate strategy through dialogue and understanding.

A key task in corporate strategy, however, is matching these two perspectives, the resolution of which has been abdicated by top management or at best has occurred outside the boundaries of their business awareness.

2.3   The Content of Corporate Strategy

The failure of companies to incorporate functional perspectives into their corporate strategy debate is reinforced by the typical content of corporate strategy statements as well as by approaches to strategy development as advocated by many leading researchers and writers in the field. In this way, current approaches are reinforced in themselves and also by the training and development of executives charged with this task and specialists providing relevant support. These characteristics manifest themselves in a number of ways including the following.

2.3.1 *Expressions of strategy are typified by their general nature*

As strategy itself is general in nature broad statements are deemed appropriate ways of expressing it. The result is that strategy statements are general and all-encompassing, typically using words with more than one meaning. Furthermore, strategic perspectives are applied in a broad-brush manner which assumes that these general perspectives are universal in both nature and relevance. But what typifies markets today is difference, not similarity. Thus, general statements are not only inaccurate but also misleading.

The outcome is that strategy statements fail to distinguish difference – a prerequisite for appropriate strategy formulation. General statements may underpin theory but strategy, like management, is an applied field. The key to understanding a business is to determine the ways in which the business competes in its different segments. And, of this you can be sure, segments will require functional strategies to reflect these differences.

2.3.2 *Strategy formulation stops at the interface between functions*

Functional strategies are typically not linked to one another. Most companies require each function to provide a strategic statement but fail to integrate them as part of its strategy formulation. The result is that corporate strategies stop at the interface between functions.

This approach is also re-enacted in many large corporations at the next level. Often, multinationals seem unable or unwilling to incorporate individual company statements into a strategy for the whole group. This failure to link, either by default or intent, is a consistent and comprehensive weakness in strategy formulation. The result is that in increasingly dynamic and competitive markets, companies are systematically failing to realise their strategic potential and consequently are outperformed.

Furthermore, this apparent lack of need to integrate strategies is paralleled in the literature. A review of books on strategic marketing and corporate strategy will confirm that the link between the marketing-related dimensions of strategy and those of manufacturing is not made. The implication is, therefore, that it is unnecessary. Or, if it is then its impact is of insufficient consequence to be an integral part of the review process. Articles and books on marketing strategy were recently reviewed. Of the 1250 pages covered by the nine articles and three books, less than 1 per cent concerned manufacturing. A similar review of ten books in the field of corporate strategy revealed that of the 4000 pages written, only 2 per cent concerned manufacturing. Thus, strategy-formulation advocated and undertaken by leading researchers in the fields of corporate and marketing strategy also stops at the interface. The result is that methodologies are put forward which lead companies into making major decisions and committing a business for many years ahead which do not require essential interface. The consequences are enormous. First, the risks associated with such approaches in today's markets are substantial, the more so when it is recognised that the high level of risk being taken is not part of the process. Second, it consistently results in the failure to create the type of strategic advantage which comes directly from embracing key functional perspectives and arriving at commonly agreed and understood corporate directions.

2.3.3 *Apparent rationale – wholes* v. *parts*

The underlying rationale for these advocated and adopted methodologies appears to be based on the assumption that corporate improvement can be accomplished by working solely on the corporate wholes. Although reshaping the whole is an important facet of strategic resolution, the necessary links to constituent parts and the role of those parts in bringing about agreed directions and change is fundamental. Unless these links are forged when making choices in terms of what is best for a business and agreeing directions to be pursued, then companies are increasingly unlikely to arrive at appropriate decisions essential for their growth and prosperity over time.

2.3.4 *Typical outcomes*

The results of this lack of integration are documents and statements which have the trappings, but not the essence, of corporate
debate. With functional strategies independently derived, the
nearest they get to one another in terms of integration is that they
sit side by side in the same binder.

Even when departments such as marketing and manufacturing
present their strategies it is not intended and does not, in fact,
spark corporate-based discussion. Those companies who justify
this procedure on the grounds of creating requirements which
necessitate executives going through rigorous, functionally orientated debate are not only guilty of false rationalisation but also are
missing the point. In today's markets, companies which fail to
harness the resources of all facets of their business will be seriously
disadvantaged. Not only will they miss out, they may well be in
danger of missing out altogether.

2.4 The Way Forward

What companies require is an orientation based neither on
products/markets nor on manufacturing but a strategy which
embraces the market/production interface, so that the degree of fit
between the proposed marketing strategy and manufacturing's
ability to support it is known at the business level and objectively
resolved within corporate perspectives.

For this to take place, relevant internal information which explains the company's manufacturing capabilities needs to be available within a business as well as the traditional information which
is primarily concerned with the customer and the market opportunities associated with the company's products and addressed
solely from the marketing perspective. It is not sufficient that such
information should be available – and often it is not. For this to
take place companies cannot, as in the past, base strategic decisions on information regarding customer and market opportunities
addressed solely from the marketing function's perspective. Information about a firm's manufacturing capabilities is also needed.
Furthermore to achieve this essential strategic link between different areas of a business is the task of senior executives, not of

heads of departments. Leaving it to others would be an inappropriate delegation of responsibilities. As with other functions, manufacturing strategy is not owned by manufacturing. It requires corporate ownership. Senior executives need to understand all the strategic inputs in the corporate debate, otherwise the conflicting or non-matching functional perspectives cannot be fully investigated and individual functions will be left to handle the trade-offs involved.

In this way, the senior management inappropriately delegates this key task and finds itself only able to exercise control over the decisions taken in a global, after-the-event way.

2.4.1 *Linking manufacturing with corporate marketing decisions*

There is no short-cut to moving forward. There are, however, five basic steps to be taken. These provide an analytical and objective structure in which the corporate debate and consequent actions can be taken.

Step 1   Define corporate objectives.
Step 2   Determine marketing strategies to meet these objectives.
Step 3   Assess how different products win orders against competitors.
Step 4   Establish the most appropriate mode to manufacture these sets of products – process choice.
Step 5   Provide the manufacturing infrastructure required to support production.

These are, in one sense, classical steps in corporate planning. The problem is that most corporate planners treat the first three steps as interactive with 'feedback loops' and the next two as linear and deterministic. While each step has substance in its own right, the really critical issue is that each has an impact on the others – hence the involved nature of strategy formulation. This is further exacerbated by the inherent complexity of manufacturing and the general failure to take account of the essential interaction between marketing and manufacturing strategies. What is required, therefore, is an approach which recognises these features and yet provides an ordered and analytical way forward.

The approach which is suggested to link manufacturing with

corporate marketing decisions is schematically outlined in Table 2.1. It has been presented in the form of a framework to help to express the stages involved in outline form. The approach to be followed provides the key to stimulating corporate debate about the business in such a way as to enable manufacturing to assess the degree to which it can support products in the market-place. It is an approach which has been researched and tested successfully in many industries and businesses of different sizes.

2.4.2 *How it works*

The objective of using this framework is to produce a manufacturing strategy for a business (Steps 4 and 5). In all cases this will include a review of existing products plus a review of proposed product introductions. Furthermore, the review will be based upon current and future market expectations. This is because manufacturing needs to 'support' a product i.e. with after-sales service and supply of spares over the whole and not just a part of its life-cycle and hence it is this total decision which the business needs to address. As product requirements change, so will manufacturing's task. The range of support requirements, therefore, will invariably affect the choice of process (Step 4) and infrastructure (Step 5) considered appropriate for the business over the whole life-cycle of each product or product family. Levels of investment will also need to reflect this total support, and the varying degrees of mismatch over the life-cycle between the product requirements and manufacturing process and infrastructure capability will need to be understood and agreed. In this way, the business will make conscious decisions at the corporate level. It will exercise its due responsibility for resolving trade-offs between the investment required to reduce the degree of mismatch and the ramifications for the business by allowing the mismatch to go unaltered.

However, to get to Steps 4 and 5 the three earlier steps need to be taken. With some understanding of what is to be achieved in a manufacturing strategy statement, it is now opportune to go through each step in turn and then to explain how the necessary interrelations between these parts come together as a whole to form a corporate strategy for a business.

TABLE 2.1
Framework for reflecting manufacturing strategy issues in corporate decisions (steps involved)

1	2	3	4	5
			Manufacturing strategy	
Corporate objectives	Marketing strategy	How do products win orders in the market place?	process choice	infrastructure
• growth • survival • profit • return on investment • other financial measures	• product markets and segments • range • mix • volumes • standardisation *versus* customisation • level of innovation • leader *versus* follower alternatives	• price • conformance quality • delivery speed reliability • colour range • product range • design • brand image • technical support	• choice of alternative processes • trade-offs embodied in the process choice • role of inventory in the process configuration • process positioning • capacity size timing location	• function support • manufacturing planning and control systems • manufacturing systems engineering • quality assurance and control • clerical procedures • work structuring • organisational structure • payment systems

Note: Although the steps to be followed are given as finite points in a stated procedure, in reality the process will involve statement and restatement, for several of these aspects will impinge on each other

Step 1 *Corporate objectives*

Inputs into corporate strategy need to be linked to the objectives of the business. The essential nature of this tie-up is twofold. First, it provides the basis for establishing clear, strategic direction for the business and demonstrates both the strategic awareness and strategic willingness essential to corporate success. Second, it will define the boundaries and mark the parameters against which the various inputs can be measured and consistency established thus providing the hallmarks of a coherent corporate plan.

For each company, the objectives will be different in nature and emphasis. They will reflect the nature of the economy, markets, opportunity and preferences of those involved. The important issues here, however, are that they need to be well thought through, hold logically together and provide the necessary direction for the business.

Typical measures concern profit in relation to sales and investment, together with targets for growth in absolute terms or with regard to market share. Businesses may also wish to include employee policies and environmental issues as part of their overall sets of objectives.

Step 2 *Marketing strategy*

Linking closely to the provision of the agreed corporate objectives, a marketing strategy needs to be developed and will often include the following stages:

1. Market planning and control units need to be established. Their task is to bring together a number of products which have closely related market targets and which often share a common marketing programme. This will help to identify a number of manageable units with similar marketing characteristics.
2. The second stage involves a situational analysis of product markets which includes:
   (a) current and future volumes;
   (b) end-user characteristics;
   (c) industry practices and trends;
   (d) identifying key competitors and a review of the business's relative position.
3. The final stage concerns identifying the target markets and agreeing objectives for each. This will include both a broad

review of how to achieve these, and the short-term action plans necessary to achieve the more global objectives involved.

In addition, the company should agree the level of service support necessary in each market, and make an assessment of the investments and resources needed to provide these throughout the business.

The outcome of this will be a declaration to the business of the product markets and segments which the strategy proposes whilst identifying the range, mix and volumes involved. Other issues pertinent to the business will include the degree of standardisation/customerisation involved within each product range, the level of innovation and product development it proposes whether it should be a leader or follower in each of its markets and the extent and timing of these strategic initiatives.

Step 3 *How do products win orders in the market place?*
Manufacturing's strategic task is to provide, better than the manufacturing functions of competitors, those criteria which enable the products involved to win orders in the market place. As stressed in the footnote to Table 2.1 the debate initiated by this methodology is iterative in nature. This is not only appropriate for, but also fundamental to, strategic resolution. Thus, the markets and segments within these markets in which a company decides to compete need to be agreed by the company as a whole.

In no way can these critical decisions be the responsibility or prerogative of a single function. Typically, however, most companies develop strategy through a marketing perspective (see Stages 1 and 2). Whilst the marketing debate is pre-eminent in corporate strategy procedures, the problem is that this is where the debate ends.

As a function, marketing will have a view and an important and essential one at that. But it is not the only view and in no way should it be allowed to dominate corporate strategy resolution. Functional dominance, no matter of what origin is detrimental to today's business needs and must be avoided (see p. 26). An essential perspective of a firm's markets has to come from manufacturing. This perspective is provided by determining those order-winners (and qualifiers* as explained later on pp. 42–5)

---

* Suffice here to say that qualifiers get and keep companies in markets but do not win orders.

FIGURE 2.2
How order-winning criteria link corporate marketing decisions with manufacturing strategy

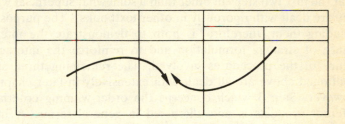

which manufacturing needs to provide. The procedure is, in reality, one of asking the marketing function questions about the market with manufacturing answers. This step, therefore, is the essential link between corporate marketing proposals and commitments and the manufacturing processes and infrastructure necessary to support them (see Figure 2.2).

However, not only will these be of more or less importance one to another but they will also change over time. The procedure to be followed and the important issues to be addressed are covered in some detail later in this chapter.

Step 4   Process choice
Manufacturing can choose from a number of alternative processes in order to make the products involved. The key to this choice is volume and the order-winning criteria involved. Each choice, therefore, needs to reflect the set of trade-offs involved for the various products in both current and future terms. The issues embodied in these trade-offs are both extensive and important. Chapter 4, therefore, has been devoted to the aspect of process choice where the implications embodied in this fundamental decision will be dealt with in detail.

Step 5   Manufacturing infrastructure
Manufacturing infrastructure consists of the non-process features within production. It encompasses the procedures, systems, controls, payment systems, work-structuring alternatives, organisational issues and so on which are involved in the non-process

aspects of manufacturing. Chapter 7 discusses and illustrates some of the major areas involved.

Whilst the five steps discussed above comprise the elements of manufacturing strategy development, it is not intended here to treat the first two steps in other than a somewhat superficial way – they are dealt with rigorously in other textbooks.[3] The purpose of including them, therefore, is both to demonstrate the integral nature of strategy formulation and to reinforce the interactive nature of the procedures involved. The remaining three steps mentioned above are all dealt with extensively in later chapters. However, Step 3 which concerns the order-winning criteria of different products is now discussed in general terms. A more detailed review is provided in Chapter 3.

2.5   Order-winners and Qualifiers

Characteristics of order-winners and qualifiers are discussed in the following section. To help to distinguish between the issues involved, it is important to recognise from the outset that some order-winning criteria do not fall within the jurisdiction of manufacturing. For example, after-sales service, being the existing supplier to a customer, technical liaison capability, brand name, and design leadership are features provided by functions other than manufacturing. It is a corporate decision whether or not to allocate resources to provide one or more of these particular features. However, within the mix of order-winning criteria over a product's life-cycle, manufacturing will normally be the most important.

The rationale for establishing the order-winners of different products is to improve a company's understanding of its markets. Before outlining the procedure for doing this some important characteristics and issues involved are now described to give essential background and context.[3]

2.5.1   *Define the meaning*

To understand a business requires that the discussion is both comprehensive and clear. As mentioned earlier, many companies, perceiving strategy to be a broadly based set of discussions, are content with arriving at statements which lack essential clarity.

Given that difference rather than similarity characterises today's markets then to understand the markets requires adequate and clear outcomes from strategic discussion. A prerequisite is that the dimensions which characterise a company's markets are clearly defined and agreed. Using words which convey more than one meaning will only lead to misunderstanding and an inadequate base on which to establish agreed direction.

Companies, therefore, which use descriptions of the success factors in their markets such as 'customer service' are ill-served. Customer service can mean any number of things. The key is to agree which dimension of customer service is the important criterion. The reason for this is simple. Without this level of clarity then executives will walk away from the strategy debate each with their own definition of which dimension of customer service (for example) is the one most critical to the business. Furthermore, reviewing the importance of the same factor in the different markets served by a company can also embody similar misunderstandings. Most, if not all, companies today are selling products into markets characterised by difference and not similarity and these essential insights need to be clearly identified as a prerequisite for sound strategy-making.

Two examples to illustrate these points are the use of the words 'quality' and 'delivery'. It is essential, for instance, to separate the word 'design' from 'quality'. Both are related dimensions but whereas the former concerns creating a product specification the latter describes the task of meeting the given specification. Whilst one is the task of the design function the other is a distinct manufacturing task. This does not imply that the perspectives do not interrelate: they do. The issue is that the tasks form part of different functional offerings.

Similarly, take the aspect of delivery. Separating the issue of on-time as opposed to that of short lead-times is an essential part of understanding the key dimensions of a market. To describe both under the one word 'delivery' will hide essential insights.

2.5.2   *Strategy is time- and market-specific*

It is not appropriate to discuss strategy as a set of stereotypes. To do so may simplify the process but will confuse the outputs. To be relevant, therefore, strategy debate needs to be time- and market-specific. Recognising this will prevent stereotypes from being applied and will help to create and sustain the essential dimension of clarity emphasised in section 2.5.1.

2.5.3   *Order-winners and qualifiers*

The last two sections have emphasised the need to distinguish differences as part of the strategy formulation. To this end, an essential perspective in terms of manufacturing's task is to recognise and apply the concept of order-winners and qualifiers.

Qualifiers are those criteria which are necessary even to be considered by a customer as a possible supplier. For example, customers increasingly require suppliers to be registered BS 5750 or ISO 9000. Suppliers, therefore, who are so registered have only achieved the right to bid or be considered. Furthermore, they will need to retain the qualification in order to stay on the short list or be considered as a competitor in the market. However, providing/ attaining these criteria do not win orders.

Order-winners are those criteria which win the order.

Order-winners vs qualifiers
The need to identify difference is further underscored by recognising the essential difference between these two dimensions in a market. Whilst with qualifiers, companies need only to be as good as competitors, with order-winners they need to be better than competitors. However, qualifiers are not less important than order-winners, they are different. Both are essential if companies are to maintain existing share and grow.
    The need to distinguish between those which win orders in the market-place and those which qualify the product to be there is highlighted in the following example. When Japanese companies entered the UK colour television market in the 1970s, they changed the way in which products won orders from predominantly price to product quality and reliability in service. The relatively low product quality and reliability in service of existing television sets meant that in the changed competitive forces of this market, existing producers were losing orders through quality to the Japanese companies, i.e. existing manufacturers were not pro-

viding the criteria which qualified them to be in the market-place. By the early 1980s, product quality was raised by those concerned so that they were again qualified to be in the market. As a result, the most important order-winning criterion in this market has reverted back to price.

Manufacturing, therefore, must provide the qualifying criteria in order to get into or stay in the market-place. But those alone will not win orders. They merely prevent a company losing orders to its competitors. Once the qualifying criteria have been achieved, manufacturing then has to turn its attention to the ways in which orders are won and ideally to provide these better than anyone else.

Also, in the case of price, if this is not the predominant order-winner, then it does not mean that a company can charge what it wishes. Whilst it needs to recognise that it does not compete on price and therefore should exploit this opportunity, it has to keep its exploitation within sensible bounds. Failure to do so will, in turn, start to lose orders increasingly to those who are more competitively priced. Hence, in this situation a company will have turned a qualifying criterion (i.e. a product highly priced within some limits) into an order-losing criterion where the price has become too high.

2.5.4   *Differentiating between order-winners and qualifiers*

Having identified and separated order-winners from qualifiers it is now necessary to distinguish between the importance of one criterion and another. This is done in two ways:

* *order-winners* – once order-winners are agreed, appropriate weightings (points out of a hundred) are allocated to each (see Tables 2.3, 2.4 and 2.5)
* *qualifiers* – less definition of importance is required for qualifiers. If a company needs to qualify in one market segment on both quality and delivery reliability then it needs to attain the necessary levels in each. However, some qualifiers will be more critical in terms of a customer's/market's requirements and these are distinguished by labelling them as order-losing sensitive qualifiers (see Tables 2.2, 2.3 and 2.4).

TABLE 2.2
The weekly volumes, order-winner weightings and qualifiers for three products considered representative of three product ranges

Order-winning criteria	Product, time-scale and weightings								
	Product A			Product B			Product C		
	1993	1994	1996	1993	1994	1996	1993	1994	1996
Design capability	–	–	–	40	–	–	–	–	–
Handling design modifications	–	–	–	–	20	–	–	–	–
Technical liaison support	–	–	–	20	20	–	20	–	–
UK-based supplier	10	–	–	10	10	10	20	–	–
Existing supplier	10	60	90	10	20	30	20	30	30
Price	60	40	10	20	30	60	30	40	40
Delivery – speed	20	–	–	–	–	–	10	30	30
– reliability	QQ	Q	–	QQ	QQ	QQ	QQ	QQ	QQ
Conformance quality	Q	Q	Q	Q	QQ	Q	Q	Q	Q
Weekly volumes	2500	1500	50	300	300	700	3000	4000	4000

Note: Q denotes a qualifier and QQ, an order-losing sensitive qualifier

TABLE 2.3
European Battery Company: order-winners and qualifiers for selected markets

	1991	1993	1995
Product Type A10			
Design	10	20	40
Conformance quality	20	20	–
Delivery – speed	70	40	30
– reliability	Q	QQ	QQ
Price	Q	20	30
Representative products A10, 60, 82 and 110			
Product Type B40			
Conformance quality	20	30	10
Delivery – speed	20	20	20
– reliability	QQ	QQ	QQ
Price	50	50	70
Technical field support	10	–	–
Representative products B40/6			
Product Type B500			
Design	50	50	50
Conformance quality	40	40	30
Delivery – speed	10	10	20
– reliability	QQ	QQ	QQ
Price	Q	Q	Q

Note: As for Table 2.2

2.5.5 *Monitoring actual/anticipated change over time*

As markets are dynamic then order-winners and qualifiers and/or their associated weightings will change over time. Thus, to monitor this change, relevant criteria and their weightings are agreed over time. The next section details how this is accomplished.

TABLE 2.4
UK food producer: order-winners and qualifiers for selected products

	1992	1995
Product A (beverage)		
Brand – image	50	60
– support	QQ	QQ
Product range	10	10
Packaging	10	–
Design	30	30
Price	QQ	QQ
Conformance quality	QQ	QQ
Delivery – speed	QQ	QQ
– reliability	QQ	QQ
Product B (food)		
Brand – image	35	30
– support	5	5
Product performance	20	20
Price	40	45
Conformance quality	Q	Q
Delivery – speed	Q	QQ
– reliability	QQ	QQ

Note: As for Table 2.2

2.6   The Procedure for Establishing Order-winners and Qualifiers

In order to create the essential interface between marketing and production it is necessary to provide a business with an understanding of its markets from the viewpoint of manufacturing, as well as marketing. Classically, companies often fail to distinguish clearly between the market (business) and marketing (function) perspectives. This lack of clarity shows itself in many ways and none more typically than the fact that, in many companies, the strategy debate ends when Steps 1 and 2 of the framework (see Table 2.1) have been accomplished. The assumption is that marketing's view of the market is how the market is. The key nature of Step 3 lies in facilitating the important distinction between the function and the business by asking market-oriented questions requiring manufacturing answers. These questions ask how different products win orders in their respective markets.

In developing a manufacturing strategy, the identification of relevant order-winners for different products is a key step. The critical nature of its role is to help companies to move from what often constitutes a vague understanding of its many markets to a new and essential level of awareness. Too often, companies describe their business as composed of relatively large segments and in so doing make the assumption that all products within a segment have similar order-winners because they have similar names, are sold to similar customers, or belong to the same segment from the viewpoint of marketing. But products win orders in different ways from one another; they will typically have more than one order-winner, and the order-winners will change over time. Unless these differences are recognised, then the level of clarity essential to increasing business understanding, and on which to base major investment decisions, will not be provided.

The procedure used to gain these insights is as follows:

- Marketing is requested to separate the business into different segments as they perceive them. The procedure, as with other aspects of strategy debate, is iterative in nature. Thus, marketing's separation of the business provides relevant insights and market distinctions as an important initial input into the debate but this is reconsidered and very often revised as the strategy formulation progresses.
- In order to focus discussion, sample products are chosen to represent these market segments. This step serves three purposes. The first is to help to test whether the segments chosen are sufficient to distinguish the market differences that exist. The second is to enable the debate from now onward to be oriented toward the particular, rather than the general. The third is to allow specific data to be collected and analyses to be completed, which, in turn, provides information giving essential

insights into the real nature of the different market segments.

- Marketing is also required to establish two time-periods in the future for each segment. Note that the chosen time-periods may not be the same for each segment.
- The next phase is to provide actual and forecast sales volumes for chosen representative products, based on current and future time-periods.
- When this information has been gathered, marketing identifies the qualifiers and order-winners relevant to each of the sample products chosen. Three illustrations are provided as Tables 2.2, 2.3 and 2.4. Weighted percentages for relevant order-winners have to be assessed for both current and relevant future time-periods.
- This information now provides the initial input into this part of the strategic debate. In turn, marketing's opinion will be contested both by the opinion of other functions and by the provision of information relating to the issues highlighted by the selection and importance attached to the relevant qualifiers and order-winners. This enables the company to have a clearer and more informed view of what it requires manufacturing to provide if it is to compete effectively in its chosen markets. Only when this is clearly understood can manufacturing strategy be formulated and appropriate decisions made in terms of process and infrastructure investments.

2.7 Understanding the Criteria Chosen and Their Relative Weightings

As explained above, marketing is asked to determine the weightings for each relevant criterion. This involves allocating percentage points to each order-winner for both current and future time-periods. In this part of the procedure, the discussion ranges around not only the individual weights but also the reasons why any changes in emphasis are anticipated in the future.

Where changes do occur, it is essential for the business to understand that the task is to support the full range of criteria together with the changes in emphasis involved. As explained earlier, whereas some of these will be non-production features, the major thrust will in fact be from manufacturing. Certainly the provision of any significant changes in emphasis anticipated in the future will typically be manufacturing-based and the need to reconcile the process and infrastructure investments appropriate to meet the changing requirements will have to be fully discussed, understood and eventually agreed by all concerned.

A final word concerns the order-winning criteria put forward by marketing and the percentage weightings proposed. There is a danger, certainly when this procedure is first adopted, that marketing will include a host of criteria and often, partly as a result of not distinguishing between their relative importance, spread the percentage points, thus failing to identify the critical order-winning feature(s). The discussions explained earlier which involve questioning and understanding the criteria and weightings selected are necessary to ensure that this situation does not arise. The need for marketing to identify clearly how orders are won is an essential prerequisite to develop an appropriate corporate manufacturing strategy.

2.7.1 *Identifying qualifiers with potential to become order-winners*

Part of Step 3 requires marketing to indicate any qualifying criteria associated with the different sets of products with the potential to become order-winning criteria (for instance, the earlier examples of the changed role of quality in the UK colour-television market). In this way, a corporate decision on whether to invest in manufacturing so as to initiate this change can be considered. The impact it would have on market share, the time it would take for competitors to catch up and the investments involved in bringing about this change would be some of the issues to be addressed in this corporate strategy decision.

2.7.2 *Identifying qualifying criteria which are order-losing sensitive*

The final phase of Step 3 is for marketing to identify any qualifying criteria which are order-losing sensitive. It is important here for manufacturing to be fully aware of any qualifying criterion which is distinctly sensitive in order-losing terms. Where these are identified, the discussion which follows is aimed at appreciating the degree of order-losing sensitivity and the degree of risk the business is prepared to accept. Trade-offs between the costs, investment and sales can then be understood and decisions based on these be taken.

2.8   The Outputs of Manufacturing Strategy

There are two outputs which accrue from the use of this framework.

The first output   This concerns a manufacturing review of the implications for manufacturing processes and infrastructure support for current and future products and volumes. As depicted in Figure 2.3 this involves assessing the implications for manufacturing processes and infrastructure of selling products in terms of current and future volumes. This will result in an assessment of the degree of match between what exists in manufacturing and those processes and infrastructure features needed to provide the order-winning criteria involved.

Similarly, this will be completed for all future product proposals as well as the essential biannual review designed to pick up any volume or order-winning criteria changes which may make a significant difference to the incremental change which has taken place over time as measured against the relevant base year. In this way,

FIGURE 2.3
Assessing the implications for manufacturing processes and infrastructure of order-winners

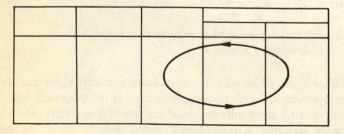

the changes in match and mismatch are monitored, thus detecting incremental marketing changes which have occurred over time and which often otherwise go unnoticed. Only by reviewing current and future requirements against the original decisions can the full change be assessed.

*   *   *

To illustrate the way in which this initial part of a manufacturing strategy is developed, a short summary of the work completed with three manufacturing companies is provided. The first is a UK company which supplies electrical and electronic parts to original equipment (OE) suppliers whose products had life-cycles varying between seven and twelve years with an agreement to manufacture spares for a further five years following the last OE orders. Table 2.2 outlines the order-winning criteria weightings for three of the products involved, each supplied to a different customer but considered to be representative of the product range as a whole.

The three examples illustrate products at different stages in their product life-cycles. Product *A* is one which by 1996 will have moved into spares volumes and reflects the change from a price-sensitive product to one where price is significantly less important. Product *B* is an example of a product scheduled to be introduced by 1994 and illustrative of the move from non-manufacturing to manufacturing order-winning criteria and the increasing price-sensitivity of the market. Product C, on the other hand, illustrates a product which will by 1994 have entered its mature phase, with orders being won mainly on price with an important element of delivery speed.

The preparation of this information enabled manufacturing to establish the appropriate way to meet the low-volume spares requirements of Product *A* and to recognise clearly the price-insensitivity associated with these volumes. With Product *B* it highlighted the emphasis which would eventually be placed on price whilst with Product *C* it signalled the need to provide a high degree of delivery speed and the process and inventory alternatives which needed to be considered. As a whole, it also drew attention to the different mix of order-winning criteria which existed throughout the product range and the different manufacturing tasks involved. In this way, manufacturing was able to establish appropriate responses to each market rather than attempting to meet these wide-ranging differences by a single strategy.

In Table 2.3, the relevant order-winners and qualifiers are given for representative products in selected markets of a European battery company. They illustrate how products with the same name (i.e. batteries) are far from being similar in terms of their respective order-winning and qualifying criteria. Establishing these clear differences allowed the company to orientate the required and different level of relevant resources to each product whilst identifying separate priorities within manufacturing. With these clearly in mind, appropriate strategic responses in manufacturing and other relevant functions can now be formulated.

Finally, Table 2.4 gives details of two products from a UK food manufacturer. It is included to illustrate how products are significantly different in terms of the way they win orders. Before the in-depth discussion took place in the company, these marked differences were not recognised and consequently not reflected in the priorities and strategic responses of relevant functions.

*   *   *

The second output Having determined the manufacturing strategy position and the necessary investments and the time-period for change involved, these now form part of the corporate strategy debate as illustrated in Figure 2.4.

The consequences of this are that the company as a whole is now required to review the business in both marketing and manufacturing terms. It changes the style and substance of corporate decisions from functionally based arguments and perspectives to ones which address functional differences by resolving the trade-offs involved at the business level. This corporate resolution therefore leads to an agreed understanding of what are the:

● business objectives;
● marketing strategy adopted;
● manufacturing strategy required.

In reality, it will lead to one of four positions based upon the degree of fit between the marketing and manufacturing strategic interface:

FIGURE 2.4
Manufacturing's input into the corporate strategy debate

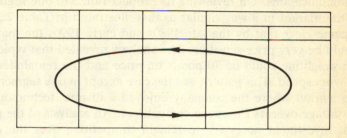

1. where the interface is sufficiently close and requires little, if any, adjustment;
2. where the interface is not sufficiently close but the corporate decision is not to invest the required time and money to bring it closer to (1) above;
3. where the interface is not sufficiently close and it is decided to change the marketing strategy so that the mismatch is reduced and moves towards (1) above;
4. where the interface is not sufficiently close and the time and investment is allocated to enable manufacturing to bring its processes and infrastructure to that required to support the marketing strategy and so move towards (1) above.

In situations (3) and (4) the company decides to reposition marketing and manufacturing respectively in order to bring about the position described in (1). In the case of (2), it is most essential that the reality of the mismatch is translated into manufacturing targets and budgets in order to present a manageable, achievable and hence controllable task. In this way, the inadequacies of manufacturing's performance against budget are separated from the consequences of the corporate strategy decision to accept the mismatch involved. The business is, therefore, able to learn the extent of the consequences resulting from the manufacturing/marketing interface mismatch and use this vital information in its future strategic decisions.

An example to illustrate the interactive nature of manufacturing strategy developments is provided by a medium-sized company involved in electronics and particularly with applications in tele-communications. On reviewing its product range in one segment of the market in a way similar to that illustrated in Table 2.2, it became clear that by the late 1980s and early 1990s the market would be very price-sensitive. The analysis revealed that typically the weighting could be 70 points on price and the remainder on delivery speed. This pattern was the case except in one segment of the market where the company enjoyed a distinct technological advantage over its European competitors. An analysis of the process investment necessary to remain competitive over the next years forced the company to select those markets in which it wished to remain. This enabled it to direct its investment, thus concentrating its limited resources in segments where it would be more able to compete or where it had a technology advantage. The consequence was that it reduced its product range and began the series of process investments necessary to enable the company to compete effectively in its chosen market segments.

2.9   Conclusion

In the past, manufacturing's role in terms of its corporate contribution has been perceived by the company as a whole as being the provider of requests. Corporate-strategy debate has stopped short at discussing the implications of decisions in terms of manufacturing. And this has been based on two incorrect assumptions, that:

1. within a given technology, manufacturing is able to do everything;
2. manufacturing's contribution concerns the achievement of efficiency rather than the effective support of the business needs.

The result for many companies is that not only have the profit margins they once enjoyed been eroded, but also the base on which to build a sound and prosperous business in the future is no longer available. Without the frequent manufacturing strategy checks necessary to evaluate the fit between the business and manufacturing's ability to provide the necessary order-winning criteria of its various products, then the absence of these essential insights leaves a business vulnerable and exposed. In times of increased world competition, being left behind can be sudden and fatal. In many cases, averting the end is the only option left. Turning the business around, however, will only be achieved by switching from an operational to a strategic mode, and one which will require a corporate review of the marketing and manufacturing perspectives involved in the alternatives to be considered and the financial implications of the proposals involved.

Notes and References

1. W. Skinner, 'Manufacturing – Missing Link in Corporate Strategy', *Harvard Business Review*, May – June 1969, p. 136.
2. This argument was put forward in T. J. Hill's article, 'Manufacturing Implications in Determining Corporate Policy', *International Journal of Operations and Production Management*, vol. 1, no. 1, p. 4.
3. These include D. A. Aaker, *Developing Business Strategies* (John Wiley, 1988); H. I. Ansoff, *Corporative Strategies* (Penguin, 1987); P. J. Below *et al. The Executive Guide to Strategic Planning* (Jossey - Bass, 1987); A. C. Hax and N. S. Majluf, *Strategic Management: An International Perspective* (Prentice-Hall International, 1984); B. Houlden, *Understanding Company Strategy* (Basil Blackwell, 1990); G. Johnson and K. Scholes, *Exploring Corporate Strategy* (Prentice Hall International, 1989); M. E. Porter, *Competitive Strategy* (The Free Press, 1980); J. Quinn *et al. The Strategy Process* (1988).

Further Reading

Buffa, E. S., *Meeting the Competitive Challenge: Manufacturing Strategy for US Companies* (Irwin, 1984).
Gunn, T. G. *Manufacturing for Competitive Advantage* (Cambridge, Massachusetts: Ballinger Publishing Company, 1987).
Mather, H. *Competitive Manufacturing* (Englewood Cliffs, New Jersey: Prentice-Hall International, 1988).

Samson, D. *Manufacturing and Operations Strategy* (Sydney: Prentice-Hall, 1991).

Skinner, W. *Manufacturing in Corporate Strategic* (New York: John Wiley, 1978).

Slack, N. *The Manufacturing Advantage* (London: Mercury Books, 1991).

Voss, C. A. *Manufacturing Strategy* (London: Chapman & Hall, 1992).

Order-winners
and Qualifiers

3

In the last chapter, the concept of order-winners and qualifiers was introduced and the rationale behind these perspectives and the characteristics and distinctions to be borne in mind were reviewed. This chapter now examines these dimensions more fully as well as explaining specific criteria in some detail.

The essence of strategy stems from companies needing to gain a detailed understanding of their current and future markets. Functions then need to develop strategies based on supporting the characteristics of agreed markets. However, this is not to imply that functions are reactive within this procedure. On the contrary, they need to be proactive in strategic debate to ensure that functional perspectives are explained and understood by the rest of the business and which then form part of the discussion and its agreed outcomes. Manufacturing strategy, therefore, consists of the strategic tasks required of manufacturing in order to support those order-winners and qualifiers which exist in a company's markets and which relate directly or indirectly to manufacturing.

3.1 Strategic Scenarios and Approaches

As highlighted in Chapter 2, an overriding characteristic of strategic formulation is that it tends to be expressed in general terms. Key reasons why the format of strategic outputs are general in nature include:

- as strategy implies a broad review then the underlying characteristic of strategic outputs is also perceived to be broad;
- companies appear to seek strategies which are uniform in nature. This offers apparent clarity in the form of a consistent strategic statement that is easy to express, explain and address and a desired level of uniformity which has inherent attractions no matter what the company's size.

It is not surprising then that typical expressions of corporate strategy (a point made earlier, see p. 33) are epitomised by general phrases such as 'service', 'responsiveness' and 'meeting the customer's needs'. In addition, researchers, writers and advisors have proffered generic statements concerning corporate strategy formulation with expressions such as 'low cost', 'differentiation' and 'critical success factors'. The use of general terms similar to these brings two major drawbacks. The first is that difference is not brought into focus but remains blurred. The second is that decisions concerning the nature of the market segments in which a company wishes to compete are not resolved at the strategic level. It is not recognised that orders for products (often within the same marketing segment) are won in different ways. As a result, this lack of clarity brings conflicting demands on manufacturing, which reinforces its reactive contribution and disperses the essential coherence necessary to provide strategic thrust, guidance and advantage.

Furthermore, this lack of clarity is considered adequate in markets which are increasingly characterised by difference and not similarity. However, ask any number of managing directors or chief executive officers whether the markets served by the group of companies under their control are similar in nature and the answer would be 'no'. Ask if the markets served by a typical company are the same and the answer would again be 'no'. How is it then that companies continue to expect or believe that manufacturing's support (in terms of process and infrastructure investments) for these would be common? If that is not so, then why do companies apply the same manufacturing approaches (often whatever is the latest approach considered appropriate or desirable) to support its different markets not only in one plant but in all its different plants?

The strategic process, therefore, needs to be based on a level of exactness in terms of understanding markets and differences within a market. As highlighted earlier, however, all too often companies debate strategy in general terms and undertake strategy using general courses of action. This invariably and increasingly leads to a lack of fit between functional strategies and corporate markets. Where this happens, companies will find themselves at a serious disadvantage.

Before moving on to how companies need to understand markets, let us review what typically happens to firms in the absence of clear, well-defined, strategic debate.

3.2 Strategic Vacuum

The absence of a manufacturing strategy within a business typically leads to a strategic vacuum, and into that void has been and currently continues to be drawn a rafter of solutions – panaceas or keys to open doors.

The reason for this response is underpinned by a basic logic. Executives recognise that manufacturing, as a significant part of the company, should make and needs to make a significant contribution to the success of the business. There is, therefore, due pressure on manufacturing to respond to these corporate demands and expectations. Without strategic context, however, manufacturing has traditionally responded by undertaking 'flavour-of-the-month' solutions. In this way, companies seek to achieve parity in manufacturing by modelling operations on best practice. The problem which companies find is that though the solutions are good in themselves it is their application which is inappropriate. Couple manufacturing's response with corporate initiatives and it is easy to see why most companies have invested regularly and significantly over the years in responses which, by and large, are now discarded. The cause of their abandonment is principally the lack of relevance of the solution in the first instance.

3.3 Understanding Markets

The essential step in formulating functional strategies (of which manufacturing is one) is to gain a clear understanding of, and corporate agreement about, the markets in which a company decides it wishes to be today and tomorrow. This initial and critical first step provides the two essential dimensions for the formulation of sound and effective strategies.

1. The in-depth debate about the markets in which a company decides to compete is a prerequisite to strategy formulation. The clear identification is based on a well-articulated understanding of market needs and the implications of these for all functions. It is through this mechanism that functional differences are reconciled one with another and the business (i.e. markets and corresponding segments) is thereby delineated. Furthermore, as markets are dynamic then the need for, and undertaking of, strategic debate is ongoing.
2. With this agreement, functions then need to be geared towards meeting the requirements of a firm's current and future markets. Thus, the role, priorities, developments and investments become the form in which each function's strategic contribution is expressed.

The first step, therefore, is to understand markets. To do this adequately companies need to set aside generic, broad-based statements and seek to identify market characteristics which recognise the level of difference which exists and the relevant dimensions in each of the segments in which they wish to compete.

3.4 Characteristics of Today's Markets: Difference and Speed of Change

As emphasised earlier in Chapter 2, whereas past markets were characterised by similarity and stability, the characteristics of current markets are their difference and high rate of change.

In addressing the task of strategic resolution, company approaches have differed. The range of alternatives is wide, and the variables which compose these differences include formality of approach, use of frameworks/approaches and the extent of the evolutionary nature of the process and outcomes. In evaluating the position to be taken on each dimension of these alternatives, however, companies need to bear in mind that improving approaches and outputs is a matter of degree and alternatives do not characteristically result in a substantial shift from their present position. In most markets it concerns incremental improvement and continuous adjustment.

The characteristics of today's markets are placing a greater need on understanding, and the strategic theme in this book is this need and the approaches to attaining this greater and necessary level of understanding. The framework outlined in the last chapter and the emphasis given to gaining more detailed market insights is illustrative of this line of argument. A wide range of methodologies has been put forward specifying approaches which would lead to strategic insights and appropriate answers. However, if any worked then all that companies would need to do would be to apply them. The problem is not that easy. The basis for a company to improve is in-depth understanding and a continuous and rigorous review of its markets.

Unless companies understand their markets better they will be unable to arrive at successful and workable strategic decisions. Only in this way will they be able to identify the strategic alternatives to meet the needs of their different markets and thus move away from prescriptive approaches and solutions. In the past researchers and consultants have offered both whilst executives have typically failed to understand what is on offer and thus have been unable to select what best suits their needs and to use these as part of their own strategic resolution. They continue, therefore, to put the cart before the horse and remain impeded by the failure to complete this fundamental task. As with most aspects of management, the essential ingredient in doing a task well is hard work. Understanding today's varied and fast-changing markets is no exception.

Identifying relevant order-winners and qualifiers, and the relative weightings to be attached to them helps companies to achieve these critical insights. The following sections describe the pertinent concepts and issues embodied in these criteria in terms of what they are and how they work.

3.5 Order-winners and Qualifiers: Basic Characteristics

This section on order-winners and qualifiers outlines important background before the specific criteria are discussed in the next section. Its purpose is to highlight characteristics and issues which need to be recognised and kept in mind when applying these concepts within a business.

- General statements about markets embody imprecise meanings. This leads to executives taking away from corporate strategy discussions their own understandings which are typically and understandably based on their own functional perspectives. Thus, a prerequisite for sound corporate-strategy development (i.e. agreement by all on what markets the company is and should be in and the characteristics of those markets) is missing.
- Order-winners and qualifiers are both market- and time-specific. Thus, the criteria relating to a market will need different levels of emphasis and will change over time. It follows, therefore, that there can be few general rules
- Following on from the last point, when developing order-winners and qualifiers there is a need to be specific in terms of distinguishing by market the level of importance for individual criteria. To do this, order-winners are weighted by allocating a total of 100 points while with qualifiers a distinction is made between a qualifier and an order-losing sensitive qualifier – one which will cause a business to lose customers' orders quickly. Examples of these dimensions were given earlier in Tables 2.2, 2.3 and 2.4 together with supporting narrative.
- Order-winners and qualifiers and their relative weightings will change over time. To assess these potential changes, weightings are assessed for the current period and two time-periods in the future. The latter will need to reflect the nature of the market and whereas for (say) a printing company the future time-periods may be next year and the year after, for an aerospace company (say) the forward look would need to be three and seven years respectively. Again, Tables 2.2, 2.3 and 2.4 illustrate these points
- In most instances, differences exist between the criteria needed to retain existing customers, and those needed to increase market-share/gaining prospective customers. These differences will need to be reflected in the relevant order-winners and qualifiers and their respective weightings
- Similarly, the criteria which relate to winning orders for a primary supplier will differ from those which relate to secondary/

other supplier categories. Although customers will tend to infer that the criteria are the same, common sense challenges that basic logic. The large percentage share of demand which typically goes to a primary supplier creates very different contractual demands and opportunities from those for other suppliers. Thus, the way in which secondary/other suppliers win their part of the contract needs to reflect this

● Not all order-winners and qualifiers are related to manufacturing. However, over time manufacturing-related criteria will typically come to the fore – for example, price and reliability of delivery.

3.6 Order-winners and Qualifiers: Specific Dimensions

As mentioned earlier, there is a range of order-winners and qualifiers and not all of them would be supported by manufacturing so they would not all form part of that function's strategic role. This section, therefore, separates the different categories and reviews typical criteria within each category. As stressed earlier, strategy is market- and time-specific and, therefore, not all order-winners and qualifiers will relate to or be of the same importance to all companies.

3.6.1 *Manufacturing-related and manufacturing-specific criteria*

This category concerns those order-winners and qualifiers which are specific to manufacturing and will, where relevant, form part of manufacturing's strategic role.

(A) *Price*
In many markets, and particularly in the growth, maturity and saturation phases of the product life cycle (see Figure 3.1), price becomes an increasingly important order-winning criterion. When this is so, manufacturing's task is to provide the low costs necessary to support the price-sensitivity of the market-place, thus creating the level of profit margin necessary to support the business investment involved and create opportunity for the future. As in many of the pertinent analyses in manufacturing, highlighting the pockets of significant cost will give direction to the areas where

FIGURE 3.1
The generalised product life-cycle

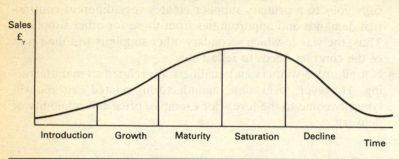

resource allocation should be made and management attention given.

In most of the manufacturing companies of Western Europe and other developed industrial nations, direct labour is only a small part of the total cost. Materials followed by overheads are usually the two main areas of cost, a factor which should be reflected in the information provision, allocation of resources and frequency of review. The likelihood, however, is that they are not.

As price has been an omnipresent factor in most markets there is often an inherent reticence to consider that this criterion may not be a relevant order-winner. This misunderstanding often stems from the fact that comparisons with alternatives will typically form part of a customer's evaluation of a product. However, for price to be an order-winner then margins will be low. Only in such situations will low-cost manufacturing be a priority task. Where margins are high then price is not an order-winner. In these types of market, customers will compare one price with another. This is not, however, to seek the lowest price but to check that the quoted price is in the broad band of what is acceptable. The evaluation described here is not unique to the criterion of price. Customers will typically cross-check all relevant criteria. In the case of qualifiers this is to ensure a 'ball-park' fit whilst for order-winners, customers will typically be looking for a 'better than' performance.

As explained earlier (p. 44), qualifiers get a company into, and maintain a company within, a market. As such, therefore, they do not win orders but are an essential prerequisite for a company to be considered as a potential supplier. Where price is a qualifier it does not mean that a company can charge whatever it wishes. It does, however, signal to the company that the key is to price a product in terms of what the market will bear and that it must keep its exploitation within sensible bounds. Failure to do so will, in turn, start to lose orders increasingly to those who are more competitively priced. Hence, in this situation a company will have turned a qualifying criterion (i.e. a product highly priced within acceptable limits) into an order-losing criterion where the price has become too high.

Returning now to a situation in which price is an order-winner then the low (or anticipated low) margins give manufacturing the clear task of reducing costs in order to maintain or improve available margins. Also, when a company decides to reduce price significantly and thus alter its role or its importance as an order-winner then related elements of manufacturing strategy will similarly have to be changed to reflect this. Companies which elect to alter the role of price would need, therefore, to assess the lead-times involved, investment implications and the extent of the cost-reduction potential. Making a strategic decision to reduce price without assessing these factors will invariably lead companies into inappropriate strategies, for the decision to reduce price, although difficult to evaluate, is easy to make. Achieving cost-reduction, on the other hand, is easy to evaluate but difficult to achieve.

● **Cost reduction** Many companies do not concentrate their efforts in the area of greatest cost. This still leads in many instances to most effort being directed by companies towards reducing direct-labour cost. Although there is still a need to improve productivity at all levels in an organisation, focusing on the area of greatest cost will tend to yield the best results. As overheads and materials typically account for some 85–90 per cent of total costs then giving these the *pro rata* attention they deserve makes sense but often is not undertaken. The traditional emphasis on the control and reduction of direct-labour cost still attracts most of the resources allocated to the overall cost reduction task. Tradition and experience of what to do still seem to reinforce these practices. (The effect of process lead-time reduction on elements of overhead costs is highlighted in a later section.)

Furthermore, concentrating on one aspect of cost rather than total costs can lead to lost opportunities. For instance, Heinz had undertaken a labour-cost-reduction plan at its Starkist tuna factories in Puerto Rico and American Samoa. With increasing competition from low-labour-cost areas, this policy seemed to make sense. But, a study revealed that the fish-workers were so overworked that each day they were leaving tons of meat still on the bone. Adding back workers, slowing down production lines, increasing supervision and retraining increased costs by $5m but cut food-waste by $15m, thus saving $10m each year.[1]

The need for companies to undertake continuous improvement as the basis for increasing productivity has been clearly identified and incorporated into the practices of many organisations. The key areas for re-evaluation, however, are broadly-based, reflecting the more significant areas of expense and cost-reduction opportunity. Typical lists include eliminating waste, product design, quality at source, process redesign, JIT production control systems, set-up reduction, overhead reduction and the involvement of people.[2]

● **Experience curves**   Evidence clearly shows that as experience accumulates, performance improves, and the experience curve is the quantification of this improvement. The basic phenomenon of the experience curve is that the cost of manufacturing a given item falls in a regular and predictable way as the total quantity produced increases. The purpose of this section is to draw attention to this relationship and its role in the formulation of manufacturing strategy. It is helpful to note that whilst the cost/volume relationship is the pertinent corporate issue, some of the examples will in fact relate price to volume because the information, not being company-derived, uses average industry price as a convenient substitute.

It is in almost everyone's experience that the price of a new product declines after its initial introduction and as it becomes more widely accepted and available. However, it is not so commonly recognised that over a wide range of products the cost follows a remarkably consistent decline. The characteristic pattern is that the cost declines (in constant £s) by a consistent percentage each time cumulative production is doubled. The effects of learning curves on labour costs have been recognised and reported over the past forty years beginning with studies on airframe production in the USA prior to the Second World War. However, experience curves are distinctly different from this. The real source of the experience effect is derived from organisational improvement. Although learning by individuals is important, it is only one of many improvements which accrue from experience. Investment in manufacturing processes, changes in production methods, product redesign and improvements in all functions in the business account for some part of the significant experience-related gains.

The experience curve is normally drawn by taking each doubling of cumulative unit production and expressing the unit cost or price as a percentage of the cost or price before doubling. So an 80 per cent experience curve would mean that the cost or price of the one-hundredth unit of a product is 80 per cent that of the fiftieth, of the two-hundredth, 80 per cent that of the one hundredth, and so on. Figures 3.2 and 3.3 shows the experience curve for random access memory (RAM) components in the period 1976 to 1984 and also illustrates the basic features of these curves which are now explained.[3]

1. The horizontal axis measures the cumulative quantity produced on a logarithmic scale. Figure 3.3 (a) and (b) shows the same information plotted on a linear and logarithmic scale, respectively. The information on Figure 3.3 (a) reveals a smooth curve and the implied regularity of the relationship between unit cost and total volume. However, Figure 3.3 (b) shows the same information plotted on double logarithmic scales. This presentation shows percentage changes as a constant distance, along either axis. The straight line on the log–log scale in Figure 3.3 (b) means that a given percentage change in one factor has resulted in a corresponding percentage change in the other. The nature of that relationship determines the slope of the line which can be read off a log–log grid.
2. Returning to Figure 3.2, the logarithmic scale shows that many doublings of production can be achieved early on, but later vastly larger quantities are needed to double the cumulative unit volumes then involved. This implies, as one would expect, that movement down the experience curve slows with time. Initially, additional growth in annual volumes can offset this but the levelling in demand associated with the mature stage in the

FIGURE 3.2

70 per cent experience curve for Random Access Memory (RAM) components in the period 1976 to 1984

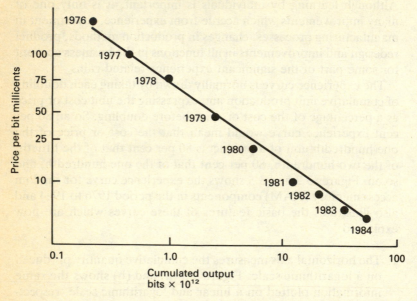

Source: P. Ghemawat. 'Building Strategy on the Experience Curve', *Harvard Business Review*, March–April 1985, pp. 143–49 (with permission)

product life-cycle and the eventual saturation and later decline through technical obsolescence will slow the rate of progress down the curve.

3. The vertical axis of the experience curve is usually cost or price per unit and is also expressed logarithmically. However, the cost or price per unit must be adjusted for inflation to allow comparisons to be drawn over time. Figure 3.2 shows that improvements further down the curve become, in absolute terms, quite small. Thus, as progress is made down the curve, each incremental movement will both take longer and yield less.

The characteristic decline in cost or price per unit was established by the Boston Consulting Group's (BCG) work in the 1960s and early 1970s as between 20 and 30 per cent for each doubling of

FIGURE 3.3
Cost/volume or price/volume relationship expressed on
(a) a linear, and (b) a log–log scale

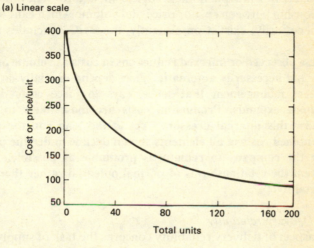

(a) Linear scale

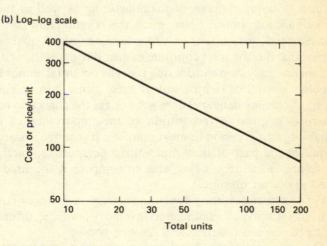

(b) Log–log scale

cumulative production. Although the BCG claim that this can go on (in constant £s) without limit and despite the rate of experience growth, in reality this tends not to happen for the reasons expressed earlier.

Furthermore, it is important to stress that the experience curve characteristics are phenomenological in nature. They portray a relationship between cost or price and volume which can, but does not necessarily, exist. Consequently, the BCG concludes that:

these observed or inferred reductions in costs as volume increases are not necessarily automatic. They depend crucially on a competent management that seeks ways to force costs down as volume expands. Production costs are most likely to decline under this internal pressure. Yet in the long run the average combined costs of all elements should decline under the pressure for the company to remain as profitable as possible. To this extent the relationship is of normal potential rather than one of certainty.[4]

(B) *Delivery reliability*
The aspect of delivery reliability concerns the task of supplying the products ordered on the agreed due date. On-time delivery, therefore, is a major concern of manufacturing as well as the distribution function. In many businesses, this criterion now constitutes a qualifier and, very often, an order-losing sensitive qualifier. This means that if companies continue to miss due dates then customers will increasingly stop considering them as potential names for their supplier short lists. Thus, unless these firms start qualifying in terms of on-time delivery, they will not get the chance to compete. There is a growing recognition of the importance of delivery reliability as a criterion in most markets. Its change towards being a qualifier is part of that competitive perspective. Increasingly, therefore, a factor in being able to compete is the fundamental need to deliver on time.[5]

For the manufacturing function this aspect involves considerations of capacity, scheduling and inventory holdings, principally in terms of work-in-progress and finished goods.

The exactness of the due date can vary from an appointed hour on a given day to delivery of the agreed quantity starting (and finishing) in an agreed week. The level of data collection, the timing and proactive nature of the feedback to customers will need to form part of this decision. As a rule, the more exact the agreed delivery is, then the more proactive a supplier should be in the collection of the data, the regularity of the performance summary and its feedback (with comments) to the customer concerned.

In addition, these data are also the source of information concerning the size of 'call-offs' (what a customer actually wants rather than the total quantities expressed in any contract or agreement) and the lead-times associated with the delivery itself. The former concerns the issue of costs and price agreements whilst the latter leads into the criterion of delivery speed.

(C) *Delivery speed*

In some markets orders may be won through a company's ability to deliver more quickly than its competitors, or when it is able to meet the delivery date required when only some or even none of the competition can do so. Products which compete in this way, therefore, need a manufacturing process which can respond to this requirement. There are two perspectives to the issue of delivery speed. The one is where the process lead-time, whilst being shorter than the delivery time required by the customer, is difficult to achieve because the current forward order load (also known as order backlog) on manufacturing capacity plus the process lead-time to complete the order is greater than the delivery time required (see Situation 1, Figure 3.4). The resolution of this is through either a short-term increase in capacity (e.g. overtime working), or by rescheduling existing jobs or using a combination of both.

The other is where the process lead-time is greater than the customer delivery requirement (see Situation 2, Figure 3.4). In these situations, manufacturing (for a given process technology), can only meet the customer's delivery requirement by either increasing short-term capacity or holding inventory and thus reducing the process lead time by completing part of manufacturing before the order point and hence in anticipation of winning these types of orders. In addition, scheduling changes may be used to facilitate the accomplishment of the task but will not in themselves resolve this type of situation.

FIGURE 3.4
Situations where delivery speed is an order-winning criterion to be provided by manufacturing

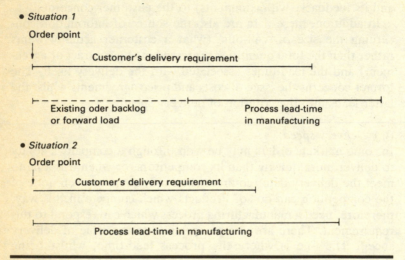

- *Situation 1*

Order point
↓

Customer's delivery requirement

Existing oder backlog   Process lead-time
or forward load   in manufacturing

- *Situation 2*

Order point
↓

Customer's delivery requirement

Process lead-time in manufacturing

FIGURE 3.5
A situation where delivery speed is not an order-winning criterion

Order point
↓

Customer's delivery requirement

Existing order   backlog   Process lead-time in
or forward   load   manufacturing

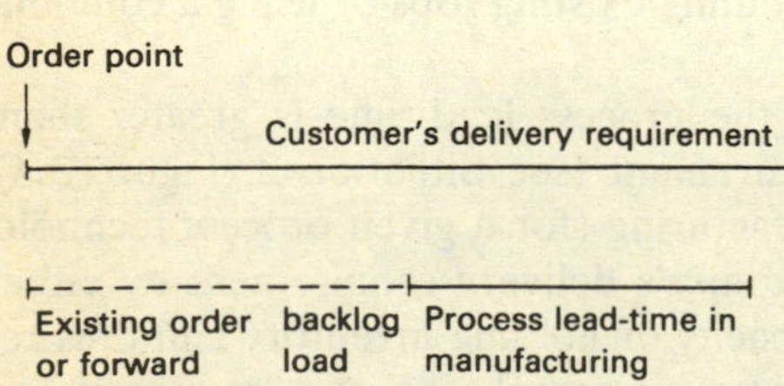

Where process lead time and existing order backlog do not exceed the customer's delivery requirement, then the criterion of delivery speed is not an issue (see Figure 3.5).

With regard to delivery, it is important to distinguish between delivery promise (that is, committing the company to deliver in line with a customer's requirements) and delivery speed. The former can be a commitment in any of the situations described by Figures 3.4 and 3.5 whereas the latter only appertains to situations similar to those given in Figure 3.4.

Increasingly, companies are finding that lead-times are reducing. Others are endeavouring to shorten them reactively, if not proactively, in line with their perception of their markets or to get a competitive edge. The levels of improvement which can be achieved are incredible, as testified by Tables 3.1 and 3.2 below. An organisation's response to reducing lead-times needs to be corporate wide. One principal contributor, however, is manufacturing. (Note that lead-time reduction in product development is addressed under the section on design covered later in the chapter.) From the moment an order reaches the factory, all elements of lead-time need to be reviewed with the aim of reducing each component involved in the total process. To succeed, companies must transform themselves and simply break the paradigms that hold current procedures and norms in place.[6]

Companies can knowingly offer short lead-times to customers by holding excess capacity, maintaining low-/zero-order backlogs/

TABLE 3.1
Superfast producers

| Company | Product | Time taken (weeks) from order to finished goods | |
		old	new
GE	Circuit breaker boxes	3.0	0.6
Motorola	Pagers	3.0	0.05
Hewlett-Packard	Electronic test equipment	4.0	1.0
Brunswick	Fishing reels	3.0	1.0

Source: B. Dumaine, 'How Managers Can Succeed Through Speed', *Fortune*, 13 February 1989, pp. 54–9 (with permission)

TABLE 3.2
Typical improvements in production flow times

	Example		Before	After	% reduction
Japan	Washing machines (Matsushita)	Hours	360	2	99
	Motorcycles (Harley-Davidson)		360	3	99
USA	Motor controllers	Days	56	7	88
	Electric components		24	1	96
	Radar detectors		22	3	86

Source: G. Stalk and T. M. Hout, *Competing Against Time: How Time-Based Competition is Reshaping Global Markets* (New York: Free Press, 1990) p. 67 (with permission)

forward loads, or holding inventory at any or all stages in the process. However, in these situations such decisions are not manufacturing-related, as they should emanate from a corporate-based agreement. Furthermore, such circumstances will not then constitute a delivery-speed requirement as defined above since manufacturing will be in a situation similar to that given in Figure 3.5. Manufacturing's role, however, would be to maintain the various elements on which such decisions are based. A supplier's promise to deliver by an agreed date then leads to the aspect of delivery reliability, which was described in the last section.

With customers typically reducing their own lead-times, many companies are finding that the element of delivery speed is becoming an increasing factor in their markets. Consequently, customer lead-times are shorter than the combined lead-times of material purchase and manufacture (see Figure 3.4). A firm's response to delivery speed, as with all criteria, can be either reactive or pro-active. By being reactive, a company will cope with the necessary lead-time reduction as and when it occurs, by some combination of priority-changing, expediting, short-term capacity uplifts or living with some level of failure to delivery on time. By being proactive, a company will reduce its own lead-times thereby obviating delivery speed from being a factor internally whilst exploiting short lead-times in the market-place. Possible scenarios in which companies may be involved are outlined in Table 3.3. This sets out a series of time-related alternatives and firms need to determine their current and preferred position by market as the first step to establishing a strategic response. Where companies are positioned their potential opportunity to reduce lead times will depend on the nature of their markets (for example, whether they sell standard or special products and offer a design-and-manufacturing, or manufacturing-only, capability) and their decisions to hold different levels of raw materials/components, work-in-progress and finished-goods inventory. As a company moves (or is able to move) from point 1 to 5 in Table 3.3 then overall lead-times will reduce. However, as explained above, any repositioning is a corporate decision directly affecting the element of delivery-speed. Adjusting its position on this continuum so as to eliminate or reduce the impact of delivery speed would then need to be supported by shortening each element of lead-time within the overall process. This would involve a whole range of decisions including capacity, inventory holdings and set-up reduction.

Finally, time-based management has a further, significant advantage. Compared with the more traditional, bureaucratic or entrepreneurial approaches it leads to reductions in overhead costs as shown in Figure 3.6.

(D) *Quality*

Quality as a competitive criterion has been thrust onto centre stage since the late 1970s. Although its importance has been recognised throughout this period many companies have failed to compete on this dimension. In part this is because the definition of the word quality has been broadened to encompass many dimensions. The result has been a lack of understanding and subsequent lack of direction, the hallmark of generic statements which characterise strategy formulation (see p. 33). Table 3.4 lists eight dimensions of quality and identifies the function(s) which would typically assume prime responsibility for its provision.[7] However in many instances and as recognised here, by separating criteria into 'manufacturing-related and manufacturing-specific', 'manufacturing-related but not manufacturing specific', and 'non-manufacturing-related', there is overlap. Single and joint provision is, therefore, the outcome.

TABLE 3.3
Alternative responses to markets and their lead-time implications

Initial positions	Length of lead-times
1. *Design to order** new product response where companies design and manufacture a product to meet the specific needs of a customer	**Long**
2. *Engineer to order* changes to standard products are offered to customers and only made to order. Lead-times include the relevant elements of engineering design and all manufacturing	
3. *Make to order* concerns manufacturing a standard product (any customisation is nominal and does not increase total lead-times) only on receipt of a customer order or against an agreed schedule or call-off	
4. *Assemble to order* components and subassemblies have been made to stock. On receipt of an order (or against an agreed schedule or call-off) the required parts are drawn from work-in-progress/ component inventory and assembled to order	
5. *Make to stock* finished goods are made ahead of demand in line with sales forecasts. Customer's orders are met from inventory.	**Short**

*Note: some customers require companies to make to print (i.e. make a product in line with a given drawing). In such markets, lead-times only include raw-materials purchase/supply and manufacturing. They do not include design, but some customer-induced redesign during the process will often be involved (see p. 81, which explains this).

FIGURE 3.6
Overhead costs incurred in time-based management approaches compared with those involved in classic structures

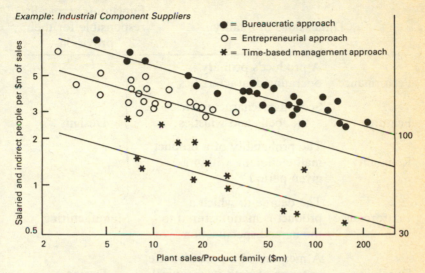

Example: Industrial Component Suppliers

● = Bureaucratic approach
○ = Entrepreneurial approach
✳ = Time-based management approach

Note: 'Indirect people' includes all hourly factory support personnel.

Sources: G. S. Stalk, Jnr, and T. M. Hout, *Competing against Time: How time-based competition is reshaping global markets* (New York: Free Press, 1990), p. 54 (with permission)

One reason why companies do not compete in the quality domain is their failure to clarify which dimension(s) of quality will provide the best results in given markets. Identifying the different dimensions involved is the first step. The next is to agree which (and to what extent each) needs addressing.

In the context of this section, the aspect of quality which concerns manufacturing provision is that of conformance – making a product to specification. Linked closely to design (which determines the specification itself – see Table 3.4) quality within this definition is a key manufacturing task. Its role in most markets has now been changed from an order-winner to a qualifier.[8] In part this has been brought about by Japanese companies who, as a facet of their competitive thrust in several industrial markets, made

TABLE 3.4
The dimensions of quality and the function(s) typically responsible for their provision

Dimensions of quality		Function(s) typically responsible for their provision
Performance	A product's primary operating characteristics	⎫
Features	Secondary characteristics: the 'bells and whistles'	⎬ Design
Reliability	The probability of a product malfunctioning within a given period	⎭
Conformance	The degree to which a product is manufactured to the agreed specification	Manufacturing
Durability	A measure of a product's life in terms of both its technical and economic dimensions	Design
Serviceability	The ease of servicing (planned or breakdown) to include the speed and provision of aftersales service	Design and After-sales
Aesthetics	How the final product looks	Design
Perceived quality	How a customer views the product	Marketing and Design

products of a high quality. The result has been similar to the colour-television example given on p. 44. Companies, in order to stay in relevant markets, needed to increase their product quality. Having done so, the role of quality then changed from an order-winner to a qualifier. Today, customers expect products to be of a high quality thus recognising (at least intuitively) that quality is a given.

The recent attention attracted by quality-based approaches in management has further highlighted the emphasis on the advantages of completing tasks correctly the first time. This, in part, has been an extension of the improvements in product quality and the significant benefits which have been secured. Much has been written on the approaches which have underpinned this success.[9]

(E) *Demand increases*

In some markets a company's ability to respond to increases in demand is an important factor in winning orders. These sales may reflect the high seasonality of customers' requirements or be of a spasmodic or one-off nature. This factor concerns the level of predictability surrounding demand itself as well as others such as product shelf-life and the frequency of product modifications in line with market requirements. All will affect manufacturing in terms of its response.

With known seasonal demand, the opportunity for agreement to be reached between supplier/manufacturer/distributor/retailer about inventory holdings throughout the process, process capacity and planned uplifts in labour (e.g. overtime working, additional shifts), is available. With one-off or spot businesses (e.g. during an influenza epidemic when the demand is for the same product which may have a short shelf-life, thus limiting viable inventory levels; or where a product is customer-specified at some point in the process and, therefore, cannot be made ahead of demand; or a significant order for a product over and above agreed call-off quantities or simply an unexpected, sizeable order for a given product) holding materials or other forms of capacity, arranging short-term uplifts in labour capacity (e.g. through overtime) re-arranging priorities, or some combination of these will typically be a supplier's response.

The phenomena described here provide another example of the way that a lack of essential clarity can lead to serious levels of corporate misunderstanding. The generalised discussion surrounding these key aspects of a business is typically enveiled in words such as flexibility.[10] However, to determine the extent to which a company intends to respond to these significant uplifts in demand is a strategic decision of some magnitude. To allow each function to respond to its own interpretation invariably leads to major areas of mismatch.

(F) *Product range*

As highlighted earlier, markets are increasingly characterised by difference, not similarity. However, the balance between levels of customisation and the volume base for repetitive manufacturing has to be addressed by bringing together the relevant parts of the organisation to select from alternatives. That markets are increasingly segmenting is a given. Manufacturing's role is to continue to develop processes that are flexible in terms not only of coping with product-range differences but also of providing low-cost results. It needs, therefore, to be able to bridge these essential differences in order to retain the volume base so essential to efficient manufacturing.

Thus, where product ranges are widening, process developments need to reflect the broadening nature of the product base and the lower-volume implications which tend to go hand in hand with these trends. The former needs to be recognised at the time when process investments are made. The latter is reflected in reduced set-up times whether manual or automated (e.g. numerically-controlled facility) so enabling companies to cope with the lower-volume nature of these changes and yet retain the necessary levels of cost.

Examples of these trends are seen in the automobile industry. The pressure on automobile-makers at the lower end of the volume scale is to continue to differentiate their products as a way of competing not only with their traditional competitors, but with makers at the higher end of the volume scale as well. BMW's 7 Series offers a marked uplift in customisation, more akin to the very low-volume luxury makers such as Rolls Royce and Aston Martin. Hand-crafted leather interiors, and its 'any colour' option are examples of this. However, BMW is also aware that Toyota is already planning a production system capable of responding speedily to individual customer requirements. However, as with all companies, to support increases in product/colour-range options successfully, manufacturing needs to develop its processes to provide these in a cost- and time-efficient way. At the moment BMW's non-standard colour option takes extra time and cost because paint lines have to be cleaned out.[11] A priority in manufacturing is, therefore, to develop a paint-spraying capability to reduce this problem.

3.6.2 *Manufacturing-related but not manufacturing-specific criteria*

Although businesses separate clusters of activities into different functions, in reality they are – and need to form – part of the same whole. Thus, many functions within a company will be directly supportive of manufacturing or will undertake tasks which link or directly affect that function in terms of both its strategic and operational roles.

(A) *Design*

The links between design, manufacturing and markets are the very essence of a business. The way that these interrelate, therefore, is a fundamental, strategic issue. Both design and manufacturing's aim is to provide products in terms of both their technical and business specification (see pp. 115–16). In addition, these two functions also combine to provide the product developments which come before the on-going selling/manufacturing activity which is the commercial substance of companies. Three of the more important dimensions are addressed in this section and have been chosen because they are fundamental to this basic corporate activity.*

• **Low cost**   Design is becoming increasingly important in providing essential support for several criteria relevant to today's markets. Products have to be designed in line with process characteristics and also with cost-reduction in mind. Thus, design not only concerns functionality but also has a critical impact on product costs. With direct materials typically accounting for some 40–60 per cent of the total then the opportunities to reduce costs at source are substantial. In addition, this essential link reinforces the need to meet the design for manufacturing requirements in terms of labour-cost reduction through increased automation and other labour-saving opportunities. For many years, Western European corporate appeals to design for manufacture have been more in the category of exhortation than accomplishment. However, in the 1990s, pressure on price will, in many segments, continue to be an

---

* The dimensions of quality listed in Table 3.4 and which relate to design function provision are addressed in a later section (pp. 92–3).

important competitive factor. Thus, design's role in the total corporate response is fundamental in more ways than one.

● **Product range** The increasing level of product diversification has already been recognised as an important factor in today's increasingly competitive markets (pp. 39–40), and central to this provision is the design function. The pressure on design will vary from market to market and the interpretation and execution of these is central to a company's ability to remain competitive. The tendency for West European designers to be more interested in functionality than the commercial facets of design is in marked contrast to competitors, particularly the Japanese. As Hiroyuki Yoshida, head of Toyota's design centre, reflected, 'Whatever the merits of a design, it has to be robust enough to go through our engineering and manufacturing system. The commercial point of design has not been lost. We are in the business to make low cost, high quality cars for a mass market. We are making cars, not art.'[12]

However, within this context markets, as highlighted elsewhere (pp. 62–3) are increasingly segmenting. Design needs to be able to meet these changes and to recognise, certainly in terms of attitude and speed of response, that change is a fundamental characteristic of today's markets and a company's essential support. For example, Honda has had to move from developing its Accord range as a world car (the same model selling into all markets) in the early 1980s to designing two distinct ranges for its home and US markets.

It is now the age of diversification and those companies unable to keep pace with this growth of diversity will decline. Many companies, therefore, are directing much more attention to incorporating the perspectives and preferences of customers into future designs. A classic example of this is provided by Toyota and Mazda. Both have built complexes in Tokyo which incorporate vehicle-design studios in which the visiting public are invited to 'design' their own cars. Backed by support staff, ideas on what constitutes a potential customer's ideal vehicle are captured as part of the input into future designs.

However, the demand for styling and product features has to be reconciled with other pressures. Environmentally-friendly products are not only a growing concern of customers but also high on the agenda of legislative bodies. For example, clean-air legislation in California is at the forefront of changing pressures on vehicle design. Its requirement for minimum percentage sales of low-emission vehicles (LEVs) and ultra-low-emission vehicles (ULEVs) has been an added stimulus for improvements on all car and emission standards. Furthermore, the legislation also requires that by 1998, at least 2 per cent of all manufacturers' sales will need to be zero-emission vehicles (ZEVs) and this will rise to 10 per cent by the year 2003. Unless there is a major breakthrough in existing engine technology, this means that companies will need to have developed an electric car towards the end of this decade.

The need to harness design capabilities to meet these environmentally-stimulated developments has been recognised by most major car-makers. In 1991, General Motors, Ford and Chrysler concluded an agreement with the US Government under which a total of $1 billion is to be spent over a period of twelve years to develop advanced battery technology. Similarly, to meet the Los Angeles initiative, the Anglo-Swedish group, Clean Air Transport won a contract to supply 3500 electric cars starting at the end of 1992, and Los Angeles City Council, LA Water and Power, and Southern California Edison have contributed about one-third of the £21m project costs as part of a joint research and development agreement. For their part, production of these vehicles will be relocated to Los Angeles from 1993.[13]

• **Lead-times**   Reducing lead-times within the manufacturing process has already been highlighted as an increasingly important order-winner (pp. 73–7). Similarly, speed to market with new product designs and developments is becoming a significant competitive factor in today's markets. The increasing priority of speed is based on the recognition that it can simply negate the competition. The results of such improvements, as shown in Table 3.5 and Figure 3.7, speak for themselves. In addition, companies receive a number of distinct sets of advantages from reducing product-design and development lead-times including the following:

1   *Benefits of double gain*   Being first in the market brings advantages of both higher volumes and higher margins – the opportunity for double gain – as explained below:

(a) **Product life-cycles are extended**   if a product is introduced sooner, rarely will it become obsolete sooner. This advantage

TABLE 3.5
Superfast innovators

Company	Product	Development time (years)	
		old	new
Honda	Cars	5.0	3.0
AT & T	Telephones	2.0	1.0
Navistar	Trucks	5.0	2.5
Hewlett-Packard	Computer printers	4.5	1.8

Source: B. Dumaine, 'How Managers Can Succeed Through Speed', *Fortune*, 13 February 1989, pp. 54–9 (with permission).

accrues even more so where customers incur high switching costs. The usual outcome, therefore, of early product introduction is to gain more customers who, in turn, stay longer – see Figure 3.8.

(b) **Increased market share**   the first producer will, in the beginning, command 100 per cent market share. Thus, the earlier a product appears then the more likely the prospects of obtaining a large market share. Link this factor to (a) above and the impact on total life-cycle volumes is marked.

(c) **Higher profit margins**   a company will naturally enjoy a higher level of pricing freedom in the early stages of a product's life-cycle. This will, therefore, provide higher margins in the early stages with the opportunity for manufacturing to provide lower costs in the light of the volume advantages highlighted above – see Figure 3.9 and also the earlier section on experience curves (pp. 68–72).

(d) **Double gain**   (a), (b) and (c) combine to give a situation of double gain – companies gain higher sales and also achieve a higher margin on each sale.

2   *Technology, consumer preference and corporate image*   Reductions in product-development lead-times also provide opportunities for companies to sustain technology leadership and corporate image:

FIGURE 3.7
Examples of reductions in product-development lead-times

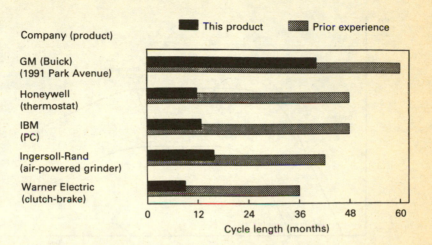

Source: Based on P. G. Smith and D. G. Reinertsen, *Developing Products in Half the Time* (New York: Van Norstrand Reinhold, 1991) p. 2, Figure 1.1 (with permission)

(a) **Exploiting technology opportunities** if an organisation can develop products quickly then it is more able to synchronise its product developments with the latest technologies and thus exploit these opportunities to the full.

(b) **Matching consumer change** short product-development lead-times help a business to match market changes thereby tracking more closely changes in consumer preferences and demands.

(c) **Corporate image** developing products more quickly will help a firm to maintain its corporate image for being a progressive front-runner in developments and technology excellence.

3 *Reduction in design costs* Compressing development lead-times also results in a reduction in design costs. This is achieved in

FIGURE 3.8
The increased sales-revenue element of double gain

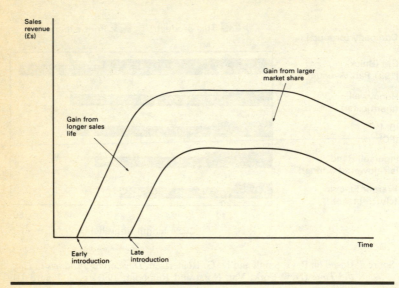

part by increased levels of cooperation and thereby reducing mis-understandings on the one hand whilst incorporating functional perspectives throughout. In addition, the changed role and contribution of design within the process also leads to less time being spent within the design stages with associated reductions in cost.

Table 3.5 and Figure 3.7 provided examples of what can be achieved whilst Figures 3.10, 3.11 and Table 3.6 show how this is accomplished. The position illustrated in Figure 3.10 compares a Japanese and Western Company making the same products, mechanical transmissions. As the figure shows, while the Western Company required 30 to 38 months to complete the development and introduction cycles, the Japanese affiliate took 14 to 18 months. A review of Figure 3.11 illustrates the source of this advantage. Whilst some elements in the process yield a substantial gain, the improvement is more cumulative in nature and emanates from two sources. Steps, at least in part, are completed not

FIGURE 3.9
The higher profit-margin element of double gain

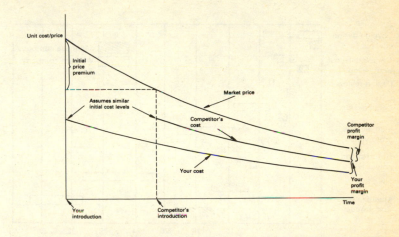

sequentially but in parallel whilst each step is typically shorter.

A review of Table 3.6 shows similar characteristics to those illustrated in Figure 3.11. It also highlights another important feature – companies within this revision do not just accelerate a stage *per se* but recognise that it may need to rethink the activities within one phase and its role in the new approach. The 'approval' phase in DEC's revised procedures illustrates this outcome.

Table 3.6 which compares development lead-times for European, US and Japanese car-makers, provides a more detailed illustration of these sources of lead-time reduction.[14]

Part of the source of this improvement stems from the changing values within the different functions involved. The expectation of Western designers is to develop a product which requires little or no modification. As perfection is rarely, if ever, achieved then the later phases identify any changes to be made. However, also part of the typical design function's attitudes is an inbuilt resistance to change which, given the perfection syndrome explained earlier, is perceived to imply failure. The result is long first-phase lead-times which are subsequently further increased due to the inherent

FIGURE 3.10
Improving response time in new-product development –
mechanical transmissions

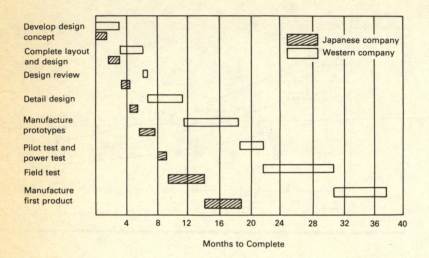

Source: G. Stalk, Jnr, and T. M. Hout, *Competing Against Time: How Time-based
Competition is Reshaping Global Markets* (New York: Free Press, 1990)
p. 188, Exhibit 4-1, (with permission)

resistance to change which increases the length of this phase of the
process.

The Japanese alternative is based on a different set of expectations. Knowing that to design perfection is impossible, designers
conclude their proposals much more quickly than their Western
counterparts and, being ready to accept change, respond to the
demands of the modification stages with appropriate expectations
and corresponding speed. The result is a significant overall reduction in development lead-times.

(B) *Distribution*
Distribution's role in quick and reliable delivery has been mentioned earlier. As part of the total process, distribution plays an
essential role in delivery.

FIGURE 3.11
**Digital Equipment Company (DEC)'s reduced competition time
for a new product development (with permission)[15]**

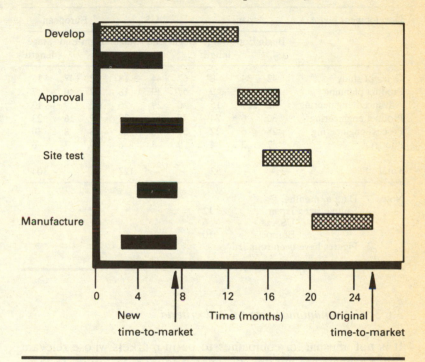

In addition, the costs of this facet of overall provision have typically been rising both in themselves and as a percentage of the total. Including the costs of storage, warehouse administration and movement, this element of cost has typically not received the same level of attention as the product itself. Classical examples of this are items which have experienced systematic and significant cost-reductions over a number of years – for example, computers. Highlighting the potential source of cost-reduction has often escaped the attention of related activities.[16]

TABLE 3.6
Average project lead-times and stage-length in US, Japanese and European car-makers[17]

Development phase	Japanese			US			European		
	Begin	End	Stage length	Begin	End	Stage length	Begin	End	Stage length
Concept study	42	34	8	62	44	18	62	47	15
Product planning	38	29	9	57	39	18	57	40	17
Advanced engineering	42	27	15	56	29	26	52	39	13
Product engineering	30	6	24	40	12	28	39	16	23
Process engineering	28	6	22	31	6	26	38	8	30
Pilot run	7	3	4	9	3	6	9	3	6
Total	–	–	82	–	–	122	–	–	104

Note: 1. Data in months
2. Sample size: Japan   12
                      USA   6
                      Europe   10
3. Figures have been rounded

3.6.3 *Non-manufacturing-related criteria*

It is not unusual for companies to be in markets whose relevant order-winners are not directly related to manufacturing. In these types of markets, manufacturing will typically be required to support one or more qualifiers. Some of the more important criteria which frequently characterise markets are now briefly discussed. In all instances, each function responsible for the criterion reviewed will have the task of providing and maintaining the required level of support.

Design leadership
The role of design and its relationship to competitive issues such as product-development lead-times and product costs have already been discussed. However, one of the design function's principal roles concerns the development of products in terms of features, aesthetics, perceived levels of design in specification and reliability

(including costs) whilst in service (see Table 3.4). Furthermore, where frequent design introductions offer a competitive edge then this requirement will be at the forefront of the function's performance priorities.

The importance of product design has always been recognised. Markets can be dominated by this dimension, and unique design, particularly in the past, has been considered the principal order-winning provision to be made by this function. However, companies are increasingly recognising the range of contributions which the design function can make in winning orders, the key elements of which have been discussed in earlier sections.

Being an existing supplier
Where a company is an existing supplier, it may continue to win orders in part, or solely, due to this factor. The criterion tends to be relevant to both low volume and spares markets. In the former, manufacturing needs to continue to support the relevant order-winners and qualifiers. In the latter market, it needs to meet relevant criteria recognising the impact which its performance on these contracts will have on orders for any new or existing products in the future.

Marketing and sales
The marketing and sales functions' principal orientation is towards the market-place. Its important links to customers and its insights into the characteristics of relevant market segments ranging from issues of pricing, competitive threats, growth and/or decline of existing segments through to the identification of new opportunities is an essential part of a company's strategic provision.

Brand name
Companies, through a variety of activities ranging from design, advertising and increasing or maintaining market share, seek to establish brand names for their products. Where this has been achieved and maintained then companies will win orders, at least in part, due to the image its products have in the markets in which they compete.

Technical liaison and support
In certain markets, customers will seek technical liaison from

suppliers during the pre-contract phase and technical support thereafter. The quality and extent of a supplier's in-house technical capability to support product development, particularly towards its introduction in the early stages of its manufacture will, therefore, be an important criterion in these markets.

After-sales support
Furthermore, companies may look for ways of differentiating their total product by offering, for instance, a high level of customer support (see Table 3.4, 'Serviceability'). One example is afforded by BMW who have a fleet of 30 cars, funded jointly with its dealers and strategically placed throughout the UK. The purpose is to go to the support of any BMW which has broken down by the roadside. The company will continue to increase this standby fleet until there are sufficient to deal with 80 per cent of the breakdowns occuring in all the BMWs in the UK that can actually be solved at the roadside.

A further example of after-sales support is the motor repairs sector. Compact discs enable a mechanic to call up information on any component or car by typing in the relevant part or the vehicle's chassis number. In repair procedure terms, the mechanic can find out which faults cause which problems and what procedures should be followed. Service sales staff are similarly able to investigate customer details and vehicle records to help in their service-support provision. Companies already using these customer support systems include Volkswagen, BMW, Opel, PSA (Peugeot and Citroen), General Motors and Toyota.

3.7 Benchmarking[18]

The failure of a company to assess and monitor its competitors is at best a mark of corporate complacency and at worst a sign of strategic naivety, and for a company, such a monitoring process has two important dimensions:

- a continuous updating of the level and dimensions of competition within its markets;
- proactivity, seeking to improve its own business performance by learning from other companies about what can be done and how to do things better.

Benchmarking is an approach which was identified and highlighted in the mid-1980s and which many companies believe is essential to help to enhance their competitive position in the 1990s. The way it does this is to redirect the corporate spotlight from assessing internal performance (typically using internal measures) to an external check on how current (albeit improved) performance compares with best practice. In this way it reinforces the clear need to identify market requirements, to differentiate importance and establish the levels of performance which need to be achieved within each competitive dimension.

As shown in the earlier section on experience curves, all companies tend to learn and improve through time but the key question is whether the rate of improvement is adequate to become and/or remain competitive. Benchmarking forces companies to look outwards and recognise this external perspective as the appropriate way to identify the levels of performance which need to become their new targets. Furthermore, checking against performance in other businesses (and particularly in unrelated sectors) leads to some distinct advantages:

- It presents the 'what' rather than the 'how'. Thus, companies are presented with targets not solutions which, in turn, increases the aspect of ownership. The 'panacea syndrome' mentioned on pp. 61 and 161 also identifies the inappropriateness of solution-oriented approaches.
- Having targets to aim for helps to create a uniform response from all parts of a business. When goals are common then improvement becomes a shared task.
- It reinforces the executive role (rather than that of support staff) as the key element for bringing about sustained performance improvements.
- External (and particularly ex-sector) comparisons are often perceived as being more objectively derived and therefore more readily accepted.
- It opens up new improvement horizons which frequently represent a stepped change in performance. In so doing it provides the opportunity to leapfrog competitors in selected and relevant dimensions of performance.

Benchmarking is concerned with the search for best practices, whatever their source, in order to identify superior performance.

It therefore involves continuously measuring a company's products, services and practices against both competitors and the leaders in any business sector. It is, however, not an end in itself but a means to help to achieve superior levels of competitiveness. In this way, it offers an important dimension within the domain of order-winners by ensuring that corporate performance against relevant criteria are measured against externally-derived, 'best-practice' norms. Benchmarking, therefore, moves a company from having an inward bias to one of incorporating external perspectives which invariably introduce a stepped change in terms of performance. These external antennae help to assess what is going on and also help a company to manage itself within its own environment.

Implementing benchmarking starts with determining the key functions within a business which need to be reviewed. When the relevant performance variables to measure these functions have been agreed then identifying 'best-in-class' performances sets the target. What follows is the task of assessing the action programmes to bring corporate performance into line with and then to surpass that achieved by the best-in-class companies.

However, for benchmarking to be successfully implemented, some key elements need to be in place. These include:

- **rigour**   it is essential that companies ensure that the targets to be achieved are set high enough. Targets, therefore, need to be derived from knowledge and not intuition;
- **overcoming disbelief**   in the initial phases of this process, companies often need to convince themselves that they can not only do better but can meet the often daunting task which benchmarking reviews typically identify;
- **accountability**   benchmarking represents an on-going procedure for measuring performance and ensuring improvement. A prerequisite for this is to instill in everyone the responsibility and authority for identifying, checking and implementing the changes necessary to achieve this improvement;
- **culture change**   managers typically spend most of their time on internal issues. Reorientating companies to be outward-looking rather than internally focused is an essential facet of the successful introduction and on-going development of this approach and associated improvement.

3.7.1 *Best-in-class exemplars*

Throughout, the need for companies to assess themselves against externally-derived standards has been stressed. Thus, examples need to be identified from a number of different company classifications including:

- direct competitors;
- companies in the same industrial sector but not direct competitors;
- latent competitors;
- companies outside-the-industry.

Recognising the different categories enables a firm to identify a broader range of potential best-in-class sources, thereby improving the quality and representative nature within this critical phase. An example which illustrates the advantages of using best-in-class exemplars is afforded by Figure 3.12. IBM's use of outside-the-industry perspectives helped it to identify its future targets.

3.7.2 *Ways to close the gap then surpass exemplars*

Improving performance is the result of a number of coordinated actions in line with the key functions already identified. The particular improvements will need to reflect the tasks on hand. However, it is important to recognise the different levels of achievement which companies will need to consider in order to ensure that they recognise the relative level which they are striving to achieve:

- try harder – a classic approach which, if adopted, implies a failure to recognise the principles underpinning benchmarking;
- emulate – setting achievement targets on a par with competitors and/or best-in-class exemplars;
- leapfrog – setting targets higher than existing exemplar norms;
- change the rules of the game – pace-setting achievements which constitute a move to driving the order-winners and qualifiers in relevant markets.

These dimensions constitute target levels of change. The difficulty many companies face at the beginning is in identifying the different levels of achievement. Many find that looking outside

FIGURE 3.12
Benchmarking quality helped IBM to identify its 'Best-in-class' six-sigma target for 1994

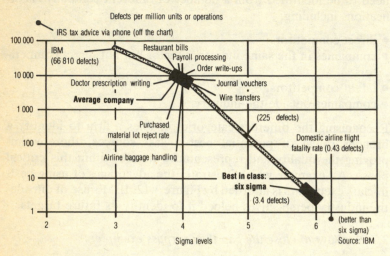

Note: At the beginning of 1990, IBM admitted its overall defect rate was around three sigma, or 66 810 defects per million operations. By 1994, IBM wants to reach six sigma.

Source: B. C. P. Rayner, 'Market-driven Quality: IBM Six-sigma Crusade', *Electronic Business*, 15 October 1990, p. 28 (with permission)

helps to more clearly identify levels of higher achievement as shown in Table 3.7.

3.7.3   *Competitors are moving targets*

Earlier, the need to recognise that order-winners and qualifiers change over time was stressed. This is because markets are dynamic and competitors are moving targets. Companies who set their sights without taking into account these dimensions may find themselves further behind. By failing to identify the rate of improvement of competitors, companies may set themselves targets only to find that the goal-posts have moved. The result is that at best they have closed the gap. However, more typically the out-

TABLE 3.7
Source and levels of targeted achievement

Exemplar	Level of achievement	
	Emulate	Change the rules of the game
Direct competitors	80	20
Industry sector but not competitor		
Latent competitor		
Outside the industry	20	80

come is that a company which fails to incorporate the future rate of improvement of its competitors will find itself even further behind and less able to catch up.

3.8 Determining Order-winners and Qualifiers

For companies to gain an understanding of their markets takes time. In fact, strategy debate has a calender time-base which cannot be circumvented. The characteristics of markets and the perspectives of functions must be allowed adequate time both in their explanation and reception. Going away for a corporate strategy weekend or arranging one-off discussions will lead to generalised statements and little insight.

The strategic facet of order-winners and qualifiers is similarly bound by these characteristics. Seeking to clarify and understand these key insights will take time and requires soundings from different sources.

- **Functional perspectives** – the internal perspectives of the functions which are engaged in the provision of products or which interface with the market-place hold important insights into customer requirements. Often, however, companies limit this internal review to that of the marketing function. In part, this is based on the historical perception that marketing's view of the market represents the market. Within this context other functions have failed to assess customers and markets in terms of what they represent from their alternative perspectives. The consequence has been that companies have given undue weight to marketing's view which has emphasised the need to respond to customer's actual or perceived wishes and demands. Checking the impact on a business has not usually been part of a firm's overall assessment of a market, segment or customer.

- **Customer's views** – checking with customers on what they believe they require can invariably lead to a distorted view of reality. Setting aside the aspect of self-interest, customers place orders on suppliers in one system and make demands on suppliers' plants in another. Furthermore, customers are unlikely to acknowledge that the business they offer to a supplier is anything other than 'favourable'. Equally, customers often fail to make distinctions concerning different criteria – it is safer to ask for anything at the highest level of provision.

   Most times, those involved in agreeing contracts do not know the critical dimensions of the contracts being discussed. Few have attempted to find out. All present their business in its best light. Thus, to seek the view of customers can only be one part of such an assessment.

- **Actual orders** – the real demands on a supplier are embodied in the characteristics of the individual orders, call-offs and/or scheduled deliveries placed by customers. Tracing these in terms of volumes, lead-times, margins and other relevant factors will bring an essential perspective into evaluating opinion. Many companies, however, fail to analyse the key data which are an inherent by-product of their systems and which contain the characteristics of the commercial transactions which represent the very nature of their markets.

3.9   Conclusion

In today's markets it is increasingly less likely that companies will have a sustainable, competitive advantage. To enable companies to compete effectively and continue to be successful, firms need to understand their markets.

However, the characteristic of strategy debate has been and continues to be its general nature. Typical outcomes, therefore, are descriptions which are general in nature and foster independent, functional responses. But companies which fail to provide coherent strategies will continue to lose out. For, unless individual functions are able, and are required, to develop strategies which directly support their markets then these firms will lose substantial and essential advantage.

Distinguishing and weighting order-winners and qualifiers forms a key element of this strategic provision. Without such insights, agreement on what constitutes markets is replaced by individual views which are grounded in the biases and preferences of different functions. However, not only does this lead to unsophisticated responses but allows, even encourages, unrelated functional initiatives to be developed.

For manufacturing, investments in both processes and infrastructure are expensive and fixed. Once commitments have been made it is difficult – sometimes impossible – to make changes, certainly within the allowable time-frames of current commercial environments. The overall effect on corporate performance is significant. In the short term it can lead to substantial disparity in performance while in the long term it can be at the root of overall corporate success or failure.

3.9.1 *The capsizing effect*

The need for companies to be proactively alert stems from the nature of today's markets. Whereas companies in the past could recover from being outperformed and strategically outmanoeuvred, this is increasingly less likely. Today's conditions result in the capsizing effect, an ever-increasing phenomenon of the current competitive environment. Companies find that one day they are confident, secure and well-directed and the next, capsized and sinking, bottom up. The capsizing effect is often due to a lack of corporate awareness of competitive performance. Not being alert to the dimensions and extent of competitive performance leaves a company vulnerable to significant reversals of fortune which increasingly leave it irretrievably disadvantaged.

An essential step to avoid being competitively outmanoeuvred (or sinking altogether) is for a company to understand its markets with sufficient insight and to undertake this task on an ongoing basis. This not only provides understanding of sufficient adequacy on which to base corporate strategic directions but gives the essential inputs from which coordinated and inherent functional strategic outputs are formed.

3.9.2   *Little is new and even less is complex*

Any third-rate engineer can design complexity. The same holds true for strategy. Moving from what is complex and uncertain to what is understood and clear is the result of hard work – just the same as a designer needs to do to get from the complex to the simple.

To build on sound foundations starts with understanding, and as markets change then knowing what to do and how to respond is equally based on knowing where you are. Companies have in the past tolerated the fact of not adequately understanding their markets with the result that they have been unable to respond and thus lost market share or even lost out all together. Complexity is an inherent feature of most aspects of business and none more so than markets. But it need not be so.

Similarly, nothing is new. The issues and criteria – even the aspect of time – discussed in this chapter are not revolutionary. For example, nearly 70 years ago Henry Ford highlighted the 'meaning of time' as an essential and integral competitive factor in all stages of his business from raw materials through to distribution.[19] With ore-extraction to sold-product lead-times at a little over four days and average shipping times between factory and branches of just over six days then the 'meaning of time' was well-understood and exercised as long ago as the 1920s. What is new is the need to identify markets in terms of what wins orders and then develop functional strategies to support these. Every long journey begins with a first step. – In strategy this first step is understanding your markets.

Notes and References

1. An example given in R. Henkoff's article 'Cost Cutting: How to do it Right', *Fortune*, 9 April 1990, pp. 40–9.
2. For example, refer to Henkoff's article (1990) and also Terry Hill, *Production/Operations Management* 2nd edn (1991) pp. 353–6.

3. The computation of an experience curve is clearly detailed in the Harvard Business School Paper, 9–675–228 (Revised 7/75) entitled 'Experience and Cost: Some Implications for Manufacturing Policy'.
4. Boston Consulting Group, 'Perspectives in Experience' (1972) p. 12.
5. Several authors have stressed the importance of delivery reliability. For example, J. E. Ashton and F. X. Cook, Jr, 'Time to Reform Job Shop Manufacturing – Organise your factory for quality and on-time delivery', *Harvard Business Review*, March/April 1989, pp. 106–11.
6. Further details and approaches are to be found in G. Stalk and T. M. Hout, *Competing Against Time: How Time-based Competition is Reshaping Global Aspects* (Free Press, 1990); R. W. Schmenner, 'The Merit of Making Things Fast', *Sloan Management Review*, Fall 1988, pp. 11–17; J. L. Bower and T. M. Hout, 'Fast-Cycle Capability for Competitive Power', *Harvard Business Review*, November/December 1988, pp. 110–18, and J. D. Blackburn, 'Time-Based Competition: The Next Battleground in American Manufacturing', Business One (Irwin, 1991). Other references include P. Goldsburgh and P. Deane, 'Time is Money', *Management Today*, September 1985, pp. 132–9, and P. Dumaine, 'How Managers can Succeed Through Speed', *Fortune*, 13 February 1989, pp. 54–49.
7. These eight dimensions of quality were first listed by D. A. Garvin in his article 'Competing on the Eight Dimensions of Quality', *Harvard Business Review*, November/December 1987, pp. 101–9.
8. C. A. Voss in his article 'Quality in a Manufacturing Strategy', *Total Quality Management*, June 1990, pp. 149–52, elaborates on the role of quality as a qualifier.
9. Books/articles which specifically address approaches to quality include R. Caplan, *A Practical Approach to Quality Control* (London: Business Books, 1971); J. M. Juran, *Quality Control Handbook* (Maidenhead: McGraw-Hill, 1974); P. B. Crosby, *Quality is Free* (Maidenhead: McGraw-Hill, 1979); J. M. Juran and F. M. Gryna, *Quality Planning and Analysis* (New York: McGraw-Hill, 1980); W. E. Denning, *Quality, Productivity and Competitive Position* (Massachusetts: MIT Press, Cambridge, 1982); A. V. Feigenbaum, *Total Quality Control: Engineering and Management*, 3rd edn (Maidenhead: McGraw-Hill, 1983); G. Taguchi, *Designing Quality into Products and Processes* (Asian Productivity Organisation, 1986); F. Price, *Right First Time: Using Quality Control for Profit* (Aldershot: Wildwood House, 1986); and B. G. Dale and J. J. Plunkett (eds) *Managing Quality* (Hemel Hempstead: Philip Allan, 1991).
10. The basic misunderstandings which surround the word flexibility are highlighted in T. J. Hill and S. H. Chambers's article, 'Flexibility: A Manufacturing Conundrum' *IJOPM*, vol: 11, no 2 (1991) pp. 5–13.
11. Reported in J. Griffiths's article 'BMW – Tailoring its Competitive Challenge', *Financial Times*, 19 October 1990, p. 16.
12. Quoted in C. Leadbeater's article 'Toyota's Conundrum: Creating a Global Car for a Niche Market', *Financial Times*, 17 July 1991 p. 16.
13. Insights in design development in cars are provided in the *Financial Times Survey* entitled 'Car of the Future', 21 May 1991.

14. Other examples of product development lead-time reductions are provided in R. H. Hayes, S. C. Wheelwright and K. B. Clark, *Dynamic Manufacturing: Creating the Learning Organisation* (Free Press, 1988); 'Time is Money', *The Economist*, 8 October 1988, pp. 90 and 95; Chapter 11 in *Managing Product and Process Development Projects*, pp. 304–39. J. D. Blackburn (ed.) *'Time-based Competition: the Next Battleground in American Manufacturing' Part II New Product Development* (Irwin, 1991) pp. 121–208; and J. Mortimer and J. Hartley 'Managing in the 90s: Simultaneous Engineering', Department of Trade and Industry Publication, June 1991.
15. Reported in R. Reeve's article 'Profiting from Teamwork' in *Manufacturing Breakthrough*, January/February 1992, p. 22.
16. For example, this issue is raised in L. McLain's article, 'Digital's Load gets Lighter', *Financial Times*, 23 April 1991, p. 12.
17. Based on data from B. Clark and T. Fujimoto, 'Overlapping Problem-Solving in Product Development' in K. Ferdows (ed.) *Managing International Manufacturing* (Amsterdam: Elsevier Science Publishers, BV (North Holland) 1989).
18. Interesting articles on benchmarking include L. S. Pryor, 'Benchmarking: A Self-Improvement Strategy', *The Journal of Business Strategy*, November/December 1989, pp. 28–32; R. Osterhoff *et al.* 'Competitive Benchmarking at Xerox', in M. J. Stahl and G. M. Bounds (eds) *Competing Globally through Customer Value* (Quorum Books, 1991) pp. 788–98; K. Perowski, 'The Benchmarking Bandwagon', *Quality Progress*, January 1991, pp. 19–24; 'First Find Your Bench', *The Economist*, 11 May 1991, p. 72; S. Holberton, 'Benchmarking – How to Help Yourself to a Competitor's Best Practices', *Financial Times*, 24 June 1991, p. 12 and A. S. Wellbeck *et al.* 'World-class Manufacturing: Benchmarking World-class Performance', *The McKinsey Quarterly*, 1 November (1991) pp. 3–24.
19. H. Ford *To-day and To-morrow* (Cambridge, Massachusetts: Productivity Press, 1988) and particularly Chapter 10, 'The Meaning of Time'.

Further Reading

Hayes, R. H., Wheelwright, S. C. and Clark, K. B., *Dynamic Manufacturing in Creating the Learning Organisation* (Free Press, 1988).
Imai, M., *Kaizen: The Key to Japan's Competitive Success* (Random House, 1986).
Schonberger, R. J., *Japanese Manufacturing Techniques: Nine Hidden Lessons in Simplicity* (Free Press, 1982).
Schonberger, R. J., *Building a Chain of Customers* (Hutchinson Business Books, 1990).
Stahl, M. J. and Bounds, G. M. (eds) *Competing Globally Through Customer Value* (New York: Quorum Books, 1991).

Choice of Process 4

The way in which a business decides to make its products is a choice which many executives believe to be based upon the single dimension of technology. As a consequence, they leave this decision to engineering/process specialists on the assumption that they, being the custodians of technological understanding, are best able to draw the fine distinctions which need to be made. By designating those specialists as the appropriate people with whom this decision should rest, a situation is created in which the important manufacturing and business perspectives are at best given inadequate weight and in many instances are omitted altogether.

This chapter describes the manufacturing and business implications of process choice and in so doing highlights the importance of these issues when making investment decisions. In this way, it helps to broaden the view of manufacturing currently held by senior executives and provides a way of reviewing the manufacturing implications of marketing decisions, hence facilitating the manufacturing input into corporate strategy. This ensures that the necessary marketing/manufacturing interface is made and that the strategies adopted are business- rather than functionally-led.

4.1 The Choice of Process

When choosing the appropriate way in which to manufacture its products, a business will take the following steps:

1. Decide how much to buy out, which in turn determines the make-in task.
2. Identify the appropriate engineering/technology alternatives to complete the tasks embodied in each product. This will concern the made-in components and bringing them together with the bought-out items in order to produce the final product specification at agreed levels of quality.
3. Choose between alternative manufacturing approaches to completing the tasks embodied in providing the products involved. This will need to reflect the market in which a product competes and the volumes associated with those sales. Existing factories will often find that their current processes are not ideal. This issue is dealt with later in the chapter when the important insights into process choice have been covered.

The choice of process concerns step 3 in this procedure. It needs to embody the decisions made in the other two steps and to recognise any constraints imposed by them. However, whilst these constraints alter the dimensions within the decision (e.g. what is involved) they do not alter its nature. The essence of the choice is linked to the appropriate way to manufacture, given the market and associated volumes involved.

However, having stressed the optimal nature of process choice, there are certain constraints which have an overriding impact on this decision. What these are and how they limit business options will be explained as part of the next section.

4.1.1   *The manufacturing function*

The principal function in the manufacturing process is to take inputs (materials, labour and energy) and convert them into products. To complete this, a business usually has a range of choices to make between different modes of manufacturing. They usually choose one or, as is more often the case, several ways. The fundamental rationale for arriving at this decision, however, must be to ensure that the choice of process is the one best able to support a company competitively in the market-place. To understand what is involved in this decision several important perspectives have to be taken into account. Each choice of process will bring with it certain implications for a business in terms of response to its markets, manufacturing capabilities and characteristics, the level of investment required, the unit costs involved and the type of control and style of management which are appropriate. To help to understand these, it is necessary to review the process choices available.* There are five classic types of manufacturing process – project, jobbing, batch, line and continuous processing. However, in many situations, hybrids have been developed which blur the edges between one process and the next. These hybrids will also be discussed in terms of what they are, how they relate to the classic types and what they mean for a business.

Before going on to describe the choices of process involved, it is worth noting here that of the process choice types, the two extremes (namely, project and continuous processing) are associated with a particular product type (e.g. civil engineering and foods/liquids, respectively), a point which will be addressed later in the chapter. However, even though a firm may find that in reality it has little option but to choose the one, appropriate process (e.g. oil-refining and continuous processesing are for all intents and purposes inextricably linked), in manufacturing strategy terms, it is still of paramount importance that a company is clearly aware of the precise nature of the business implications involved in the choice it is 'forced' to go along with, and that the trade-offs associated with these dimensions are fixed.

4.1.2 The 'classic' types of process choice

(A) Project
Companies which produce large-scale, one-off (i.e. unique) complex products will normally provide these on the project choice of process. Examples include civil engineering contracts and aerospace programmes. A project concerns the provision of a unique product requiring large-scale inputs to be coordinated so as to achieve a customer's requirement. The resource inputs will normally be taken to the point where the product is to be built since it is not feasible to move it, once completed. All the activities,

---

* There is confusion surrounding the use of words (and their definitions) to describe 'processes'. The more common sources of misunderstanding are addressed throughout.

including the necessary support functions, will usually be controlled in the form of a total system for the duration of the project. Resources will be allocated to the project and reallocated once their part of the task is complete or at the end of the project.

The selection of project as the appropriate process is based upon two features. The product is a one-off, customer-specified requirement and, second, it is often too large to be moved or simply cannot be moved once completed. The latter criterion is such an overwhelming facet of this decision that products of this nature will always be made using the project choice of process. However, businesses will also be concerned with determining how much of the product to make away from site and how best to provide the parts or sections which go into the structures made on site. These will, in turn, often be produced using a choice of process other than project. These decisions need to be based upon other criteria which will become clear in the descriptions of these other choices which now follow.

Some confusion arises in the use of the word 'project'. Its common use – to describe a one-off complex task and/or the managerial style used to control such an event – needs to be distinguished from its use here which identifies a distinct process of making a product the very characteristics of which (for example, moving resources to and from a site) are detailed above.

(B) *Jobbing, unit or one-off*

A jobbing process is used to meet the one-off (i.e. unique) order requirements of customers – for example, purpose-built tooling. The product involved will be of an individual nature and requires that the supplier interprets the customer's design and specification whilst applying relatively high-level skills in the conversion process. A large degree of this interpretation will normally be in the hands of the skilled employee whose experience in this type of work will be an essential facet of the process. The design having been specified, what happens in jobbing is that one, or possibly a small number of skilled employees if the task is very time-consuming, will be largely responsible for deciding how best to complete the task on hand and for carrying out the work. It may also include a level of responsibility over scheduling, liaison with other functions and some involvement with the arrangements for outside subcontracted phases where necessary.

This one-off provision means that the product will not again be required in its exact form or, if it is, the demand will tend to be irregular with long time-periods between one order and the next. For this reason, therefore, investment in the manufacturing process (e.g. in jigs, fixtures and specialist plant) will not normally be warranted.

It is worth noting here that confusion often arises around the terms 'jobbing' and 'jobshop'. Whilst the former is a description of a choice of process as explained above, the latter is a commercial description of a type of business. For example, a small printing business may often be referred to as a 'job shop' or even a 'jobbing printer'. What this is intended to convey is the nature of the business involved or market served. That is, it describes the fact that the printer undertakes work which meets the specific needs of a whole range of customers and is typically of a low-volume nature. However, printing is, in fact, a classic example of a batch process, the explanation of which follows in the next section. Thus, from a commercial standpoint such a firm takes on low-volume orders (hence the phrase 'job') from its customers and, from a manufacturing perspective, uses a batch process to meet these requirements.

Finally, it is also important to distinguish between special, customised and standard products. The word 'special' is used to describe the 'one-off provision' mentioned earlier in this section (i.e. 'the product will not again be required in its exact form or, if it is, the demand will tend to be irregular with long time-periods between one order and the next'). The phrase 'standard product' means the opposite – the demand for the product is repeated (or the single customer order is of such a large-volume nature) and thus warrants investment.

The world 'customised' refers to a product which is made to a customer's specification. However, the demand for a customised product can be either 'special' (i.e. not repeated) or standard (i.e. repeated) in nature. An example of the latter is a container of a particular shape and size, as determined by a customer. Although customised, the demand for such a container (e.g. Coca-Cola or other soft-drink products) will be high and of a repeat nature. The appropriate choice of process will, therefore, be determined by volume and not the customised nature of the product.

Furthermore, some businesses are by their very nature the

producers of customised products. The earlier example of the printing firm is such a case. Here, products will normally be customised in that the printed material will include the logo, name, product and other details of the customer in question. However, to a printer, there will be a significant level of similarity between the demands placed on manufacturing of the different customer orders in question. In fact, the differences will be provisioned in the plate or mat containing the specific images and writing and the ink colours and paper-size in question. To manufacturing, therefore, the jobs (though customised) are not specials (as defined earlier) but standards. Thus, it will select a process other than jobbing as one better able to meet the requirements of these markets. In the printing example this would, as mentioned earlier, be batch and the rationale for this and what is involved become clear in the next section.

(C) *Batch*

When a company decides to manufacture using batch processes it does so because it is providing similar items on a repeat basis usually in larger volumes (quantity $\times$ work content) than associated with jobbing.* This type of process, however, is chosen to cover a wide range of volumes as represented in Figure 4.1 by the elongated shape of batch compared to the other processes. At the low-volume end, the repeat orders will be small and infrequent. In fact, some companies producing very large, one-off items will adopt a batch rather than a jobbing process approach to their manufacturing. When this happens, the work content involved will be high in jobbing terms and often the order quantity is for a small number of the same but unique items. At the high-volume end, the order quantities may involve many hours, shifts or even weeks of work involving the same product at one or more stages in its designated manufacturing route.

The procedure followed in batch is to divide the manufacturing task into a series of appropriate operations which together will make the products involved. The reason is simply to determine the most effective manufacturing route so that the lower cost require-

---

* Note that companies do manufacture order quantities comprising only one item on a batch basis. In this instance, what underpins their decision on which process to adopt is the repeat nature of a product, not the size of an order quantity.

ments of repeat, higher-volume markets can be best achieved. At this stage, suitable jigs and fixtures will be identified in order to help to reduce the processing times involved, the investment in which is justified by the total product throughput over time.

Each order quantity is manufactured by setting up that step of the process necessary to complete the first operation for a particular product. The whole order quantity is now completed at this stage. Then, the next operation in the process is made ready, the total order quantity is completed and so on until all the stages required to make a product are completed. Meanwhile, the process used to complete the first operation for the product is then reset to complete an operation for another product and so on. Thus, capacity at each stage in the process is used and reused to meet the different requirements of different orders.

Examples (in addition to printing mentioned earlier) include moulding processes where one mould to produce an item is put into a machine. The order for that component or product is then produced, the mould is taken off, the raw materials may have to be changed and a mould for another product is put into the machine and so on. Similarly, in metal-machining processes, a machine is set to complete the necessary metal-cutting operation for a product and the whole order quantity is processed. When finished, the machine in question is reset to do the required metal-cutting work on another item while the order quantity of the first product goes on to its next stage which is completed in another part of the process. At times, an order quantity may have more than one stage completed on the same machine. Here the same principle applies with the process reset to perform the next operation through which the whole order quantity will be passed.

(D) *Line*

With further increases in volumes (quantity × work content), investment is made to provide a process that is dedicated to the needs of a single or normally small range of products. The width of the product range will be determined at the time of the investment. In a line process, products are passed through the same sequence of operations. The standard nature of the products allows for this and hence changes outside the prescribed range of options (which can be very wide, for example, with motor vehicles) cannot be accommodated on the line itself. It is the cumulative volume of the product range which underpins the investment. Hence, the wider the product range then normally the higher is the investment required in the process in order to provide the degree of flexibility necessary to make these products. Where the options provided are very wide and the products involved of high cost or of a bulky nature then the more likely is the company to make these on an order basis only. Thus, for example, there will normally be a longer delay when purchasing a motor vehicle (especially if several options are specified)* than say a domestic appliance. The underlying reason for this is the different degree of product standardisation involved. The motor vehicle, therefore, will be made against a specific customer order and the domestic appliance to stock.

In summary, to a line process all products (irrespective of the options involved) are perceived to be standard. Thus in line, the process does not have to stop in order to meet the requirements of the products made on the line. However, in batch the process in order to accommodate another product (which may only constitute a different colour as in moulding) has to be stopped and reset.

(E) *Continuous processing*

With continuous processing, basic material(s) is passed through successive stages or operations and refined or processed into one or more products; for example, petrochemicals. This choice of process is based upon two features. The first is very high-volume demand, and the second is that the materials involved lend themselves to be moved easily from one part of the process to another; for example, fluids, gases and foods.

The high-volume nature of the demand justifies the very high investment involved. The processes are designed to run all day and every day with minimum shutdowns because of the high costs of starting up and closing down. Normally, the product range is quite narrow and often the products offered are purposely restricted in order to enhance volumes within the other products in the range. For example, UK oil-refining companies now offer only four-star and lead-free petrol and diesel. In this way, companies have

---

* Note that whereas this is typically the case in West European motor vehicle plants, Japanese automobile/makers schedule their manufacturing plants in accordance with sales forecasts, and make to stock rather than order-backlog, make-to-order principles.

restricted the range of octanes and hence increased the volumes associated with the grades that are provided.

In continuous processing the other feature is the nature of the materials being processed. Whereas in line there are manual inputs into the manufacture of the products as they pass along, in continuous processing the materials will be transferred automatically from one part of the process to the next, with the process monitoring and automatically adjusting flow and quality. The labour tasks in these situations are predominantly involved in checking the system and typically do not provide manual inputs into the process as they would on a line.

4.1.3   *Choices of processes within a business*

The five classic processes have been described separately because they are discrete choices. However, most businesses will select two or more processes as being appropriate for the products they manufacture. A typical illustration of this is the use of batch processes to make components for products and the choice of line to assemble components into final products. The reason why this occurs is that the work content associated with most components is insufficient to create the level of volume which would justify a more dedicated process, such as line.

(A) *Markets and product volumes*
The explanation of the five classic processes stressed throughout that the underlying factor when choosing the process most appropriate to manufacturing the products is *volume* (i.e. *quantity × work content*). The link between the demand for a product and the investment in processes to complete this task is fundamental to this decision. It is important, therefore, to distinguish clearly what is meant by volume.

Though companies express forecast sales in terms of a period (typically a year), manufacturing does not make annual volumes – it makes order quantities. Thus, contracts that agree on period sales, but not the size of actual orders (or call-offs), can be very misleading. On the other hand, manufacturing often cumulates orders from different customers (using order backlog/forward load principles), or decides to make products for finished goods inventory to be sold in a future time-period, in order to enhance

FIGURE 4.1
Choice of process related to volume

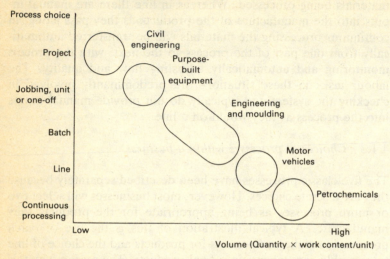

Note: Volume on the horizontal axis refers to order-quantity size.

Source: Hill, *Production/Operations Management*: *Text and Cases* (Prentice-Hall International, 1991) 2nd edn, Chapter 4.

volume. The choice is restricted by the degree of customisation of the product concerned, and factors such as current forward load, seasonality of sales, and lead-times in supplying customers' requirements. Hence, the horizontal axis in Figure 4.1 concerns order quantities placed on manufacturing. In project and jobbing, products are only made to customer order. In batch, decisions to cumulate demand, or make to inventory, relate to appropriate 'volumes' in terms of the process investments in place, and the actual sales-order volume required.

The term 'flexibility' is used to describe several different requirements. Two of these relate to volume. The one concerns demand increases, and the other alludes to the ability of a process to manufacture low quantities at required levels of cost. In turn, the latter concerns the relationship between set-up and process time. Hence, a high-volume process designed to manufacture products at fast output speeds will need appropriate investment, if it is to ensure that it can keep set-up times sufficiently short to maintain this ratio at an acceptable level. Current research work in many manufacturing companies provides numerous illustrations of where annual sales for a product may be similar to those in the past, but actual order quantities (or call-offs) have reduced significantly. The link between this section and the previous one is fundamental in terms of process investment.

(B) *Technical specification versus business specification*

As volumes increase, the justification for investing in processes dedicated to make that product(s), increases. High utilisation of plant underpins the investment. Similarly, if processes will not be highly utilised by one product they need to be sufficiently flexible to meet the manufacturing needs of other products. When choosing processes, therefore, businesses need to distinguish between the technology required to make a product and the way in which the product is then manufactured. On the one hand, the process technology choice concerns the engineering dimension of providing a process which will form, shape, cut , etc. a product to the size and tolerances required (the technical specification). On the other hand, the manufacturing dimension concerns determining the best way to make a product. This decision rests on the basis of volumes and relevant order-winners and qualifiers (the business specification). As volumes rise, the appropriate choice will change as illustrated in Figure 4.1.

When companies invest in processes, they usually specify the technical requirements, as this is recognised as fundamental, and appropriately so. However, typically, what they fail to do is to specify the business requirement the process investment has to meet. But it is this requirement that is crucial to the success of a business. In the past, manufacturing has failed to develop these critical, strategic arguments and insights. The consequences for many companies have been serious, leading to premature reinvestment of a considerable size, or even the closing down of parts of its business. Leaving the choice of these investments to be made against the single dimension of the technical specification has led to inappropriate decisions, based on the narrow base of technology. Manufacturing's failure to realise that it is the custodian of these decisions has indirectly contributed to this.

The choice of process needs to be understood, not in engineering terms (the technical specification), but in terms of manufacturing constraints and other dimensions of the business specification. Understanding how well a process can support the order-winning criteria of a product, the implications for a company in terms of its infrastructure, and other relevant investments, are fundamental to this strategic decision, and are dealt with in the following section.

4.2   The Business Implications of Process Choice

It has already been explained that market characteristics (i.e. order-winners and qualifiers) and product volumes are the underlying factors in choosing the appropriate process. The nature of the product is also a factor in this decision in terms of the two extremes in Figure 4.1, namely, project and continuous processing.

Hence, the procedure used is first to assess the market/volume dimension. This then forms the basis for choosing the most appropriate process to meet these critical business needs. The engineering dimension provides the initial set of alternatives concerning the ways to meet the technical requirements specification of the product. However, it is at this juncture that the engineering dimension finishes and the manufacturing and business dimensions (i.e. the provision of the business specification) start. Phase 1 links the market/volumes to the process choice (the manufacturing dimension which also takes into account the engineering dimension described earlier) – $A1$ and $B1$ in Figure 4.2. Phase 2 automatically picks up the corresponding point on each of the various manufacturing and business implications given in Table 4.1; $A2$ and $B2$ respectively in Figure 4.2. However, what tends to happen in many companies is that whilst the engineering dimension is recognised the manufacturing and business dimensions are unforeseen. In companies the engineering proposal currently underpins the major part of a process investment decision and this in turn, is based upon the forecast market/volumes which form part of the corporate marketing strategy. However, the manufacturing and business implications embodied in a proposal are given scant recognition. But it is these issues which bind manufacturing and hence regulate its ability to respond to the business needs. Once the investment is made not only are the processes fixed, but also the whole of the manufacturing infrastructure is fixed. The result is that this decision dictates the extent to which manufacturing can

FIGURE 4.2
The engineering, manufacturing and business dimension phases involved in process choice

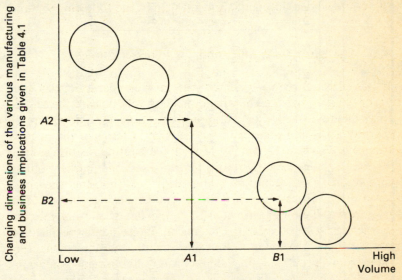

Phase 1 which links the market/volume to the process choice.

Phase 2 which picks up the corresponding manufacturing and business implications of the many dimentions given in Table 4.1, and which go on the vertical axis. The above diagram shows volumes *A*1 and *B*1, the appropriate process choice and their corresponding points on the manu-facturing and business implications dimensions, *A*2 and *B*2.

support the needs of the market-place, the essence of business success.

When Phase 1 in Figure 4.2 is completed, the choice of process is designated. However, at the same time it stipulates the position on the vertical dimensions which will accrue as a result. Hence, Phase 2 is inextricably tied to Phase 1. Therefore, the decisions in Phase 1 cannot be taken in isolation. The choice has to embrace both Phase 1 and Phase 2. Only in this way will an organisation avoid falling into the Cyclopean trap from which it will take years to extricate itself. Only in this way will a business take into account the short- and long-term implications which emanate from the

TABLE 4.1
Selected business implications of process choice

Aspects	Typical characteristics of process choice				
	Project	Jobbing, unit or one off	Batch	Line	Continuous processing
PRODUCTS AND MARKETS					
Type of product	Special/small range of standards	Special	→	Standard	Standard
Product range	Wide	Wide	→	Narrow: standard products	Very narrow: standard products
Customer order size	Small	Small	→	Large	Very large
Level of product change required	High	High	→	Low and within agreed options	None
Rate of new product introductions	High	High	→	Low	Very low
What does a company sell?	Capability	Capability		Products	Products
How are orders won?					
Order-winners	Delivery speed/unique design capability	Delivery speed/unique design capability		Price	Price
Qualifiers	Price/delivery reliability/quality	Price/delivery reliability/quality reliability	Quality/delivery	Quality/design/delivery reliability	Quality/design/delivery reliability
MANUFACTURING					
Nature of the process technology	Orientated towards general purpose	Universal	→	Dedicated	Highly dedicated
Process flexibility	High	High	→	Low	Inflexible
Production volumes	Low	Low	→	High	Very high

	Mixed	Labour		Plant		Plant
Dominant utilisation	Mixed	Labour		Plant		Plant
Changes in capacity	Incremental	Incremental		Stepped change		New facility
Key manufacturing task	To meet specification/ delivery schedules	To meet specification/ delivery dates		Low cost production		Low cost production
INVESTMENT AND COST						
Level of capital investment	Low/high	Low	↑	High	↑	Very high
Level of inventory						
Components/raw material	As required	As required/low	Often medium	Planned with buffer stocks/low		Planned with buffer stocks
Work-in-progress	High[1]	High[1]	Very high	Low		Low
Finished goods	Low	Low		High[2]		High[3]
Percent of total costs						
Direct labour	Low	High	↑	Low	↑	Very low
Direct materials	High	Low	↑	High	↑	Very high
Site/plant overheads	Low	Low	↑	High	↑	High
INFRASTRUCTURE						
Appropriate organisational						
Control	Decentralised/centralised	Decentralised		Centralised		Centralised
Style	Entrepreneurial	Entrepreneurial		Bureaucratic		Bureaucratic
Most important production management perspective	Technology	Technology		Business/people		Technology
Level of specialist support to manufacturing	High	Low		High		Very high

[1] This would depend upon stage payment arrangements.
[2] However, many businesses here will only make against customer schedules, or on receipt of a customer order.
[3] The finished goods inventory in, for instance, oil-refining is stored in the post-processing stages of distribution and at the point of sale.

decision to manufacture using one choice of process as opposed to another.

To help to explain the business implications of process choice, the perspectives involved have been placed into four categories – products and markets, manufacturing, investment and cost, and infrastructure. Furthermore, the issues for illustration and discussion have been chosen on the basis of their overall business importance. However, there are many other issues which are equally important to understand but which have distinct operational rather than strategic overtones.[1]

The critical issue embodied in Table 4.1 is to illustrate how each perspective reviewed changes between one choice of process and another. Thus, when a company decides to invest in a process, it will also have determined at the same time, the corresponding point on each dimension within these four categories. It is necessary, therefore, for companies to understand this and to be aware of the trade-offs embodied in that choice.

Table 4.1 contains many generalised statements which are intended to relate the usual requirements of one type of process to the other four. It can be seen that in almost all cases there is an arrow drawn between jobbing and line. This is intended to indicate that as a process moves from jobbing/low-volume batch through to high-volume batch/line then progressively the particular characteristic will change from one form to the other. The reason for this approach is to help to explain the implications of these choices and to examine the consequences which will normally follow.

It is important to bear in mind that companies selling products which are typically made using the project process will also need to make decisions on how much is made away from the site and then transported in. Today, many parts of a civil-engineering structure, for instance, are made off-site by jobbing, batch or line processes and then brought in as required. Similarly, products with the fluid, semi-fluid or gaseous characteristics necessary for a continuous processing choice may also be made on a batch process basis. Thus, the changing business characteristics displayed to Table 4.1 illustrate the sets of alternatives embodied in these choices as well.

Finally, Table 4.1 has been so arranged as to illustrate the linked relationship between jobbing, batch and line choices as opposed to the more distinct process/product relationship existing in project and continuous processing which was described earlier. As a consequence the next section adopts this division.

4.3   Selected Business Implications of Process Choice

This section of the chapter takes the dimensions provided in Table 4.1 and further explains the implications involved. In order to help to link the four categories of products and markets, manufacturing, investment and cost, and infrastructure, these are explained under each of the process choice headings. Furthermore, in order to emphasise the separate nature of project and continuous processing, and the linked nature of jobbing, batch and line the order in which these are discussed is project, followed by jobbing, batch and line with continuous processing at the end. Jobbing, batch and line nevertheless differ from each other. Each is dealt with under a separate subsection but as batch often links the change in dimensions between jobbing and line, the latter two processes are dealt with first in order to help to describe batch within this overall perspective.

4.3.1   *Project*

(A)   *Products and markets*
Companies choosing project processes sell capability. They sell their experience, know-how and skills to provide for a customer's individual needs. Hence, they are in a market which will require a high level of product change and new product introductions. Its product range will be wide with low unit sales volumes. It will win orders on aspects such as unique design capability, or delivery speed, with price normally acting as a qualifier rather than an order-winner. Through the competitive nature of today's markets, criteria such as quality and delivery reliability have typically changed in nature from order-winners to qualifiers, a fact signalled by their presence in all types of market.

(B)   *Manufacturing*
Orientated towards general-purpose equipment with some specialist plant to meet particular product, design or structural features, project processes are highly flexible coping with the low product volumes of the market and the design changes which will occur during production. Changes in capacity-mix or in total can be made incrementally with the key tasks being on-time completion and meeting the specification as laid down by the customer.

(C) *Investment and cost*

The capital investment in plant and other processes will tend to be low but with some high-cost items which may be purchased or hired depending upon their potential usage, availability, costs and similar factors. Due to the opportunity to schedule materials, the inventory at this stage will be on an as-required basis. Work-in-progress levels will be high but normally much of this will be passed on to the customers by stage payment agreements. In a make-to-order situation, finished goods are small with immediate delivery on completion. The key cost will normally be materials, and sound purchasing arrangements and work-in-progress usage and control will be essential.

(D) *Infrastructure*

Because of the uncertainties in the process and the need to respond quickly to any changes made by the customer, the organisational control should be decentralised and supported by an entrepreneurial rather than a bureaucratic style. In addition, however, once the business grows there will also be a need to control key items of plant, internal specialist/engineering skills and other purchased commodities/skills centrally to ensure that they are effectively scheduled by project and between projects. It is essential for the production manager to have a grounding in the relevant technology in order to appreciate and respond to unforeseen difficulties and problems of a technical as well as a non-technical nature and to use the local and centrally based specialist support effectively.

4.3.2 *Jobbing*

(A) *Products and markets*

In essence, a jobbing business sells its capability to manufacture to a customer's requirements. The only restrictions it has concern the range of skills provided by its workforce or limited by its processes. Thus, it handles a wide product range competing on aspects other than price. This does not mean that the business can charge any price it decides. But providing the price is within what is reasonable for the market (and that includes provisions for additional delivery speed or post-start modifications) then price is a qualifier rather than an order-winner.

(B) *Manufacturing*

As a consequence of the products it provides and markets it serves, the manufacturing process is flexible and needs to be geared to this flexibility with its major concern surrounding the utilisation of its labour skills, with processes being purchased to facilitate the skilled operator to complete the task. Changes in capacity can be achieved incrementally. The order backlog/forward load position which exists in make-to-order markets will allow manufacturing the opportunity to look ahead and make any foreseen adjustments in capacity ahead of time. The key manufacturing task is to complete the item to specification and on time, as normally this one-off item forms an integral part of some greater business whole as far as the customer is concerned.

(C) *Investment and cost*

Although many items of equipment in jobbing can be very expensive, this investment is generally low compared with batch and line. In addition, material will tend to be purchased only when an order has been received, with material delivery forming part of the total lead-time. Work-in-progress inventory will be high with all jobs, on average, being half-finished, while the make-to-order nature of its business means that products are despatched once completed. There will tend to be few specialist and other support functions which leads to a relatively lower plant/site overhead cost. These functions will be largely part of the skilled worker's task which together with the high labour content normally makes this the highest portion of total costs. Materials will tend to be low; where expensive materials are involved, these will invariably be on a customer-supplied basis.

(D) *Infrastructure*

On the organisational side, it is important to recognise that the control and style needs to be decentralised in structure and entrepreneurial in nature so as to respond quickly and effectively to meet the inherent flexibility requirements of this market. For this reason, the production executive has to understand the technology involved as this forms an important part of his contribution to business decisions (e.g. in accepting an order, confirming a delivery quotation or providing part of the specialist inputs into a business).

4.3.3   *Line*

(A) *Products and markets*
When a line process is chosen, it reflects the other end of the
spectrum to jobbing. The business sells standard products which,
to be successful, are sold on price and are associated with large
customer-orders. The level of product change is usually prescribed
within a list of options and outside this, the product is not normally
available. Product design and quality are determined at the outset
to meet the perceived needs of the customer with delivery reliability typically a qualifier in today's markets.

(B) *Manufacturing*
In order to provide low manufacturing costs the process is dedicated to a predetermined range of products and is not geared to be
flexible outside this range because of the high costs of change. In
addition, this provides the opportunity to maintain the necessary
quality levels throughout the process. Production volumes are high
and need to be so in order to achieve the high level of plant
utilisation necessary to justify the investment and to underpin the
cost structures involved. Output changes are more difficult to
arrange because of the stepped-change nature of capacity altera-
tions.

(C) *Investment and cost*
The key to low manufacturing costs is the high process investment
which goes hand-in-hand with line. The volumes involved allow
schedules of raw materials and components to be planned with
associated buffer stocks to cover the uncertainty of supply. Work-
in-progress inventory will be low. Finished goods will normally
tend to be high. But many businesses, as part of a decision to keep
overall inventory investment as low as possible, will only make
standard products against customer schedules or on receipt of an
order. Also, products offering many optional extras (e.g. motor
vehicles) will tend to have a policy of only being made against a
specific order. Hence, even in times of relatively low sales, if the
new car you decide on has an unusual set of options and thus is
unlikely to have been built in anticipation of an early sale, you will
have to wait. Finally, the high areas of cost tend to be in materials/

bought-out components and site/plant overheads, with direct labour a relatively small part of the total.

(D) *Infrastructure*
As the choice of a line process represents a high-volume business then a more centralised organisation, controlled by systems, is more appropriate. On the manufacturing side, the key production executive task concerns the business/people aspects of the job with specialist support providing the technical know-how involved in terms of both products and processes.

4.3.4 *Batch*

(A) *Products and markets*
In between jobbing and line comes batch. This is chosen to cover a very wide range of volumes (as illustrated by the elongated shape depicted in Figures 4.1 and 4.2) and links the low/high volume, special/standard product and make-to-order/make-to-stock businesses. In most cases the choice of batch rather than jobbing as the appropriate way to manufacture the products involved, signals the fact that the production volumes (i.e. quantity $\times$ work content) have increased, are of a repeat nature but are insufficient to dedicate processes solely to them as would be the case in line. Some unique orders with a high-volume content may also be done on a batch basis.

At the low-volume end of batch, the processes are able to cope with a high degree of product change and a high level of new production introduction. Here the business is orientated towards selling capability with price starting to become a more important order-winner because of the volume and repeat nature of the products. At the high-volume end of batch, products have become increasingly standard, order sizes are becoming larger, product change is lower, all of which illustrate the shift in product/market characteristics towards line. As mentioned earlier, market pressures have typically created a requirement to meet the qualifying needs of both quality and delivery reliability criteria which in earlier times would have often been order-winners.

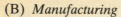

(B) *Manufacturing*

It can be deduced from the product/market features that batch processes usually have to cope with a wide range of both products and production volumes. In order to be able to handle this task, these processes will be of a general-purpose nature offering a high degree of flexibility. With some items of equipments, the utilisation will be low; with other items, plant will have been purchased to meet the needs of a product or to offer distinct process advantages (e.g. numerical control (NC) machines, machining centres and flexible manufacturing systems); each of which will be described in a later section. In these cases, high investment will normally be justified on a usage basis and the aim will be to utilise the capacity to the full.

In order to help to underpin the total process investment, many companies adopt a deliberate policy of increasing the utilisation of plant in three ways:

1. putting a wide range of products through the same set of processes;
2. usually manufacturing many of the same products in a single order quantity or batch quantity (hence the name). In this way, the number of set-ups are reduced which both decreases the setting costs and increases effective capacity;
3. making products wait for processes to become available. This policy, together with the order quantity decisions above, leads to a work-in-progress inventory investment which, in relation to the size of the business, tends to be very high compared with jobbing and particularly line.

(C) *Investment and cost*

As the products/markets move towards the high-volume end of the spectrum then a business, in order to be competitive, will increasingly invest in its batch processes in order to achieve the low manufacturing-cost requirement of these markets. As explained earlier, many companies exploit this still further by putting more products through the same processes and hence increasing overall utilisation. However, the major trade-off associated with this policy is the very high investment in work-in-progress inventory. The raw materials/components and finished goods inventory levels will, in turn, be associated with the make-to-order or make-to-stock nature of the business. As with all companies in these mid-volume markets, the nearer it is to a make-to-order situation the more the characteristics of that market will prevail, and *vice versa*. The make-up of total costs is no exception.

(D) *Infrastructure*

As the business moves away from the low-volume end of the continuum then centralised controls and a bureaucratic style become more appropriate. The increasing complexity of this growth will change the nature of the specialist functions where design and production engineering will be an ever more important support to manufacturing. The production manager's role will be bound up with appreciating and recognising the critical business issues involved, providing coordination throughout and spearheading the development of manufacturing systems.

At the low-volume end of batch the characteristics, though not the same, will be, in many situations, more akin to those in jobbing. It is important, therefore, to recognise the extent and trends in these changes and ensure that the necessary adjustments take place.

4.3.5 *Continuous processing*

(A) *Markets and products*

At the other end of the volume spectrum, companies choosing continuous processing will be selling a narrow range of standard products in markets where product change and the rate of product introductions are low. The company will be selling products rather than capability and the large customer-orders will be won principally on price.

(B) *Manufacturing*

In a price-sensitive market, the key manufacturing task will be low-cost production. To help to keep costs low, the process will be highly dedicated where the cost structure is based upon high production volumes leading to a need to achieve high plant utilisation. The fixed nature of capacity also creates restrictions when increases or decreases in output are required, with the decision based upon whether or not to build a new facility on the one hand or how often to run the plant (known as 'campaigning') on the other.

(C) *Investment and cost*

The high plant investment and high volume throughput associated with continuous processing offers the opportunity to keep raw-material inventory on a planned usage basis with built-in buffer stocks to cover uncertainties. Work-in-progress will be relatively low in total throughput terms with inventory in finished goods high. This is because of the need to maintain throughput levels at all times against fluctuating sales patterns. In many cases, however, finished goods are held in the extensive distribution system of a business and sometimes at its own retail outlets (e.g. on garage forecourts).

Because of the high process investment, direct labour costs are small with the highest cost usually in materials. Site/plant overheads in this process will be high because of the need to support the process and handle the high throughput levels involved.

(D) *Infrastructure*

The high volume nature of these businesses lends itself to a centralised, bureaucratic organisation control and style. Manufacturing performance is measured against budgets, variance analysis is the order of the day and investment proposals are centrally monitored. An understanding of the process and product technology is important when running a production unit together with the ability to coordinate the high level of specialist support provided for manufacturing.

4.4 An Overview of Process Choice

In order to help to clarify the issues involved in process choice, an overview of the way these alternatives link to one another is now described. The first important fact to stress is that each of the choices embodies a totally different approach to manufacturing a product. Although described in some detail in the chapter, a short explanation of these differences will serve to reinforce this important point.

Project   used for one-off products which have to be built on site because it is difficult or impossible to move them once they have been made. Consequently, the resources involved need to be brought to the site and released for re-use elsewhere when they are no longer needed.

Jobbing   used for one-off products which can be moved once completed. The responsibility for making the product is normally given to a skilled person who decides how best to make it and then completes all or most of the operations involved including checking the quality at each stage.

Batch   with an increase in volumes and the repeat nature of products, companies select batch as the effective way to meet the requirements involved. Because the products are repeated, companies can consider investment at each of the manufacturing steps necessary to make them. This includes engineering time to decide how best to make a product, jigs and fixtures to facilitate the completion of certain operations, and equipment purchased with an eye to making these and other products with similar characteristics. However, the volumes involved do not warrant the purchase of dedicated equipment. The operations necessary to complete a product, therefore, are not linked and are said to be decoupled.

Thus, a product to be completed will move from one process to the next in a predetermined sequence. At each stage, the process in question will be set up to complete the required operation. Once completed, the process then becomes available to undertake either the next operation on the same product or a relevant operation on another product. In each instance, however, the process will need to be reset each time.

Line   when demand is sufficient to justify dedicating equipment solely to making a specified range of products, then a line process is normally chosen. The operations necessary to complete a product are linked together so that each product goes from one operation directly to the next and so on. The operations necessary to complete a product in this instance are said to be coupled. As a line is designed to handle all products allocated to it, there is no need for set-ups. To the line all products are the same and thus it copes with product differences without having to stop the process.

Continuous processing   when the demand for a product is such

FIGURE 4.3
Potential transitions between the different choices of process

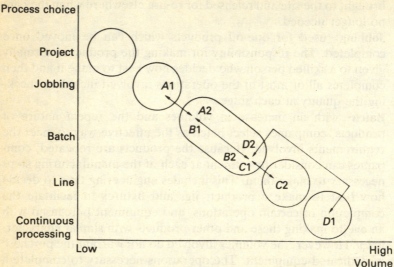

← → This shows four potential volume transitions which typically may face a business. The first example shows a move from one-off, *low-volume demand (A1) to repeat order, low-volume demand (A2) for a product of vice versa and the change in manufacturing process which should ideally accompany this movement. Examples *B*1 to *B*2, *C*1 to *C*2 and *D*1 to *D*2 show similar demand changes at different points on the volume scale and requiring similar decisions concerning the realignment of the process choice.

* One-off is a description of uniqueness, not order quantity.

that the volumes required necessitate a process being used all day and every day then further investment is justified. The equipment in this instance is designed to transfer the product automatically from one stage to the next, check the quality within the process and make adjustments where necessary. However, the transferring of products throughout the process limits its application to materials which can be easily moved, for example liquids and foodstuffs. The investment associated with this is warranted by the volumes involved.

Therefore, as also illustrated in earlier diagrams, Figure 4.3 shows a gap between the five choices outlined in order to emphasise the distinctions made above. Furthermore, it also makes the point that whereas there will sometimes be a transition from jobbing to low-volume batch, from low-volume to high-volume batch, from high-volume batch to line or from continuous processing, to high-volume batch, the same will not apply between project and jobbing or from line to continuous processing. Similarly, when volumes reduce towards the end of a product's life cycle the reverse movement will take place, but again it will only go as illustrated in Figure 4.3.

Transition in these instances refers to the possibility that as volumes increase or decrease, a business may change its choice of manufacturing accordingly. Project and continuous processing however, are prescribed by the nature of the product itself and the volumes involved. In this way, businesses with these characteristics are precluded from considering any other choice of process in terms of a transitional movement as described here and shown in Figure 4.3. However, those products which lend themselves to being produced using continuous processing (e.g. fluids, gases and foods) can and often are produced on a batch basis where the production volumes involved are not adequate to justify the high investment associated with continuous processing.

When product volumes increase or decrease, then companies should ideally realign their choice of process in keeping with that which is more appropriate to the new level of volumes. Many companies, however, find themselves unable or unwilling to commit the fresh investment necessary to complete this realignment especially where the volume movement experienced is downward.

4.5 Hybrid Processes

As mentioned earlier, many companies have developed hybrid processes, in order to provide a process which better enables them to support the characteristics of their markets. Some consist of a mix of two of the five classic processes, others are developments within an existing process type often based on the use of numerical control (NC) machines.[2] Some of the more important hybrid developments are now explained, and to help to position these in relation to the classic processes, they are included together in Figure 4.4. However, the list includes some (for example, machining

FIGURE 4.4

The position of some hybrid processes in relation to the five classic choices of process

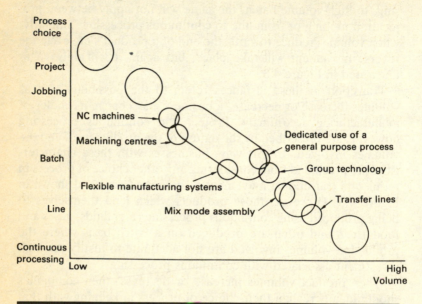

centres) which have received general application and are provided as standard items from a supplier's catalogue. In reality, some customisation may be offered but the substance of this equipment is standard.

Finally, as with all hybrids, there is a 'root stock'. Thus, although each hybrid format will consist of a mix of two process types, it will still be classified as belonging to one or the other. This phenomenon is highlighted by the headings of 'batch-related' and 'line-related' which follow. Within these sections the hybrids described have batch and line roots respectively. What happens is that they alter some of the trade-offs described in Table 4.1. Some will improve and some will get worse. What a company seeks is an overall set of trade-offs which are better for the business as a whole than those provided by the current process(es).

4.5.1   *Batch-related developments and hybrids*

(A) *NC machines*

An NC system describes a process which automatically performs the required operations according to a detailed set of coded instructions.[3] As mathematical information is the base used, then the system is called numerical control. The operation of machine tools (the first applications were applied to metal-cutting processes such as milling, boring, turning, grinding and sawing but in recent years the range of NC applications includes tube-bending, shearing and different forms of cutting) is from numerical data stored on paper or magnetic tapes, tabulating cards, computer storage or direct information. Compared with conventional equipment, NC machines offer increased accuracy, consistency and flexibility even with the need to meet very complex manufacturing requirements. Thus, design changes and modifications require only a change in instruction, nothing more.

In reality, an NC machine is a development of a batch process and one which is low-volume in nature. It is batch because the machine stops at the end of one process and is reset for a new job or new program being loaded. It is low volume because the set-up times are short hence providing an acceptable ratio between set-up times and the length of the run-time before the next set-up. The position of NC machines on Figure 4.4 illustrates this.

However, the trade-off against conventional plant is the increased investment associated with NC processes. In addition, it brings with it variations for the operators, setter and supervisor in terms of their role, the level of specialist support and skill requirements together with the problems involved in the introduction of new technology and associated changes.

(B) *Machining centres*

Machining centres, which first appeared in the late 1950s, combine NC operations previously provided by different machines into one machining centre. With tool-changing automatically controlled by instructions on the tape, and carousels holding up to 150 tools and more, the underlying rationale for this development is to maximise the combination of operations completed at a single location. A machining centre typically embraces several metal-cutting facilities (for example, milling, boring and drilling), which are applied to a given piece of work in a predetermined sequence which the NC program reflects. Storing the relevant range of tools in the form of a magazine, the appropriate tool is then selected and the particular operation completed. The hybrid nature of this process is that several operations are completed before the item of work is removed. Thus, a machining centre completes many operations in sequence and without removing the items from the process. This reflects aspects of line within what is, in reality, still a batch process (i.e. the process stops and resets itself not only between operations but between one item and the next). However, if the pre- and post-machining operations are performed on another process choice (e.g. batch) then, as with most companies, a combination of processes would be in use and the relevant point on the dimensions in Table 4.1 would reflect these differences. Machining centres as with all NC-based processes provide a higher level of flexibility (in terms of reduced set-ups and the resulting ability to meet the low-volume requirements of products) than do alternative non-NC process because of the nature and level of the capital investment involved. This is reflected in Figure 4.4.

Thus, machining centres are a hybrid between batch and line and, as a consequence, the position on some trade-offs (see Table 4.1) changes. For instance, work-in-progress inventory within the machining centre will go down compared with completing the same operations at individual and unconnected work stations, whilst the relative level of investment will increase. Similarly, lead-times will reduce as will the complexity of the manufacturing planning and control system. As you will note, all these changes are more towards a line process. However, the 'root' process is still batch.

(C) *Flexible manufacturing systems*
Whereas a machining centre is best suited to low volumes, a flexible manufacturing system (FMS) is appropriate for mid-volume requirements as shown in Figure 4.4. This too is designed to complete a given number of operations on an item before it leaves the system. However, rather than the item being contained in a single centre, in an FMS the workpiece is transferred automatically from one process to the next. Besides volume differ-

ences, the physical dimensions of the items to be machined are typically much larger than those completed by machining centres.

Flexible manufacturing systems (FMS) are a combination of standard and special NC machines, automated materials handling and computer control in the form of direct numerical control (DNC)[4] for the purposes of extending the benefits of NC to mid-volume manufacturing situations.[5] Whereas NC equipment and particularly machining centres cater for relatively low volume demand, much less attention has been given to improving manufacturing's approach to mid-volume, mid-variety products, although this accounts for a large part of the products which would fall into the batch range of volumes.

FMS are designed around families of parts. It is the increased volumes associated with the range of products which justifies the investment on the one hand and the inherent flexibility of the NC equipment on the other which combine to create the rationale of FMS in this mid-volume segment of demand. Classical families of products are:

1. By assembly: grouping parts together that would be required to make a single assembly (e.g. an engine assembly). The system would be designed to allow the user to order against an assembly requirement, rather than scheduling order quantities for each part through an appropriate series of functionally laid out processes.
2. By type: categorising parts by type in terms of a range of similar products. This would then relieve higher-volume-production processes of the low- to mid-volume part numbers and thus reduce the number of change-overs involved. This aggregate family demand justifies the capital investment with the inherent flexibility within the FMS allowing a relatively wide range of products to be considered and facilitating the balancing and rebalancing of the workload as product mix and volumes change.
3. By size and similar operations: the specification of the FMS in this situation reflects the physical size of the parts and the particular operations which need to be completed. Again, the flexibility within the system extends the range of work with which it can cope and allows high utilisation owing to its ability to handle product-mix and volume changes.

A typical series of events in processing a part in FMS (see Figure 4.5) is as follows:

- A DNC system directs a cart carrying an empty fixture to a load station and also advises the loader which part is to be loaded.
- On completion the loader signals that it is now ready and the computer directs the part to the first operation selecting, if available, the lowest backlog potential.
- The part is automatically unloaded, the appropriate NC program selected and the work completed.
- This procedure will be followed until the part is finished whence it goes to the unloading area and out of the system.

The hybrid nature of FMS is based on similar logic to that described in the section on machining centres, i.e. maximising the combination of operations completed at a single location. The additional capital investment will bring with it both lower cost and lower work-in-progress inventory advantages, combinations of trade-offs more akin to line. However, the root process (see earlier) is still batch.

(D) *Group technology*

The first three hybrid processes concerned the use of NC equipment as the basis for the process change. However, there are alternative hybrids which can be adopted using conventional or non-NC equipment. Three are described here. The first concerns a batch/line hybrid known as group technology.

The underlying difference between the choice of batch and line processes is one of associated volumes. What group technology does is to gain for batch processes some of the advantages inherent in high volume, line situations. It does this by changing the process or functional layout associated with batch manufacturing, into the product layout associated with line (see Figure 4.6).

The approach adopted is to separate out those processes which do not lend themselves to the application of group technology because of factors such as the level of investment involved and health considerations (e.g. noise or process waste/fumes). The next step is to group together families of like products. The criteria for this selection are similar to those outlined under the section on FMS. However, note that the process flexibility inherent in group-technology applications is not of the same order as in FMS.

FIGURE 4.5
Layout and general view of the flexible manufacturing system at R.A. Lister

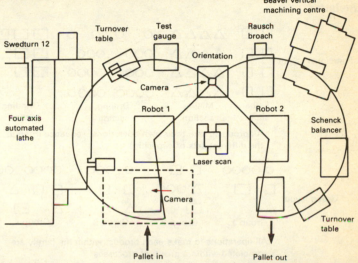

Source: M. Dooner and J. Hughes, *Structure and Design of Manufacturing Systems, Unit 2, Flexible Automation* (Milton Keynes: Open University Press, 1986) (with permission)

FIGURE 4.6
Group layout, its relationship to functional (batch) and line (product) layouts to illustrate the transition from the former to the latter

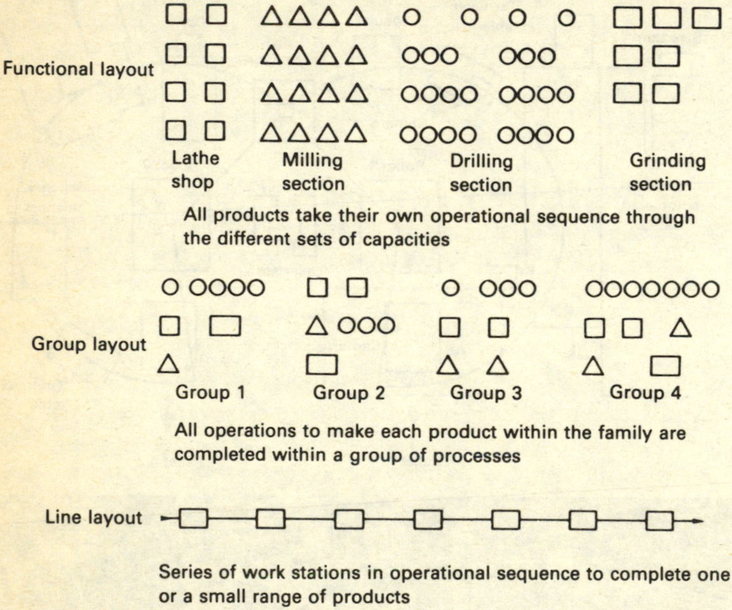

Functional layout

□ □   △△△△   o o o o   □□□
□ □   △△△△   ooo ooo   □ □
□ □   △△△△   oooo oooo □ □
□ □   △△△△   oooo oooo

Lathe   Milling   Drilling   Grinding
shop   section   section   section

All products take their own operational sequence through
the different sets of capacities

Group layout

o oooo   □ □   o ooo   ooooooo
□ □   △ ooo   □ □   □ □ △
△   □   △ △   △ □

Group 1   Group 2   Group 3   Group 4

All operations to make each product within the family are
completed within a group of processes

Line layout →□—□—□—□—□—□—□→

Series of work stations in operational sequence to complete one
or a small range of products

Source: Terry Hill, *Production/Operations Management: Text and Cases*, 2nd edn,
p. 141 (with permission)

The third step is to determine the process configuration necessary to manufacture each product family involved and to lay out the cell or line to reflect the manufacturing routings involved. The final stage is to complete a tooling analysis within each family, with a twofold aim. The first is to group together those parts within the family which can use the same tooling. This then forms the basis for scheduling in order to reduce setting time. The second is to include this feature as part of the design prerequisites for future products.[6]

The implications of group technology for a business are that the enhanced volumes have moved the point on the horizontal axis in

Figure 4.4 towards the higher-volume end. In so doing, the process choice of group technology substitutes the point on many of the Table 4.1 dimensions associated with a batch process, to that of line. Most importantly, it creates an inherently less flexible process in that to re-use any spare capacity brought about by a decrease in product-family volumes will not be easy or even possible without moving the location of the plant, itself a form of process investment. The key advantages to be gained from group technology include reduced lead-times and lower work-in-progress inventory together with a series of advantages associated with any form of small-scale manufacturing unit. A detailed review of these issues is provided elsewhere (see note 5 at the end of the chapter).

(E) *Linked batch*

As with most of the developments discussed in this section, linked batch is a hybrid of batch and line. However, linked batch does not need to encompass a large number of processes (which is more typical in the examples given earlier). In some instances, only two or three sequential processes may be linked, in others (for example, food packing) the whole of the process may be coupled. Whereas in the other examples the investment decisions are typically made as part of a complete process review, linked batch is often undertaken on a more piecemeal or evolutionary basis (i.e. where only two or three processes are linked, decisions are typically piecemeal in nature and, where the whole set of processes are coupled, this is quite often the result of changing volumes over time and of adaptive use of existing capacity to meet the process requirements of other products). The sequential processes though physically laid out in line (i.e. one operation following another), are run as a batch process (i.e. when product change is required, all the linked operations have to be stopped and reset to accommodate this change). Irrespective of the length of the set-up changes, the fact that the process has to be stopped makes it a batch process.

(F) *Dedicated use of general purpose equipment*

Where the volume of a specific part is such that it can justify the allocation of a process to its sole use, then manufacturing does so. In this instance the dedication is not in the plant itself but in the use of a general purpose process. Thus, the potential flexibility and other characteristics illustrated in Table 4.1 of a general-purpose process are still retained and when volumes reduce will be re-claimed.

You will deduce from this description that characteristically the process is not altered. Hence, the process is still batch (and, therefore, general purpose in nature). What becomes dedicated is the use of the process, which reflects the volume requirements for the product in question.

Thus the nature of the hybrid is one which stems from a change in use (as explained earlier) to reflect the high-volume demand for a product and not a physical change to the process itself. Thus, it still remains a batch process even though during the period in which its use is dedicated to the manufacture of a given product it may (for example, for colour changes) or may not be reset.

4.5.2   *Line-related developments and hybrids*

Just as the last section related to developments and hybrids based on batch processes and which had continued to have their 'root' in that process, so this section reviews hybrids related to line.

(A)   *Mix-mode assembly lines*
By investing in order to broaden the range of products with which a line process can cope without stopping, companies purposefully move towards what is known as a mix-mode assembly line. In reality, the product range for all line processes is determined at the time of the process investment. However, the term 'mix-mode' has been used to reflect processes where systematic and purposeful investment has been made to increase the product range accommodated by the process, whilst typically programming the line to make small quantities of different products in a predeter-mined sequence.

The origins of a 'mix-mode' assembly line are twofold. On the one hand, an existing line process can be developed to accommo-date other products because of a reduction in demand for the existing products. This, in turn, releases capacity which a company may wish to re-use. On the other, a 'mix-mode' assembly line can be developed to handle the operations necessary to complete a number of products currently completed in other ways (e.g. using linked batch processes). What makes the root here a line process is that it does not have to be stopped and reset in order to accommodate the next product.

Mix-mode assembly lines are designed to cope with a range of products in any scheduled combination. This is achieved by the use of computer-controlled flow lines which schedule work in terms of the overall production requirement and the short-term workloads at the various stations. The increased range of products which can be catered for and which, in turn, justify the investment, is achieved by the increased expenditure necessary to obtain a higher level of this aspect of flexibility. In this way, mix-mode assembly lines are an alternative process to batch which could be used to meet the level of volume associated with the products in question.

As you will have deduced from this explanation, a mix-mode assembly line is not technically a hybrid, in that the characteristics of another process have not been combined with those of line. What you have here is a line process which can accommodate the requirements of a wider range of products than can typically be made on a classic line process. It has been included here to provide a further illustration of the way process investment can change certain relevant trade-offs in a business.

(B) *Transfer lines*

The last hybrid process to be discussed is transfer lines. Where the volume demand for products is very high, further investment is justified. Transfer lines are a hybrid between line and continuous processing. However, their root process is still line because it can be stopped without major cost being involved. The position of transfer lines on Figure 4.4 illustrates the features involving this process where the high demand justifies investment designed to reduce the manual inputs associated with a line process and move more towards a process which not only automatically transfers a part from one station to the next but also automatically positions, completes the task and checks the quality as an in-built part of the process. Furthermore, deviations from the specified tolerances will be registered and automatic tooling adjustments and replacements will often be part of the procedure involved. In order to achieve this, the process is numerically controlled in part or in full which provides the systems-control afforded, in part at least, by the operator in the line process.

4.6 Review of the Use of Numerical Control (NC) in Hybrid Processes

Whereas linked batch, group technology and the dedicated use of a general-purpose process are derived from alternative uses of conventional non-NC processes, the other four hybrid processes are based upon the concept of numerical control in one form or another.[7]

The last section explains and Figure 4.4 illustrates that the basis for the choice between one NC hybrid process and the other is volume. As with the choices between the five classical processes which were outlined in Table 4.1, the implications for these choices have to be understood and taken into account at the time of their selection (see Figure 4.7). It is important here to recognise that the NC base of these processes brings with it a level of flexibility which is far greater than that inherent in non-NC alternatives. This means, therefore, that the process is more able to cope with a wider range of products and to handle product-mix changes over time. However, dedication in these alternatives starts to be introduced when processes are brought together to meet the needs of a given range/family of products. In order thereafter to re-use these, further and often substantial investment will have to be made to relocate, adapt or change existing processes and their configuration to meet the needs of other products. This change is illustrated by the gap between machining centres and FMS. As the choice moves to the other end of the spectrum, the implications of dedication will begin to take hold.

Figure 4.7 illustrates the rationalised use of NC-based processes as they relate to volume. Thus, in the same way as with the classic processes described earlier, whilst volume is the basis for choice, two other equally important dimensions must be a part of this decision. The first is the changes in volume expected over time. The second is the host of implications to the business which need to be understood and to be taken into account when arriving at this decision. Some of these are shown in Figure 4.7 but Table 4.1 provides a more complete list.[8]

FIGURE 4.7
Hybrid NC process choice related to volume

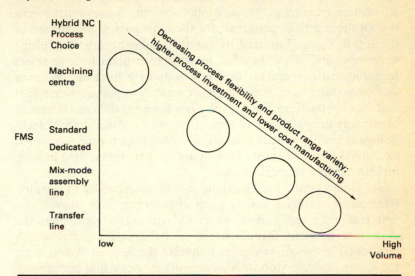

4.7   Technology Strategy

Advances in computer control have brought fresh opportunities for Western manufacturers. The potential for innovation in manufacturing is greater now than it has ever been. Advanced manufacturing technologies (AMT) have provided a viable option to sourcing manufactured components and products from other parts of the world. There is no doubt about the potential, and recent reports indicate an expected boom period, with 'some sectors, such as robotics and computer-aided design, growing at over 30 per cent a year. By 1990, the entire AMT industry is expected to have annual sales of more than $30 billion.'[9]

However, it is the approach to the use of technology and ensuring the suitability of its application that creates most concern. Tripping over engineering white elephants from the past should make companies understandably wary, not of technology improvements themselves, but of the approach adopted that leads the company to make sizeable investments in inappropriate technologies. However, the preoccupation with the search for panaceas may well lead companies to duplicate yesterday's mistakes. Indeed, the case for a technology strategy in itself should sound warning bells. Articles advocating technology/strategy links abound. However, the content of these articles concerns, for the most part, a description of the technologies illustrated by specific applications and resulting improvements. What they fail to do is to explain how to select technological investments that best support a business. Without this conceptual base, companies are unable to make assessments and draw distinctions. As a result, they have to fall back on hunch, or support the judgment of specialists, who are devotees of technological innovation and advantage, rather than business-oriented executives trying to ensure fit with the market and viewing process investment in a supportive role.

To some extent, the emerging call for companies to develop technology strategies has its roots in recent process innovations and computer applications in manufacturing. Historically, the clear link between manufacturing and the marketplace, which developed in the growth years following the Second World War, led to a well-understood manufacturing strategy that was appropriately reflected in the activities and developments within the process, production, and industrial engineering functions. Not only was the status of engineering clearly reinforced, but it also evolved that engineers were perceived to be the decision-makers determining appropriate process and relevant elements of infrastructure investments.

This post-war role also led to, or reinforced, the low status in manufacturing management with the attendant difficulties discussed in Chapter 2. These role characteristics in manufacturing were established in relation with other specialist functions, with similar consequences, some of which are discussed in later chapters on process positioning, infrastructure, and accounting.

4.7.1 *Flexibility – a strategic cop-out?*

For many businesses, past investments in dedicated processes have proved inappropriate in terms of current markets. While this has been brought about, in part, by pressures of competition faced with new investment requirements, the response has often been to purchase new equipment with a high level of flexibility in terms of width of product range, and coping with low-order quantity requirements. However, where such decisions are not based on an assessment of the market-place and an evaluation of alternatives, then they have degenerated into what is tantamount to a strategic cop-out! If in doubt, resolve the doubt has become, if in doubt buy flexibility!

One company, after witnessing an overall decline in volumes throughout the parent group, committed itself to the purchase of flexible processes to cope with an environment of change. An analysis of processes, product life-cycles, and order-winners clearly showed that the purchase, in part, of dedicated plant would best meet these requirements, and eliminated $0.25 million investment on unnecessary flexibility. Another illustration is provided where in three companies, each manufacturing in different segments of engineering, it was found that expensive NC machines were being primarily used on high-volume products. Discussions revealed a failure in the company to separate comparisons of process capability, in terms of holding tight tolerances (current *versus* early 1970s technology), and the business needs of the process (low cost based on high volumes).

4.7.2   *Technology push* v. *pull strategies*

It is essential that companies recognise that process investments can be based on either technology push or pull strategies. A push strategy reflects the position where the rationale for process investments comes from technology-based arguments, whereas pull strategies reflect technology investments based on defined market needs. Where companies are faced with push strategies it is critical that arguments concerning the corporate potential to sell the spin-offs available from the proposed technology investments are only accepted as part of the evaluation, if a clear market need has been determined. Otherwise, such investments must be evaluated on their own merits.

4.7.3   *Manufacturing strategy and technological opportunities*

The rate of current process innovation presents an important opportunity for companies to compete effectively against world competition. However, committing scarce resources to investments based primarily on the perspectives of specialists, or in search of a panacea to update and realign manufacturing, presents enormous and unnecessary risks. It is essential that technology alternatives form part of manufacturing strategy developments, as discussed in this and the last chapter. Linking investments with a well-argued understanding of its markets must be the procedure for a business to follow, if it is to avoid inappropriate major capital expenditure.

4.8 Product-profiling

A company needs to have a comprehensive understanding of the changing implications to its business as alternative processes are chosen, and then to use this concept as an important input into the corporate strategy debate. In fact, it forms the blocks on which to build the strategic, manufacturing dimension. Assessing how well existing process choices fit an organisation's current market requirements and making appropriate choices of process to meet future products are critical manufacturing responsibilities, because of the high investment associated with the outcomes of these decisions.

The purpose of this assessment is to evaluate and where necessary improve the degree of fit between manufacturing's ability to support the different manufacturing-related order-winning and qualifying criteria of the company's products in terms of the current and future ways in which they will win orders, i.e. manufacturing's strategic response within the business. In many instances though, companies will be unable or unwilling to improve the degree of fit, because of the level of existing investment, executive energy or time scales involved. Instead they will be prepared to live with the existing trade-offs. In such circumstances, however, product profiling will enable these decisions to be based on an increased awareness of the corporate position and to be taken as a conscious choice between alternatives. It is this level of strategic alertness to which many companies have not aspired.

Inconsistency between the market and manufacturing process capability, in terms of supporting the business specification of its products, can be induced by changes in the market or process investments, or a combination of the two. In all instances, the mismatch is created by the fact that the investments within manufacturing are both significant and fixed in nature (once a company has purchased them, then it will have to live with them for better or for worse for many years to come). On the other hand, corporate marketing decisions can often be relatively transient in nature, should a company so decide. While this allows for change and repositioning, manufacturing decisions bind the business for years ahead. Thus, linkage between these two parts of a business is not just a felt need, but a reality requiring strategic awareness, recognition, and action.

Product-profiling is a way to ascertain the degree of fit between the choices of process, which have been or are proposed to be made, and the order-winning criteria of the product(s) under review. The next sections provide an example of the use of product-profiling. But first, let us review the procedure to be followed which is given below.

- Select relevant aspects of products/markets, manufacturing, investment/cost and infrastructure. The basis for the selection will be to reflect the critical dimensions of the market-place, manufacturing, investment, cost and infrastructure as they appertain to a business and the product(s) under review. Table 4.1 provides many relevant dimensions. However the potential number of perspectives is far larger than those given here, some of which may be highly relevant to the company under review, a fact somewhat illustrated by the examples included later in this section.[10]
- Display the characteristics of process choice that would be typical for each chosen dimensions. This provides the backdrop against which the product or products are to be profiled.
- Profile a product or group of products by positioning it on each of the dimensions chosen. This is to test the level of correlation between the market needs and manufacturing's current or proposed response to their provision.
- The resulting profile illustrates the degree of consistency between the characteristics of the market, the business specification of the process and chosen features of investment, cost and infrastructure. The higher the consistency, the straighter the profile will be. Inconsistencies between the market and manufacturing's inherent ability to meet the related performance criteria (order-winners and qualifiers) of the markets being

assessed will show in the dog-leg shape of the profile that will result. It is not aligned.

Thus, product-profiling is a way of checking the level of alignment between manufacturing processes and infrastructure and a company's markets. The straighter the line, the higher the level of alignment. Causes of non-alignment and steps to re-align market and manufacturing strategy are now discussed.

Where the marketing needs have changed over time then the effect on the degree of fit between manufacturing's support for, and the market itself can be assessed and described. One such illustration is provided by Table 4.2 which shows the 1986 and 1990 profiles for a company and its products. The incremental marketing changes in this five-year period had had the cumulative effect of moving, in a leftward direction, this company's position on several of the relevant product/market dimensions. However, the order-winning criteria had remained the same and without the required process and infrastructure investment and change, manufacturing had increasingly been less able to cope effectively. The result was that profits tumbled. Furthermore, given the 1990 product-profile which existed, manufacturing would be unable to improve its performance, and hence redress this situation without the necessary reinvestment involved. As Table 4.2 illustrates, the level of inconsistency between the actual 1990 position on the vertical axis and where it should have been (see Figure 4.2, which explains the Phase 1 and Phase 2 steps in manufacturing strategy development) has resulted in a profile mismatch. This, therefore, explains and illustrates the level of inconsistency involved. In such situations, companies face a number of alternative choices:

1. Live with the mismatch.
2. Go some way to redressing the profile mismatch by altering the marketing strategy.
3. Go some way to redressing the profile mismatch by investing in and changing manufacturing and its infrastructure.

Alternative (1) affords companies the opportunity to make a conscious decision on the trade-offs involved. It does not in any way imply this to be an incorrect strategic choice. What it does do is to bring a company's expectations more in line with reality, makes it aware of the real costs of being in different markets, changes the measures of performance by distinguishing between those which are based upon business-related decisions and those which are based upon functional achievement, and raises the level of corporate consciousness about the overall consequences of maintaining product-profile *status quo* or the decision to improve or widen any *mismatch* which may exist. Furthermore, future decisions concerning new products are now more able to incorporate these essential perspectives and hence arrive at decisions which reconcile the diverse functional perspectives under the mantle of what is best for the business.

Alternatives (2) and (3) concern ways of straightening existing or consciously avoiding the creation of new mismatches which may be taken independently or in unison. *Alternative (2)* represents the influencing of corporate policy through changes or modifications to existing or proposed marketing strategies. In this way, the implications for manufacturing or marketing decisions are addressed and included as an integral part of the corporate strategy debate. Thus, manufacturing is able to move from the reactive stance it currently takes to a proactive mode, so essential to sound policy decisions.

Alternative (3) on the other hand, involves a company in the decision to invest in the processes and infrastructure of its business either to enable manufacturing to become more effective in its provision of the order-winning criteria and support in the marketplace for existing products, or to establish the required level of support for future products. As in *Alternative (2)* therefore, it enables manufacturing to switch from making a reactive to making a proactive response to corporate marketing decisions. Thus, by receiving pertinent inputs at the strategic level, the business now becomes more fully aware of the sets of implications involved and is thereby able to arrive at strategic options based upon the relevant and comprehensive inputs necessary to make sound judgements at the strategic level.

4.9   Conclusion

Establishing the level of mismatch between its current processes and current business and the adjustment it must, or is able to, achieve, or making the appropriate choice of process for future

TABLE 4.2
A product profile for a company in which the mainstream products have been profiled. The 1990 profile illustrates the dog-leg shape which reflects the inconsistencies between the high-volume batch process and infrastructure and the 1990 market position

Some relevant product/market, manufacturing and infrastructure aspects for this company	Typical characteristics of process choice[1] and the company's 1986 and 1990 product profile		
	Jobbing, unit, one-off	Batch	Line
PRODUCTS AND MARKETS			
Product range	Wide		Narrow
Customer order size	Small		Large
Frequency of change product schedule	Many		Few
	Many		Few
Order-winners	Delivery speed/ unique capability		Price
MANUFACTURING			
Process technologies	General-purpose		Dedicated

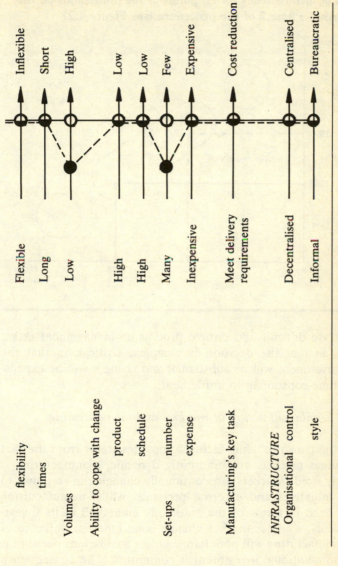

[1] The process choices open to the company whose profile is represented here did not include project or continuous processing.

○ ○ 1986 company position on each of the chosen dimensions and the resulting profile ——
● ● 1990 company position on each of the chosen dimensions and the resulting profile ------

FIGURE 4.8
The level of inconsistency on all points of the dimensions on the vertical axis – Phase 2 of the procedure (see Figure 4.2)

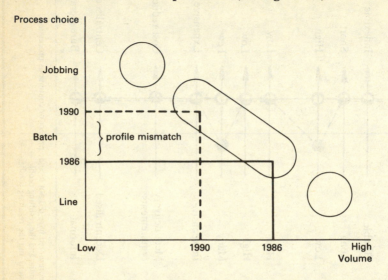

products are difficult and critical production-management tasks. Difficult, in that the decision is complex. Critical, in that the process investment will be substantial and changes will be expensive and time-consuming to implement.

4.9.1   *The inherent nature of markets and manufacturing*

One of the core problems facing companies stems from the fact that whereas markets are inherently dynamic, manufacturing is inherently fixed. Markets are continually changing in response to internal initiatives and external pressures whilst manufacturing remains fixed in terms of the trade-offs embodied in its investments. Thus, whereas market change is an inherent outcome of time, manufacturing will not change unless a conscious decision is made and additional investment is committed. The consequence for a company which fails to make these commitments is a manufacturing function which is less able to support its markets.

4.9.2 *Manufacturing's strategic response*

Typically, companies have responded to the need to make manufacturing changes by leaning solely on the engineering/technology dimension for the choice of process answer. But, it is not an engineering solution that is required. The engineering input concerns providing alternative, technological options which will enable the product to be manufactured. However, the choice of process concerns how manufacturing is then completed. This will involve the product/market, investment/cost and infrastructure besides the manufacturing dimensions all of which have been examined in this chapter.

Engineering prescriptions, technology solutions seeking problems or the belief that panaceas are on hand, have been instrumental, in part, for UK manufacturing's current uncompetitive position. Couple this with a marketing-led strategy in some businesses which has overreached itself or the more universal impact of incremental marketing changes which, over time, have altered the business without a strategic recognition of the consequences involved, and the result has been to facilitate the erosion of large, traditional markets by our competitors. Other companies, persuaded by the apparent desirability of new markets or the short-term solution to get out of tough manufacturing industries have also left the way clear in these high-volume, established markets. However, there is no long-term future in easy manufacturing tasks. The short term may appear attractive but tomorrow matters.

Successful manufacturing nations have been picking off the markets of many well-established industrial nations by a combined marketing/manufacturing strategy so creating, at the expense of its competitors, a sound industrial base essential to a nation's long-term prosperity and growth. The Japanese have, in fact, built their manufacturing base on traditional smoke-stack industries.

Corporate decisions on process choice entail going through the initial conceptualisation, justification and finally implementation of the procedures described here. There are no short cuts. Understanding the complexity of a business and determining the strategic direction so necessary for its success are by-products of hard work and basing decisions on informed insights. The manufacturing inputs into the corporate strategy debate and its outcomes have invariably been too little and too late, but to compete effectively in the future this will have to be redressed. Only when an informed corporate resolution of the interfunctional differences within a business is achieved will a company be in charge of its own destiny.

Notes and References

1. Many of these additional issues are illustrated and discussed in Hill, *Production/Operations Management: Text and Cases* (1991) 2nd edn, pp. 61–9.
2. More advanced NC systems were introduced in the late 1960s in the form of computer numerical control (CNC) which replaced the hard-wired control unit of the NC system with a stored program using a dedicated minicomputer. Hence, the memory storage rather than paper-tape input makes the process more reliable and more flexible in terms of program changes. Direct numerical control (DNC) systems consist of a number of NC and/or CNC equipment connected to a centralised computer. The centralised source of information provided by DNC helps in the control of manufacturing. Flexible manufacturing systems (FMS) combine the DNC principle with the other features described in the relevant section on pp. 134–6.
3. Ibid.
4. Ibid.
5. P. R. Haas, 'Flexible Manufacturing Systems – a Solution for the Mid-volume, Mid-variety Parts Manufacturer' SME Technical Conference, Detroit, April 1973 and J. J. Hughes *et al.*, 'Flexible Manufacturing Systems for Improved Mid-volume Productivity', *Proceedings of the Third Annual AIEE Systems Engineering Conference*, November 1975.
6. A fuller explanation is given in Hill, *Production/Operations Management* (1991), pp. 140–5; also refer to G. A. B. Edwards, *Readings in Group Technology* (Machinery Publishing Company Ltd, 1971), and J. L. Burbidge, *The Introduction of Group Technology* (Heinemann, 1975).
7. NC refers to the operation of machine tools from numerical data stored on paper or magnetic tape, punched cards, computer storage or direct information. The development of machining centres result from the concepts of NC. In a machining centre, a range of operations are provided. A carousel with up to 150 tools (i.e. embodied in the centre) from which the program will select as required and with some taking place simultaneously as required. Consequently, a machining centre is able to cope not only with a wide range of product requirements but it can also be scheduled to complete one-offs in any

sequence desired. More advanced NC systems include computer numerical control (CNC) systems using a dedicated mini computer to perform NC functions and direct numerical control (DNC) which refers to a system having a computer controlling more than one machine tool. A DNC system includes both the hardware and software required to drive more than one NC machine simultaneously. To do this, DNC uses a computer which may be a mini computer, several microcomputers linked together, a mini computer linked to a large computer or a large computer on its own.

8. A fuller range of operational issues is provided in Hill, *Production/ Operations Management*, (1991) pp. 60–9.
9. I. Rodger, 'Pressure to Innovate', in 'Manufacturing Automation', *Financial Times (London) Survey*, 5 February 1985, p. 17.
10. Hill, *Production/Operations Management*, pp. 60–9.

Further Reading

Blois, K. J. 'Market Concentration – Challenge to Corporate Planning', *Long Range Planning*, vol. 13, August 1980, pp. 56–62.
Bolwijn, P. T. *et al. Flexible Manufacturing: Integrating Technological and Social Innovation* (Amsterdam: Elsevier Science Publishers BV, 1986).
Burbridge, J. L. 'The Simplification of Material Flow Systems', *International Journal of Production Research*, vol. 20, no 3, pp. 339–47 (1982).
Dale, R. G., Burbidge, J. L. and Cottam, M. J., 'Planning the Introduction of Group Technology', *International Journal of Operations and Production Management*, vol. 4, no 1, pp. 34–7.
Goldhar, J. D. and Jelinck, M. 'Plan for Economies of Scope', *Harvard Business Review*, November/December 1983, pp. 143–8.
Harvard Business School, 'Types of Production Process and Their Characteristics' 8-678-071 (revised 1978).
Hyer, N. L. and Wemmerlov, U. 'Group Technology and Productivity', *Harvard Business Review*, July/August 1984, pp. 140–9.
Leonard, R. and Rathmill, K. 'The Group Technology Myths', *Management Today*, January 1977, pp. 66–9.
Malpas, R., 'The Plant after Next', *Harvard Business Review*, July–August 1983, pp. 122–30.
Miller S. S., 'Making Your Plant Manager's Job Manageable', *Harvard Business Review*', January/February 1983, pp. 69–74.
Slack, N. *The Manufacturing Advantage* (London: Mercury Books 1991) chap 5.
Zelenovie, D. M., 'Flexibility – a Condition for Effective Production Systems', *International Journal of Production Research* (1980) vol. 20, no 3, pp. 319–37.

Focused Manufacturing 5

Manufacturing is inherently a complex task and managing this complexity is one of the key corporate roles. The complexity involved, however, does not emanate from the intrinsic nature of the individual tasks which comprise the job. In all but highly technical, customised, market segments, it is not difficult to cope with the technology of either the product or the process. In most situations, the process technology and wherewithal to make the product involved have been brought in from outside, with appropriate engineering and technical know-how provided inside to support the manufacturing requirement and underpin any necessary development. In a similar way, product design and the associated technology fall under the auspices of the customer and/or the design function. Hence, neither the process nor product technologies are generally either difficult to understand or manage from the viewpoint of the manufacturing function.

What creates the complexity then is not the technology dimension but the size of the task in terms of the number of aspects and issues involved, the interrelated nature of these and the level of fit between the manufacturing strategy task and the internal process capability and infrastructure.

In all instances, the level of complexity involved is derived largely from, or can be controlled by, the corporate strategy decisions made within the business itself. However, whereas the number and interrelated nature of the tasks and issues involved are more readily identified as a fundamental characteristic of complexity (the small-is-beautiful syndrome)[1] the fit between the manufacturing-strategy task and the internal-process capability and infrastructure has only recently received close attention. And it is these latter issues which come under the heading of 'focused manufacturing'.

5.1 Focused Manufacturing

Focused manufacturing deals with the issue of linking an organisation's manufacturing facilities to the appropriate competitive factors of its business(es) with the aim of enabling that company to gain a greater control of its competitive position. However, one of the most difficult tasks in managing manufacturing is responding to the different demands made on the facilities in terms of the market-place. This is not only due to the wide and often diverse nature of these demands but also to the level of complexity generated in the corresponding parts of the manufacturing function, including suppliers. Many companies are now finding that focusing the demands to which individual facilities must respond can achieve a marked reduction on the level of complexity involved in managing those operations. This, in turn, results in an improved overall performance.

When explaining 'focus' the word narrow or narrowing is often used as part of this description. For example, Skinner, who was the first to expound the benefits of focused plants, argues that 'a factory that focuses on a narrow product mix for a particular market niche will outperform the conventional plant, which attempts a broader mission'.[2] However, taken at face value this argument can be misleading. Many companies do not have the 'narrow product mix' alternative alluded to here. The issue of focus, therefore, is more accurately explained in Skinner's fuller definitions which formed part of his fourfold view for effecting basic changes in the management of manufacturing. Two of these were:

Learning to focus each plant on a limited, concise, manageable set of product, technologies, volumes and markets.
Learning to structure basic manufacturing policies and supporting

services so that they focus on one explicit manufacturing task instead of on many inconsistent, conflicting, implicit tasks.[3]

The emphasis here is on a limited and consistent set of tasks, which will often be far from the layman's definition of narrow. So, to avoid confusion and the implication of a simplistic resolution of the infinitely complex reality of business, the dimension of narrow should be omitted. It is the homogeneity of tasks and the repetition and experience within manufacturing of completing these which is the basis of focused manufacturing. Thus, focusing the demands placed on manufacturing will enable resources, efforts and attention to be concentrated on a defined and homogeneous set of activities, so allowing management to identify the key tasks and priorities necessary to achieve a better performance. However, in most plants the recognition, let alone the achievement of a meaningful level of plant focus, is rarely understood. There are several factors which have contributed to this position over the past twenty years.

5.2   Applying the Principle of Economies of Scale in Markets Characterised by Difference rather than Similarity

For many years it has been (and still is) argued that the principle of economies of scale is a sound and appropriate way of organising and managing businesses. As an underlying approach, the principles involved are highly attractive. However, the problem facing most organisations today is that this approach no longer works well. The advantages which accrue from applying the principle of economies of scale are no longer being realised. The reason for this is simply that the markets and necessary corporate response to, and support for, these has changed. Whilst markets in the past were characterised by similarity, today's markets are characterised by difference.

These principles are most appropriate for, and best applied to, markets which are characterised by high volumes and are steady-state in nature (i.e. where similarity is the hallmark). The problem is that for most companies these conditions no longer reflect the nature of their businesses.[4] For many, these prerequisites are far from their own realities. In fact, if anything, the opposite applies. Their markets are characterised by low volumes and are dynamic and changing in nature (i.e. where difference is the hallmark).

To appreciate why the conditions have changed, the key issues involved are now discussed.

5.2.1 *Marketing*

Marketing-led strategies are usually based on the principle of growth through extending the product range. Invariably what happens is that new products (even those requiring new technologies) are manufactured, partly at least, on existing processes and almost always within the same infrastructure. The logic for this is based on the principle of the economies derived from using existing plant capacity where possible and being supported by the existing overhead structure. Over time, the incremental nature of these marketing changes will invariably alter the manufacturing task. 'The result is complexity, confusion, and worst of all a production organisation which, because it is spun out in all directions by a kind of centrifugal force, lacks focus and a doable manufacturing task.'[5] The factory is increasingly asked to provide the different order-winning criteria for a range of products with the result that it makes a series of compromises.

5.2.2 *Increases in plant size*

Faced with a shortage of capacity, the attractions of on-site expansion prove irresistible. The tangible arguments of cost and overhead advantages plus the provision of a better hedge against future uncertainty provide the basis against which the alternatives are measured. Rarely argued or taken into account are the costs of the associated uplift in complexity, and the resulting bureaucracy that develops as factories try to cope. The piecemeal or incremental nature of these changes further hides or disguises the changes which are taking place. Schmenner concludes that:

> **big plants usually have formidable bureaucratic structures. Relationships inevitably become formal, and the worker is separated from the top executives by many layers of management. All too often managers are shuffling the paperwork that formal systems**

have spawned . . . Although there has to be some formality in plant operations, too much can wipe out the many informal procedures that keep plants nimble and able to adapt to change.[6]

5.2.3   *Manufacturing*

To aggravate the situation of compromise described in the last section, manufacturing in these circumstances will almost always not have a definition of its task. It will be required to perform on every yardstick with these often changing from one day to the next depending on the pressures from both within and outside the business. The result is that manufacturing, without an agreed strategy, will respond as best it can, independently deciding on the best corporate compromises or trade-offs involved. The result invariably is reduced plant performance.

5.2.4   *Plant utilisation*

Embodied in these scale principles is the argument concerning the high utilisation of plant. As capacity is released due to a fall-off in demand for a product(s), companies typically re-utilise the spare capacity now available by making new products. In other circumstances, the justification for purchasing new processes/equipment will often, in part, be based on total volumes. To achieve this requirement companies plan, therefore, to complete some or all of the operations needed to make a product for several (often many) products using the same process. Invariably when evaluating the suitability of processes for a product the only check made concerns meeting the technical requirements (specification). What is rarely checked is the consistency of the business requirement (i.e. manufacturing task) for each of the products involved, and this check is necessary not just for current requirements but over time as products go through their life-cycles and relevant order-winners correspondingly change.

5.2.5   *Specialists as the basis for controlling a business*

The use of specialists is the hallmark of the way in which management perceives the appropriate basis for controlling a business. 'These professionals, quite naturally, seek to maximise their contributions and justify their positions. They have conventional views of success in each of their particular fields. Of course, these objectives are generally in conflict.'[7] Furthermore, the essential link between the activities of specialists and the major functions of a business requires close cooperation and understanding. Too often that is not present. The failure of companies to define the focus of their business clearly exacerbates this problem. Without this direction there is insufficiently shared understanding of what is required. Thus, support systems, controls, information provision and other features of infrastructure are not developed in line with the appropriate and agreed corporate needs. Trade-offs are not made, therefore, against the shared understanding of the business. They are assessed on the fragmented and uncoordinated views and advice of specialists and based on what seems best at the time, rather than an agreed strategic appreciation of competitive performance.

5.3 Looking for Panaceas

Emanating from the last point is the underlying tendency of many businesses to seek the resolution to problems through the application of panaceas. Most companies will be able to point to examples of this syndrome by recalling their own versions of redundant solutions. The latest example in a long line is that of exhorting businesses to adopt the 'best' of the Japanese system as a matter of course rather than as one effective way of meeting a defined need. Although in themselves such developments are not without their potential and often substantial contribution to business success, they need to be derived from strategic discussion and to be in line with the appropriate focus. To achieve this potential there are two prerequisites both of which relevant Japanese companies followed. The first is that developments in manufacturing, as well as other functions, need to fit the market needs of a business. Japanese companies' developments were undertaken as a direct consequence of a requirement placed on the manufacturing function to improve given dimensions of its activities recognised as being critical to the overall success of the business. The result was the Just-in-Time, Total Quality Management and other concepts and approaches which many Western companies now treat as panaceas.

The second dimension is that of time. To undertake, develop and fit major initiatives into existing structures requires adequate time. After all, it took those Japanese companies who have developed these approaches some thirty years to 'perfect' their ideas and to adapt these approaches carefully to the needs of their business. The characteristic approach of Western companies is to expect and even demand their implementation, and successful adoption to be achieved 'overnight'. The rushed nature of this approach results in inappropriate applications and unrealistic expectations.

The panacea approach will at best only distract management from the essential resolution of its strategic direction, and at worse will imply that there is no longer any need to be concerned – all is in hand.

5.4   Trade-offs in Focused Manufacturing

Choice of focused manufacturing implies trade-offs. In arriving at this decision, however, it is important to distinguish between the gains associated with size reduction and manageable units and those which accrue from the approach adopted towards achieving focused manufacturing. Whilst a reduction in size may well go hand-in-hand with the decision to focus, it is important to separate those advantages which will be shared by any decision to reduce size and those which will be unique to each choice.

5.4.1   *Down-sizing* v. *focused plants*

It is important to separate the concepts of down-sizing (i.e. reducing the size of plants) and focusing. When companies rearrange their manufacturing businesses based on the concept of focus it will invariably lead to a reduction in the size of the plant. However, the two dimensions of this approach will bring very different sets of advantages and disadvantages. Smaller plants will bring advantages associated with size reduction. These advantages include the potential for improved communication, being more orientated towards a well-understood and agreed set of business objectives, simpler and more appropriate forms of control and managerial style, higher levels of employee participation, the potential for a higher level of employee motivation, shorter process lead-times, lower work-in-progress inventory, reduced complexity of the production-control task and a more accurate assessment of financial performance. On the other hand, smaller plants run contrary to the concept of economies of scale and may well lead to the need to increase/duplicate certain processes or parts of the infrastructure provision such as procedures and specialist capabilities.

As these sets of advantages and disadvantages are a direct result of the change in size itself, then the basis for selection needs to be made on the characteristics that emanate from each alternative approach. There are three approaches to focusing facilities. A list of the characteristics of each approach is provided as Table 5.1 and is now summarised below.

(A) *Based on products/markets*

This orientates relevant parts of the manufacturing facilities towards a particular customer or generic group of products, with this aspect providing the base for focus, thus reflecting the breakdown of actual or forecast sales. It typifies the marketing view of the market often, in fact, becoming the mirror-image of this function's view of the business.

(B) *Based on processes*

This groups products together on the basis of the processes necessary to meet the technical specification of those products. The principal rationale is to gain advantages such as concentrated expertise and in particular the improved utilisation of manufacturing processes by minimising the need for process duplication. It accomplishes this by identifying like products on the basis of their process requirements.

As you may recall, companies which make repeat/standard products which have insufficient volume to go to line (a situation which is most common) will choose batch as the appropriate process. In this way it will enable spare capacity to be utilised and reutilised by any product requiring an operation(s) to be completed by the process in question. The approach to focus described here is based on a similar rationale. Products needing the same process will go into the same manufacturing unit thereby avoiding the potential duplication of investment. However, when plants are broken down into two or more focused units, no matter what the basis for achieving this, the process capacities allocated to the smaller units will never be as fully utilised as they are when using batch as the choice of process. For, the latter arranges processes on a functional basis (i.e. all equipment providing similar technical capabilities to be put into the same geographical area and managed as a whole unit). In this way, the utilisation and reutilisation of process capability is facilitated by this arrangement.

However, breaking plants down on the basis of processes enables a company to minimise plant duplication as shown in Table 5.1. This principle is known as Group Technology which was identified as a hybrid process in the last chapter (pp. 136–9).

(C) *Based on order-winners*

This approach allocates products to a particular unit based on the different order-winners and qualifiers which manufacturing needs to provide. Thus, it focuses parts of a manufacturing unit on the basis of these critical manufacturing differences. In that way it creates conditions where the manufacturing task (i.e. what manufacturing has to do well in terms of supporting the particular order-winners and qualifiers) is consistent. Often this orientation is paralleled by differences in volume levels but this link is by no means always the case. As shown in Table 5.1, when breaking down plants into two or more units, this approach provides the best conditions for creating a consistent and coherent set of manufacturing requirements, tasks and priorities.

5.5 Steps to Achieve Focus

Before discussing the steps to achieve focus, it is important to consider from where plants will normally be coming. Typically, plants would currently be larger units, developed and organised on the basis of the principle of economies of scale. In this way, processes would often be shared (to increase overall utilisation) and the organisation would have a combination of line/executive functions together with an appropriate provision of specialists undertaking advisory and supporting roles.

The rationale supporting economies of scale arguments has been referred to earlier. The concept of focus challenges the appro-

TABLE 5.1
Characteristics of alternative approaches to focusing facilities[8]

Characteristics		Alternative approaches		
		Product/market	Process	Order-winners*
Orientation	basis	Product/market name	Process	Manufacturing task
	rationale	Marketing's views of the market	Plant utilisation	Order-winners to be provided by manufacturing
	principal functional stimulus	Marketing	Engineering	Manufacturing
Minimum duplication of plant involved			√	
Range of volumes produced	widest	√	√	
	narrowest			√
Conflicting order-winners to be provided		√	√	
Products stay in the same unit for all or most of their life cycle		√	√	
Greatest potential for orientating and evaluating appropriate levels of infrastructure within the units				√

*Often related to volume

priateness of the trade-offs which the scale principle provides in terms of the needs of today's markets. What is being sought, therefore, is an approach which brings overall corporate improvement. Thus it is essential that companies apply these approaches with a clear recognition that pragmatism and not the pursuit of a theoretical alternative is the task on hand.

As with all approaches, focus has many facets. If, however, extending part of the principle of focus to a situation does not bring improvement then that facet of focus should in no way be applied. What in reality will happen in most businesses is that a combination of the principles of economies of scale and focus will be the best approach in terms of securing the highest level of overall improvement. However, a company needs to test the extent of change by achieving what is best overall for a business and be wary of the inertia and resistance to change which typically exists in many organisations. Furthermore, the process of change is ongoing. As markets will continually change so manufacturing's response will need to reflect fresh demands. In the past, many companies have failed to question existing approaches in part because of the fundamental logic of the current approach but also because there has not been a viable, well-argued and well-articulated alternative. Focus provides one such challenge and the steps involved to bring this about are now explained.

5.5.1 *Process review*

The first task is to review the existing manufacturing processes in order to identify any which are too expensive to duplicate.* Examples of these will differ from one business/industry to the next. On the one hand it may be a particular process such as heat treatment or cleaning/coating/finishing facilities, while on the other it could be the whole of a process requirement to make particular products. This technical sweep, therefore, identifies the realistic constraints in moving from economies of scale to focus as a basis for plant configurations. Those processes which result in not being

---

* There may, in some instance, be others, for example, space constraints. But often these also constitute cost-related reasons for not duplicating existing capabilities.

allocated will, therefore, retain their batch-process features and will still be based on the principle of economies of scale.

5.5.2 *Identification of manufacturing-related order-winners and qualifiers*

The next step is to identify the manufacturing-related order-winners and qualifiers which relate to the business. These will form the basis for determining any rearrangement of manufacturing given the constraints identified under Step 1.

These criteria need to be carefully evaluated, then matched to the relevant plant focus. Failure to do this will often lead to an inappropriate choice being made on the one hand and result in a failure on the other to understand the rationale on which to base future decisions in line with ever-changing market needs. Throughout, the principle is to create (within the constraints of reality and what is best for the business) a coherent set of tasks for manufacturing within each plant configuration. The manufacturing task, therefore, needs to be based upon a set of similar order-winners and qualifiers wherever possible. Once the split is agreed then considerations of hardware (processes) and software (infra-structure) can proceed.

5.5.3 *Process rearrangement*

Process rearrangement is then completed in which processes are allocated to the agreed units in line with product requirements regarding capability and capacity. Those which it has been decided not to duplicate will, as explained earlier, retain their batch-process features, still based on the principle of economies of scale. In this way, companies need to arrive at pragmatic decisions which best suit the business overall. Some processes are too expensive to duplicate given the level of utilisation which would result and to do so would not be considered a sound investment. These would need, therefore, to retain their process lay-out and be managed, organised and controlled on a batch-process basis.

5.5.4   *Infrastructure*

The final stage concerns reviewing the infrastructure requirements of the different manufacturing units. The selection must also reflect the market needs of each manufacturing unit but will have to be tempered by sensible constraints and principles. These are addressed in Chapter 7 which concerns infrastructure provision within the context of manufacturing strategy.

What happens is that companies reshape existing overheads by allocating relevant support/specialist functions (in terms of both capability and capacity) to each focused unit. The purpose is to enable overhead support to orientate its activities to the particular needs of each different part of the business. To this end, the overhead resources allocation needs to be on a physical (i.e. for relevant staff to be located in the same geographical area of the site) and not a nominated-only basis.

In reality, companies decide that a combination of these approaches best suits their needs. The reason for this is that the constraints typically associated with the duplication of investments alter the trade-offs under review such that certain advantages need to be foregone as this makes better sense for the business overall. Similarly, companies ideally could argue for green-field provision in order to create the ideal response to the market differences which are at the root of these proposals. However, companies have existing sites and this investment-based argument is usually an overpowering factor in what is eventually decided. Approaches to meet these different realities include plant-within-plant configurations, a concept dealt with in a later section. Before we go any further, some examples will prove a useful way to illustrate some of the issues raised so far.

Suffice it to say at this stage that identifying those aspects of a support function's tasks which are truly specialist in nature and those which are candidates for being completed in manufacturing is the first step. This then enables consideration to be made of who would best complete the latter, their appropriate reporting structures and where they should be geographically situated.

The importance of this part of an organisation's review is two-fold.

- Overheads are typically a very large part of an organisation's total resource provision. Thus, orientating this to support the needs of its various markets will be a significant factor in the level of corporate success.

● Whereas process reallocations are constrained by factors such as investment, the opportunity to reshape and reposition overheads is not as restricted by such factors. Therefore, this aspect of strategic review will often provide more opportunities to make the sizeable gains associated with the changes brought about through focus.

*   *   *

A major UK supplier of components and products to the private, commercial and off-highway home and export vehicle markets was reviewing one of its principal manufacturing facilities. The accumulated complexity derived from its attempts to cope with product range increases, volume changes and the growing original equipment (OE)/spares mix had created a factory which was difficult to manage, had high work-in-progress investment and yet was increasingly unable to meet either the delivery needs of its customers or a satisfactory level of return on its investment.

In order to reduce the manufacturing task to a manageable size, it decided to create several 'units' based on a product/market split. In this way, it argued, it would best be able to reflect the needs of its customers whilst reducing its work-in-progress investment requirements. In order to test the validity of the approach it initially took the smallest manufacturing unit within the product/market split and, as it was convenient, relocated the processes and infrastructure for this within an unused part of the existing site. The first review highlighted a series of gains which, when analysed, were predominantly to do with the small-is-manageable philosophy. A more testing analysis, however, showed that the order-winning criteria for different parts of this and the other product/market units were not being addressed any more specifically than before the reorganisation. What had happened was that the company had merely created smaller versions of the larger whole which, in fact, mirror-imaged the problems of the bigger manufacturing units except those associated with plant size. The high and low volumes linked to OE and spares demand respectively called for different order-winning criteria. The appropriate split here would have been to separate out units based on volume in order to create the necessary link between the manufacturing task and the market. The gains owing to small size would automatically follow.

*   *   *

A large European company involved in the manufacture of electronics was facing the decision on where to site its thick-film facility. At the time it had a manufacturing unit in two geographically separate sites and needed to double its overall capacity in the near future in order to meet the anticipated growth in thick-film application. The alternatives were either to spread the increase over both sites or to re-examine its process needs and reflect these in the plant selection. On reviewing this problem two issues were recognised as being fundamental to the choice. The first concerned the widening quality demands of products, and the second the extent to which each location could attract an adequate level of infrastructure support in terms of engineering and development. Discussions on the effects of these implications provided the company with the opportunity to recognise that in its case the process requirements associated with more exacting product specifications, low volumes, development activities and the necessary high calibre of engineering and specialist support came together to form a coherent set of process and infrastructure requirements. Whereas, the demands on the process and support staff for the low product specification and high volumes required a different set of processes and infrastructure. With this now clearly established and the availability and likelihood of attracting sufficient engineering and specialist staff at each location identified, the choices fell into place. In addition, by keeping the process capabilities separate for the two groups of products the problems of establishing, identifying and maintaining the quality requirements for items with very different levels of product specification were considerably reduced. In this way, therefore, the plant focus choice based upon process split enabled the company to recognise, appreciate and take account of the key practical constraints involved, to reflect these within the focused manufacturing decision, thus aligning the plant to the different market segments.

*   *   *

A large food company had grown from its very early beginnings on the same manufacturing site. Over the years it had developed an organisational structure with the purpose of realising the benefits of having had the foresight to select a position which was sufficiently large to contain expansion and well-placed to facilitate access in terms of the local labour pool and relevant distribution channels.

Like many other companies, although enjoying good profits and steady growth in terms of real sales, it was always questioning its cost base and the appropriateness of its organisational set-up. In the early 1990s it decided to consider moving away from its traditional and well-established style of centralised support functions and apply the concept of focus. In process terms it found that the technical requirements of groups of products prevented any opportunity to cross-link different products either in terms of markets or order-winners. Furthermore, it could not justify duplicating plant because of the equipment, buildings and space costs involved. However, in questioning its current set-up it reviewed its product-mix in terms of appropriate order-winners and adjusted what it made so as to create a consistent manufacturing task within its chosen market segments. The real gains, however, came when it reviewed its infrastructure. The outcome was a recognition that the centralised specialist and other overhead functions were not aware of the distinct differences within its markets nor, consequently, of the different manufacturing tasks required. A review of information provision and supporting activities and priorities revealed a marked inconsistency between what was needed and what was provided. Reallocating specialist and other support staff, where appropriate, to the separate manufacturing units resulted not only in support tailored to the particular needs of each part of the business but also in significant reductions in overheads resulting from the unnecessary duplication of procedures and systems as well as the unwanted provision of support staff resulting from the lack of adequate direction in the centralised approach followed in the years before.

5.6   Plant-within-a-plant Configurations

As stressed throughout this chapter an important trade-off implicit, if not explicit, in focused manufacturing is that of plant-size *versus* the economies of organisational scale. Although the ideal would be plants individually focused to the needs of the markets and arranged on the basis of the alternatives given in Table 5.1, this is often not practical on two counts. First, many companies own existing sites together with the sizeable investment in the bricks and mortar, utilities, plant, offices and other facilities they have provided over the years in line with the needs of the business. Second, as businesses change, there is a real danger that the type of manufacturing complexity associated with lack of focus could gradually permeate some of the plants. Where rearrangement is constrained because of the size of initial plants, their geographical location, the distribution difficulties involved, process and infrastructure support considerations and the like, then the flexibility of overall size (i.e. the larger the factory then the greater the permutations available) can often be to a company's advantage. However, although this second aspect may not be a major issue for many companies, the first constraint is.

As inferred in the earlier examples above, the way to proceed in these situations is to adopt the plant-within-a-plant (PWP) resolution to providing focus. In this way, sites are physically divided (i.e. with walls, different entrances and other facilities) thus providing a 'separate' plant within which manufacturing is focused to the needs of different parts of its total business. This reduces units to a more manageable task, attracting the advantages of both focus and smaller size.

Whilst the trade-off for these distinct and often critical gains is the apparent loss of economies of organisation size, what happens in addition is that PWP provides the opportunity to review overheads in line with each focused manufacturing plant similar to the manufacturer referred to earlier. In this way, these judgements are found to be much easier to make because of the improved clarity between business needs/direction and overhead requirement. The amorphous mass takes on shape which in turn allows each part of the business to reflect its needs with its overhead provision whilst the total business now has the opportunity to assess the relative contribution of each part to its overall success.

Focused manufacturing creates a structure in which each plant or PWP has it own facilities in which it can concentrate on every element of work that constitutes the manufacturing task. Each part of the facility has its own processes and infrastructure which are developed in line with each task. This not only provides significant gains in terms of sustaining the qualifying and meeting the order-winning criteria but also decreases the likelihood of *focus regression* (in which the agreed focus is undermined).

5.7 Focus and the Product Life-Cycle

In an earlier section the three principal ways on which to base a focus split were examined and the key approaches summarised in Table 5.1. However, where possible companies should seek to base focused plants on the principle of providing manufacturing with a consistent task (i.e. supporting similar order-winners). Splitting on the basis of products/markets and/or process typically results in the creation of a smaller version of the previous larger whole as explained in the earlier example on p. 169. Bearing in mind the fact that down-sizing will always result in the advantages of being smaller, the key is to gain, as much as possible, the many other advantages available, some of which were given in Table 5.1

As mentioned earlier, separating plants on the basis of order-winners and qualifiers will often be 'parallelled by differences in volume levels' (p. 164), and the link between volume and order-winning criteria as presented in Table 5.1 (p. 165) was clearly established and explained. An important illustration of this concerns the nature of the product life cycle and the changes in volume and order-winning criteria which take place over time.

*   *   *

Over a number of years a European-based telecommunications switchgear company had moved from Product *A* to Products *B* and *C* with Product *D* to be introduced in the near future. These changes reflected product technology developments moving from mechanical (Product *A*) to electromechanical and finally electronic (Product *D*).

All four products basically performed the same task for the

TABLE 5.2
Changes over time in production volume and the main manufacturing task for current and future products

Aspect	Product			
	A	B	C	D
Production volumes				
Current	Low spares volumes	Large	Low	–
In two to three years	Low – little change	Decreasing	Increasing	Low
Manufacturing task based upon agreed order-winners and qualifiers				
Current	Delivery speed	Cost reduction	Quality/ delivery reliability	
In two to three years	Delivery speed	Cost reduction	Cost reduction	Quality/ delivery reliability

customer – more sophisticated, but the same task. As is often the case, there was a considerable overlap between the life of one product and that of another. As a result, there was a need to manufacture more than one range at a time, plus spares for each range. The spares service was part of the company's commitment to the past, as well as demonstrating to its current customers that they would be provided for in the future. In order, therefore, to establish the whole of the manufacturing task it was necessary to review the whole of the corporate marketing requirements as this would provide a true picture of the issues involved. A review of these products is summarised in Table 5.2

Product *A*, based upon a mechanical technology, was no longer sold as part of a new contract. Sales were restricted to spares or replacement equipment in existing installations. The processes required to make this product were specific to this range as the other three products were based upon eletronic product technology and required different processes. Products *C* and *D* emphasised the trend in product development reflecting the rapid advance in microtechnology.

The company whilst maintaining the process capability unique to meeting the spare parts and replacement equipment sales of Product *A*, currently produced both Products *B* and *C* on the same processes. With Product *D* already being earmarked as the next stage in the product development, the question facing manufacturing was, which processes were appropriate to meet both the technical and market requirements of the three products based on similar technology? The decision concerned the principle of *process and product focus**.[9] This concept helps a company to look at its present and future product decisions in terms of manufacturing, by considering what type of focus would best suit the corporate marketing needs. Being process focused** means that the manufacturing facility is designed on a general-purpose basis and is thus able to meet the needs of a relatively wide range of volumes. These requirements would typically include product development, low volumes, intermittent, uncertain demand patterns and delivery speed. When a plant is product-focused,† it is designed to meet the needs of what is often (compared with a process-focused plant) a relatively narrow range of products, normally with high volumes and/or similar process requirements. Such a plant is, therefore, specialised in order to meet the low-cost requirements of what would typically be a price-sensitive market.

The manufacturing strategy adopted by this company for its electronic products had been based on the provision of a general purpose production process and it was manufacturing Products *B* and *C* and intended to manufacture Product *D* in this way. This decision had been taken to meet three main objectives:

---

* These different types are broad descriptions of approaches to focus. Though they do not always provide an appropriate 'strategic fit' between the market and manufacturing, they are sound, generalisable explanations and, in that way, a most useful insight into the key differences which exist for many products throughout their life-cycles.

† The first edition of this book used the phases product and process focus in the opposite way to their use here. This earlier decision was made in order to be consistent with early writers in the field. However, finding that practitioners were confused by a use of terms which appeared to be the wrong way round, I have altered the terminology accordingly.

1. To cope with known product development with an existing facility and so avoid the need to plan for new facilities at each stage.
2. To minimise total product costs for all items, accepting that this may not be possible for individual products.
3. To be better able to handle volume fluctuations due to variable demand patterns from major customers.

However, by the very nature of general-purpose processes, each product will be assumed to have similar order-winners and hence, a similar manufacturing task will be appropriate. In this situation, these processes would be suboptimal in meeting the cost-reduction requirements of Product *B* and later those of Product *C*.

A facility to provide the existing and future market requirements would need to encompass the characteristics of both a process- and product-focused plant as described earlier. To provide these in one process will always lead to a compromise through a series of trade-offs. However, where this trade-off is between the key order-winning criteria of different products, it is necessary to make alternative focused manufacturing provision.

This distinction is shown in Figure 5.1 by a product focus/process focus continuum. Establishing where a production facility

---

FIGURE 5.1
Orientation of a particular manufacturing facility[10]

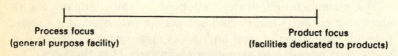

Process focus
(general purpose facility)

Product focus
(facilities dedicated to products)

---

stands on this spectrum and in which direction it is evolving will provide a firm with the opportunity to review where it is and where it should be in terms of manufacturing's support of its markets. In this way it provides one of the essential inputs into the corporate strategy debate by highlighting the degree of match between the marketing and manufacturing strategies bringing the company's attention to any current levels of difficulty and the possible ways forward to provide what is best for the business as a whole.

In the example described earlier the company in developing its

FIGURE 5.2
A typical product life-cycle and its relationship to focus

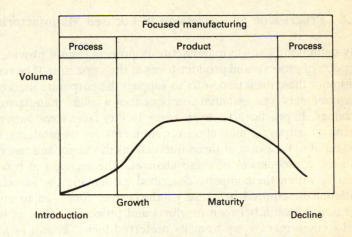

manufacturing strategy became aware of the type of focused manufacturing appropriate to its products as they went through their life-cycles and as illustrated in Figure 5.2.

In the early stages of growth, the implications for manufacturing will be towards handling less predictable sales volumes, product and process modifications, customer orientation with varying levels of delivery speed. The provision of these will usually best be met by the capability and flexibility characteristics which are inherent in process focus. In the period of maturity, the high-volume sales and the product technology having been fixed, attention is totally directed towards processes, with low cost manufacturing becoming predominant (i.e. product focus). Finally, in the period of product decline, the manufacturing requirements revert back to a process focused facility due to the change in volumes and order-winning criteria.

A look back at Table 4.1 (p. 118) and relevant discussion will not only further illustrate these differences but also help to underpin the underlying rationale for focus. Companies will continue to find themselves needing to support different markets and their position will be one of continuous change. Effectively supporting these differences is the strategic role of manufacturing which will constitute a key factor in overall corporate success.

5.8 Progression or Regression in Focused Manufacturing[11]

By definition, a single manufacturing process cannot provide the aspects of process- and product-focus at the same time. The recognition of the critical trade-offs to support the corporate marketing requirements is an essential component of a sound manufacturing strategy. In practice, however, every facility faces some variety in terms of corporate marketing requirements for its products. It is essential to be aware of these fluctuations in variety and to evaluate the consequences of these changes. The increase in product variety within the company described earlier and the associated differences required by these products over time, led to an increased diffusion between products and processes. This, in turn, led to movement away from its preferred focus, known as *focus regression*. On the other hand, for a facility to become increasingly competitive it needs to take appropriate steps to achieve greater movement towards its preferred focus, known as *focus progression*. For this to take place it would be necessary for the company described earlier to align Products *B* and *C* and later Product *D* to their appropriate focus. For, only in this way could the key task be addressed by manufacturing for the different products at the respective stages in their product life-cycles.

5.9 Conclusion

Achieving and maintaining focused manufacturing needs to be an overt corporate activity. Focus does not occur naturally and, in fact, there are normally forces at work that militate against it. These need to be recognised so action may be consciously taken to ensure that improved focus is not inhibited through corporate neglect or traditional views of what is best for the business.

1. *Marketing* often stimulates the desire to create and maintain a broad product line. This is largely because this feature is, and has been for some time, an integral part of its own strategy.

Thus it has become a felt need, with overtones of image and frequently constitutes an important measure of the function's own performance.

2. *Sales* holds the understandable view that it is easier to sell a broader line, a fact reinforced by commission schemes for salesmen, normally based upon total sales value (£s). This implies that sales of all products are of equal value to the business, and fails to recognise the need to differentiate one product sale from the next. This function will also argue that a review of total competition reveals a wide variety of features on offer, affording wider selection for the customer. It follows that as customers' preferences vary, then a wide range better meets the total diverse needs. However, although this may well be true for some of the time, it does not usually hold true for all the time. Often customers' preferences are based upon unsubstantiated and/or non-technical rationales. In these circumstances, it is much harder to sell to customers a product which meets their actual as opposed to their perceived needs. Finally, in businesses experiencing seasonal or cyclical demand, there is often a strong argument to increase variety to help smooth out such patterns.

3. *Manufacturing* also inhibits focus for reasons such as being bound by past union agreements on work practices, high investment costs associated with the purchase, movement of processes, and the risk of uncertain benefits.

4. *Accounting and finance* similarly stimulate forces that work against focus. These include capital restrictions and rationing, the overriding emphasis on short-term earnings, and the prevalence of cost information, which distorts reality by failing to provide data that allow sensitive insights to be gained.

5. *Corporate* forces also limit the steps taken, because of a general resistance to including the manufacturing perspective in the corporate strategic development and a reluctance to increase the interaction between marketing and manufacturing. The reason for this trend is based largely on the divisions between specialists and executives within management, and the predominance, at different times, of a single function in formulating strategy. The background and perspectives brought to strategy discussions by key managers, therefore, have been too narrowly based. This leads to corporate imbalance, in the first

instance, and insufficient breadth in the second, on which to base appropriate revisions. The changed economic circumstances of the late 1970s to mid-1980s has only now forced the corporate hand to arrive at strategy decisions based upon what is best for the business as a whole. This change has been brought about by the increased level of corporate consciousness within the business as a whole. Strategies developed out of a single functional perspective, which were then superficially overlaid by particular perspectives as and when they arose, are rapidly being replaced by genuine corporate debate. However, until that happens, corporate forces will drive out focus and other manufacturing strategy arguments, placing these functional perspectives in their customary reactive position.

5.9.1   *Supporting markets characterised by difference rather than similarity*

Failure to challenge existing concepts in terms of how well they apply to the current and future needs of a business is at the root of today's problems for many companies. By continuing to use concepts and approaches developed for markets, the characteristics of which are very different from the needs of today and tomorrow, companies are finding increasing difficulty in competing effectively. With manufacturing measured on every yardstick and corporations failing to address the size and relevance of its enormous overhead expense, the process of determining appropriate, strategic direction (and its effective pursuit) is inadequately managed.

However, substituting one approach for another is not the answer. Making better use of large key resources is the aim. With markets being characterised by difference rather than similarity, it is essential that firms learn to effectively compete in market segments which are different to one another.[12] Markets based on different order-winners will present conflicting requirements for manufacturing to support only if facilities (processes and infrastructure) are not organised to meet these differences. The concept of focus, therefore, is an appropriate response to meet the increasing levels of difference which characterise today's markets. Thus, focused approaches make more sense and lead to substantial improvements on every significant corporate dimension. Being able to fashion manufacturing facilities and supporting activities to the particular needs of various markets enables companies to compete effectively in the relevant and diverse segments which reflect the requirements of most businesses. Corporate approaches based on reducing or eliminating diversity within corporate port- folios as a strategy in itself are unsound. Advocates of these policies are not only turning their backs on today's reality (i.e. diversity) but also on opportunities. Competing in diverse markets is not in itself strategically unsound. What makes such a business- mix unsound is the failure to recognise and reflect the very differ- ences that exist. Being competitive and successful in different types of markets is a prerequisite for a company today, and the concept of focus offers key insights and principles on which to achieve this.

5.9.2 *Ways forward – halting the drift into unfocused manufacturing*

The development of a manufacturing strategy, as outlined in Chapter 2, provides one overriding advantage: it offers a meaning- ful and realistic way for manufacturing to communicate with the rest of the business. By doing this, it provides the base on which to build, creating a positive move to halt the drift into unfocused manufacturing.

The first step is to concentrate management attention and effort onto the core business areas. As a company adjusts to market- place changes, then product lines, customer characteristics, cus- tomer preferences, and order-winning criteria all change. There must be a reference point from which, or around which, to build the corporate strategy. This reference is the existing core of the business in which a company has a clear competitive advantage. Concentration by production and marketing on the core business is essential. However, there are several aspects, general and speci- fic, that need to be addressed, and these are outlined below.

Overall, it is important to use the opportunity created by the strategic development procedure to redress some of the general inhibitors detailed earlier. The development of an appropriate manufacturing strategy will, in itself, induce a corporate strategy, which embodies the marketing and manufacturing perspective. In so doing, it will get both these functions to pull in the same corporate direction, by matching production and marketing with the corporate need and measuring the achievement of both against the same corporate yardsticks. Similarly, capital budgeting needs to be couched within the long-term corporate plan, and each expenditure measured in terms of the agreed focus. Revisions need also to be made in the accounting system, in order to provide data more relevant to these decisions and the necessary information on which to base them and monitor future performance.

Now it is time to consider the tasks essential to achieving focused manufacturing. The fundamental purpose behind focus is to establish a plant mission, based upon the development of an appropriate manufacturing strategy. In many instances, it will result in a split of existing facilities in terms of processes and infrastructure and the establishment of plant-within-a-plant configurations. Where these steps are principally to do with refocusing existing plants, it is also important for manufacturing to establish and agree an optimum plant size. By doing this, not only will it restrict the task to what is meaningful and manageable, but also it will limit the future potential for focus regression. But this is not enough. Manufacturing's task is to ensure that focus progression becomes an integral part of their strategic task, and this is facilitated in two ways. The managerial consciousness of the importance and strategic strength derived through focus, and an annual programme to give direction to ensure its achievement.

Notes and References

1. Brought to prominence in E. F. Schumacher's book, *Small is Beautiful* (Blond & Briggs, 1973).
2. W. Skinner, 'The Focused Factory', *Harvard Business Review*, May–June 1974, pp. 113–21.
3. Ibid, p. 114.
4. The need for differentiated strategies is also identified by R. G. Schroeder, J. C. Anderson and G. Cleveland in their article 'The Content of Manufacturing Strategy: An Empirical Study', *Journal of Operations Management*, vol. 6, no 3 (1988) pp. 405–16 and by A. Roth in 'Differentiated Manufacturing Strategies for Competitive Advantage: An Empirical Investigation' (Research Report Series, School of Management, Boston University, 1987).
5. Skinner, 'The Focused Factory', p. 118.
6. R. W. Schmenner, 'Every Factory has a Life-Cycle', *Harvard Business Review*, March–April 1983, p. 123.

7. Skinner, 'The Focused Factory'.
8. Based on Table 5.1 in T. J. Hill *Manufacturing Strategy: Text and Cases* (Irwin, 1989) p. 103.
9. Product and process-focused plants are examined by R. H. Hayes and R. W. Schmenner in their article 'How Should You Organise Manufacturing?', *Harvard Business Review*, January/February 1978, pp. 105–18, and R. J. Mayer and K. U. Agarwal in their article 'Manufacturing Strategy: Key to Industrial Productivity', *Outlook*, Fall/Winter, 1980, pp. 16–21.
10. The company example described in this section (together with Figure 5.1) was first detailed in an article by T. J. Hill and R. M. G. Duke-Woolley, 'Progression or Regression in Facilities Focus', *Strategic Management Journal*, vol. 4 (1983) pp. 109–21.
11. This concept was first introduced in Hill and Duke-Woolley, 'Progression or Regression in Facilities Focus', p. 118.
12. See also Shroeder *et al.* (1986), Roth (1987), and D. A. Garvin, 'Quality on the Line', *Harvard Business Review* (1983) vol. 1, pp. 65–75.

6

Process
Positioning

An important facet of a company's manufacturing strategy concerns the question of process positioning. This consists of the width of a firm's internal span of process, the degree and direction of vertical integration alternatives and its links and relationships at either end of the process spectrum with suppliers, distributors and customers. The process-positioning decision, therefore, has major ramifications within the business itself. As an integral part of corporate strategy it can, on the one hand, be crucial to survival as in the Texas Instruments and Bowmar example referred to in this chapter. On the other hand, however, it can restrict a company's ability to change direction in the future because of the investment involved in earlier integration moves, often justified on the short-term rationale of profit return.[1]

6.1 Reasons for Choosing Alternative Strategic Positions

Although in theory, every item is a candidate to be made or bought, in reality the choice is far more restricted. Many businesses, however, when taking stock find that rarely has their current position been reached as part of some strategically based set of arguments over time. A review of current process positioning will often reveal a number of reasons which have persuaded a company to change its process position or which have contributed to its current stance. Some of the reasons are now outlined. They have been chosen to reflect not only important factors but also to illustrate the different levels of corporate awareness involved.

6.1.1 Core elements of the business

Most companies choose to keep in-house those processes which represent the core elements of their business. For instance, in the situation where a company manufactures its own finished items then it will invariably retain the assembly-onwards end of the production process. The reasons include the wish to retain product identity within its own immediate control, design security, to enable it to exercise final product quality and to provide control over the penultimate link with its customers.

6.1.2 Strategic considerations

Ideally process positioning is chosen in response to the strategic requirements of the business. This decision will include a manufacturing strategy input concerning aspects such as lower cost and improved control. It will also take into account non-manufacturing arguments concerning the market-place and the competitive conditions in which a business operates.

6.1.3 Span of process and product technology

Often, a significant increase in product technology can lead to a corresponding decrease in the internal span of process. This arises where a company applies technology changes to its existing products or on the introduction of new or similar products within its range. Not having the process capability in-house to meet all of the new and more complex product technology requirements, it takes the practical step of buying-in the technology in the form of components. Normally, this narrowing takes place in the earlier stages of the process where the new technology developments are the most radical, the later stages of the process being kept in-house. This is because the technology associated with these later processes is more in line with existing manufacturing expertise and is closer to the final product itself. Figure 6.1 provides an example of this in the strategy adopted by the telecommunications company

FIGURE 6.1

To illustrate (not to scale) the reduction in span of the process with increases in the technology of the product

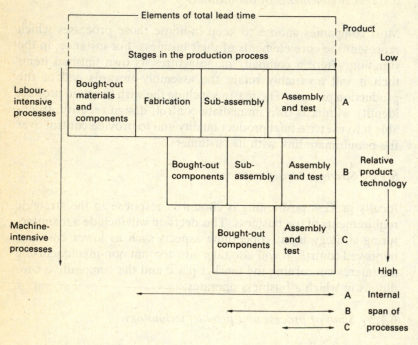

Source: T. J. Hill and R. M. G. Duke-Woolley, 'Progression or Regression in Facilities Focus'.[2] With permission

referred to in Chapter 5 (Table 5.2). When the company only produced Product *A*, it had developed the in-house processes necessary to complete most of the manufacturing involved. However, the advent of Product *B* and later Product *C* heralded a distinct product technology change from mechanical (Product *A*) to electro-mechanical (Product *B*) and electronic (Product *C*). Not having the manufacturing-process capability to provide these new requirements, the company bought them in from outside in the form of components. The narrowing of the internal span of processes which resulted is shown in Figure 6.1.

In these situations, the decision on when and by how much to widen the span of process after the initial narrowing is a significant strategic issue, whereas in practice it is often treated as an operational decision. In the 1970s, the hand-held calculator market provided an example of how Bowmar, one-time market leader, failed to integrate backwards into integrated circuit production and eventually withdrew from the business, whereas Texas Instruments (TI), successfully integrating forward into calculators, took over the market leadership. One major reason for TI eventually displacing Bowmar was that its comparative process position gave it more opportunity to reduce costs and exploit the potential experience curve gains. And that is what it did. Bowmar, restricted to assembly-cost gains, was limited by its suppliers' price reductions for a large part of its costs. TI, on the other hand, had no such limitations. In a related example, *Business Week* in 1974 provided a survey within the calculator market.[3] Part of this concerned the stated strategy of Commodore at this time; one which was to change within a couple of years. It quotes Commodore's President arguing that backward integration was neither necessary nor desirable. To retain the ability to get into and out of a technology as and when necessary was considered by Commodore to be well worth the higher component costs associated with this strategy. However, in 1976 Commodore's purchase of MOS Technology – an ailing manufacturer of calculator chips – is sometimes credited with Commodore's later success in small computers.

6.1.4 *Product volumes*

Where companies are faced with the different tasks involved with manufacturing high and low volumes the strategic decision of adopting a plant-within-a-plant alternative has already been reviewed in Chapter 5. A company may also consider buying out those products with a low-volume demand, for instance, which would, in turn, normally lead to a narrowing of the internal span of process. An example of this decision involved a manufacturer of engine parts for agricultural and diesel trucks. When the low-volume spares demand was reached in a product's life-cycle, the company increasingly subcontracted component manufacturing where the machining processes involved were only used on operations for components for that product or products with similar low volumes. In that way it reduced its span of processes and kept the manufacturing task within agreed bounds.

6.1.5   *Yesterday's strategies*

It is not unusual for companies' process positions today to be a direct result, at least in part, of yesterday's strategic decisions. Reduction in product life-cycles, changes in product and process technology development and an acceleration in world-wide competition over the past twenty years have all contributed to companies taking their eye off the ball. Unless periodic revision is made of this important strategic area, the impact on costs and manufacturing complexity will go unnoticed until a radical overhaul is necessitated. The damage meanwhile, especially in times of accelerating change, can be irreparable.

6.1.6   *Shedding difficult manufacturing tasks*

Over recent years the trend involving corporate responses to difficult manufacturing tasks has been to shed them by subcontracting or divestment. The area of concern is that many companies approach this decision with an eye more on the difficulties embodied in the task rather than on the strategic consequences of the make or buy decision they are about to take. Short-term gains taken on their own look most attractive. However, the accompanying loss of skill and essential manufacturing know-how and infrastructure may limit a company's ability to respond in the future. A maxim to bear in mind is that if the manufacturing task is easy, then any company can do it! The key to manufacturing success, therefore, is resolving the difficult manufacturing issues, for this is where high profits are to be made.

Furthermore, some companies have, in the ongoing evaluation of these decisions, omitted related costs and investments, thus distorting the picture. One large company established an offshore manufacturing capability to avail itself of the low-costs inherent in that decision. However, its subsequent assessment of that investment failed to recognise that the established costing and financial procedures did not allocate appropriate costs and inventory holdings to the offshore site. Consequently, all re-work costs and in-transit inventory were charged against the home-based plant.

The distorted figures reinforced this, and pointed the way to similar decisions in the future. However, when the accounting rules were changed, future options became less attractive.

Thus, this type of decision often gives inadequate weight to important strategic issues. Issues concerning surrendering the ownership of costs and quality and the need for an appropriate infrastructure base from which to launch changes in direction are ignored, and thus lost to a business in terms of future options. Proponents of such strategies typically have the superficial understanding of business development associated with the analysis of figures, rather than a grasp of reality.

6.2   Issues Involved in Process Position Changes

While in the past, process position changes have principally been associated with the widening of a company's initial span of process, more recently the decision to reduce process spans has been a necessary option to be considered by many businesses. Faced with a decline in demand and the associated reduction in capacity requirements, companies have – possibly for the first time in their recent histories – been confronted with the necessity of decreasing parts of their span of process, often on many major business fronts.

However, when repositioning whether for growth or contraction, it is essential for a business to assess fully the issues involved. Particular attention needs to be given to ensure that the real costs and investments in both process and infrastructure have been fully assessed on the one hand, and will be achievable on the other. Additional, quite sizeable, investments are often incurred after the event which, although not included in the original decision, form an integral part of securing the benefits of the original undertaking. In the same way, cost and investment reductions assumed to accrue from divestment may well not be achieved when anticipated, and sometimes not at all. An illustration which typifies this concerns the support functions within a firm's overhead structure. Often, the extent of overhead support necessary to sustain effectively the new process investment and/or growth into new products is understated whilst the anticipated reduction in overheads associated with a narrowing of a firm's internal span of process is generally overestimated.

It is also necessary to separate the issues involved in these decisions between those which essentially support strategy and those which do not. To ensure that the span of process decisions are consistent with key corporate objectives (or if not, is recognised as not being consistent) is an important management task. Decisions can all too often be taken without this appropriate level of clarity. This differentiation of issues provides the opportunity to review these critical manufacturing decisions in the light of relevant corporate strategy considerations, by allowing comparisons between options to be made on the basis of appropriate information. Separating the strategic arguments into their functional derivatives will add further clarity to corporate understanding of the basis on which these important manufacturing decisions need to be addressed.

Recognising that particular issues will differ from one case to another and that the level of importance of issues will vary, some of the more important advantages and disadvantages are listed here. How effectively a business is able to achieve the mix of benefits and risks involved and yet offset costs wherever possible depends upon a functionally capable and alert management team together with the level of understanding and agreement they have reached on the strategic issues involved.

6.2.1   *Costs and investments*

One of the fundamental sets of trade-offs involved in span of process decisions concerns costs and investments.[4] The level of investment will determine the width of process internal to the business and in so doing will have a direct bearing on the levels of cost involved. (The link between span of process and experience curves was discussed in Chapter 5). The principal areas of cost associated with span of process decisions are:

- Transaction costs concerned with the buying, selling and physical handling activities involved in the supply of materials throughout the relevant processes.
- The costs associated with improving the coordination between the supply, production and distribution activities.
- The combination of similar overhead activities is afforded where firms widen their span of process. However, where centralised

FIGURE 6.2
To illustrate the corresponding overhead support to the process under review which will form part of the corporate decision on process narrowing – known as *vertical slicing*

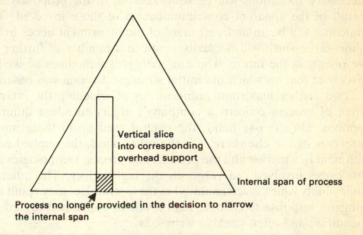

Vertical slice
into corresponding
overhead support

Internal span of process

Process no longer provided in the decision to narrow
the internal span

activities exist, it is really difficult to achieve the apparent over-head gains where internal span of process is narrowed. In these situations, companies need to be aware that unless the *vertical slicing* into those overheads attributable to a proposed reduction in span are in fact achievable then the cost rationale for this decision will need to be reassessed (see Figure 6.2).

• The investment linked to span-of-process changes not only in-volves the hardware but also the controls, procedures and other relevant infrastructure requirements. Although the tangible costs of plant and equipment are both readily identified and at least in principle agreed to, the costs resulting from changes in the less tangible areas are not as apparent and do not lend themselves to being as easily quantified. In turn, they become the decisions which are subject to judgement, often have to bear the brunt of close vetting, and invariably become the areas where projected costs are cut on the assumption, or based on the argument, that the existing infrastructure can or will have to cope.

In situations of process widening, many companies neither clearly identify all the investment and associated requirements involved, nor hold a shared view of the strategic relevance of the proposed span-of-process changes. Invariably in these circumstances, sufficient allowances will not have been provided or the necessary allocations will be squeezed out of the proposals as a result of the apparent conscientiousness of those involved. The outcome will be an underestimate of the investment needs in the short-term which will normally result in a number of further investments in the future. The final tally will sometimes be well in excess of that on which the initial strategic decision was based.

Two further important ramifications of widening the internal span of process concern a company's ability to adopt different options. On the one hand, the capital used up in these moves prevents its use elsewhere. On the other hand, the implied commitment to a market and the product and process technologies and life-cycles involved can verge on the highly risky. The inherent inflexibility which is accumulated in these strategies may result in a sluggish response to change, high levels of unplanned capital expenditure and often sizeable write-offs.

6.2.2 *Strategic considerations*

Although decisions on process repositioning usually embody their own set of specific strategic considerations, there are some important general considerations which help to form the basis for strategic action.

- *High entry barriers* In industries where a wide span of process brings with it a set of distinct advantages, then increasing the internal span will raise the financial and managerial resources required to enter and compete effectively with existing businesses. Established companies may, therefore, raise the stakes thus discouraging new entrants.
- *Supply assurance* The supply of critical materials may well be of such importance to a company, that this gain alone will be the basis for the investment involved. However, as with all forms of backward integration, the issue of whether or not a company aims to keep the supply capacity solely in balance with its internal needs raises its own set of advantages and disadvantages.

- *Secured outlets*   In the same way as supply can be assured by integrating backwards, securing outlets can result from integrating forwards. Additional advantages also accrue with this move from improved feedback which leads to the position of being more aware of demand changes and provides the opportunity to increase the accuracy of forecasts.

6.2.3   *The managerial task*

Changes in span of process will invariably lead to a change in the total management task within the business. These come under three broad headings:

- *The level of complexity*   One important consequence which invariably comes from a widening of process span is the increase in complexity and the hidden costs associated with these incremental uplifts. The associations of synergy are probably more apparent in the level of complexity than elsewhere. Here, one and one really are greater than two.
- *The question of balance*   When companies increase their span of process they face the questions of the trade-offs involved between whether or not to keep the supply or outlet in balance with the rest of the business. A large group of manufacturing companies, deciding on a policy of expansion, asked the individual companies involved to put forward proposals relevant to their own business. One such company, a cable-maker, put forward a proposed strategy of integrating backwards into wire-drawing. In order to limit the investment involved it purchased a local site and installed capacity roughly in line with its own needs. With the high price of copper, neither part of the business wanted high material inventory. As a consequence, the production runs on which the drawn-wire cost-structure had been based and which also sustained the investment rationale could not be maintained. This was because of the programme changes necessary to meet cable sales and the low inventory planned for in the overall investment. As one part of the business was not adequately decoupled from the next, even shorter runs and overtime working in the wire-drawing plant could not prevent cable delivery dates being missed. Eventually, issues of capacity balance and decoupling inventory levels had to be re-examined.

- *The manufacturing task* Span-of-process changes bring corresponding changes in the manufacturing management task. The
cable-making/wire-drawing example had one further important
rider. The management team assumed that their knowledge of
cable-making together with existing internal organisational and
control systems would be sufficient to anticipate likely difficulties and to cope with any that were unforeseen in the processes
involved in drawing wire. They underestimated the change in
the manufacturing management task which partly contributed to
the wire-drawing unit's failure to break even in the first twenty
months let alone meet the projected return on investment.

The traditional argument for ownership has been based, at least
in part, on the economies of large scale. In the last two or three
decades this argument has been a major thrust within existing
accounting perspectives. Based on inadequate analysis of what the
new reality would bring, the economies-of-large-scale rationale
has often been the principal distorting factor in these critical
decisions. In many companies the impact has been further dis-
guised by the build-up of complexity associated with incremental
process widening. In most situations, it is not the technology
considerations but the control and other infrastructure features of
the manufacturing task which are affected.

6.3 Level of Vertical Integration

The previous sections introduced some of the important perspectives, issues and context concerning process positioning. The sections which follow address the more important considerations
concerning the alternative strategies which can be followed. This
first section concerns dimensions of vertical integration, what is
entailed and the benefits and disadvantages involved. Section 6.4
flags up a growing problem for many industrialised nations, that of
the hollowing of its manufacturing sector. Finally, in Section 6.5 a
company's alternatives to widening the span of processes are explained. These offer a mix of the advantages associated with the
approaches discussed in the two previous sections.

6.3.1 *Dimensions involved*

The principal dimensions of vertical integration are the breadth and level of activity as well as the form it takes. *Breadth* addresses decisions on which of the principal activities a firm decides to perform in-house. This involves functions such as design, manufacturing and distribution. Closely linked to this is the decision on the amount (i.e. level) of each chosen activity which is to be undertaken in-house and how much will, therefore, be subcontracted. Finally, the *form* concerns the nature of the provision in terms of the level and type of ownership, trading partnership arrangements and other issues which are addressed in the following sections.

6.3.2 *Benefits of vertical integration*

All process-positioning decisions bring a mix of internal and external benefits and costs. In particular, decisions on vertical integration offer a company a number of inherent competitive advantages which are linked to increased intelligence in terms of markets and technology, improved control over its environment and increased opportunity to support the characteristics of its markets. These include:

1. Improved market and technological intelligence by offering an increased ability to forecast more accurately trends concerning key aspects of a business from demand patterns to cost changes. Furthermore, it provides guarantees both in terms of supplies and markets which, in turn, strengthens a firm against known and opportunistic competitors in given areas.
2. More readily available technological innovations and options through greater coherence and transfer within the total organisation, sharing technology initiatives and opportunities by collaboration. In addition, it also enables companies to transfer experience, thereby increasing the level of knowledge of events and so reducing some areas of uncertainty.
3. Increased control over relevant aspects of a firm's environment. These opportunities can take the form of background integration to reduce dependency of supplies, and forward integration to help to gain market penetration or acceptance. Instances of the latter range from overcoming strong entry (even monopoly)

barriers on the one hand to gaining acceptance of new products on the other. With regard to the former, St Gobain, a French glass-maker, purchased the UK-based glass-processor and merchant, Solaglass, in 1990 as one way of entering the UK glass market which, at the time, was dominated by Pilkington Glass. The advent of both aluminium and rayon provide examples of the way that vertical integration facilitated the acceptance of the use of these new materials as substitutes in existing markets.

4. The provision of low-cost opportunities by generating internal demand and thereby contributing to the high-volume requirement for low-cost manufacturing. One example of this is the semiconductor market. Destined by the year 2000 to exceed $100 billion in sales, Japanese companies such as Fujitsu, Hitachi, Mitsubishi, NEC and Toshiba have progressively out-competed their US rivals partly through the high level of integration which characterises their businesses. Semi-conductors were invented in the 1950s and since then three decades of accelerating growth produced by 1990 a world-wide industry of $56 billion, more than double what it was in the mid-1980s. However, the highly integrated Japanese semiconductor manufacturers are able to make their products at increasingly lower costs than their competitors throughout the rest of the world. A substantial part of this is the result of the high-volume base created by internal, corporate demand. Japanese giant *zaibatsus* make semiconductors along with everything else from robots to cars and satellites. The result is that Japan currently has 50 per cent of the world semiconductor market with the USA at 37 per cent and Western Europe at 11 per cent.

5. Finally, being vertically integrated may help a company to differentiate its products in all aspects from product customisation through to the availability and use of alternative new materials as a way of meeting a product's technical and other requirements more effectively in terms of cost and specification.

6.3.3 *Costs of vertical integration*

The degree of success of vertical integration depends on how well it has been thought through and fits the needs of the enlarged business. In some instances, the strategic rational for integration may not have been thought through. Where this is so, rationalisation tends to replace strategic rationale. To secure the benefits of vertical integration there is an implied assumption that not only was the rationale for the decision well thought through and appropriate but also the potential benefits are tangible and achievable rather than illusory. In some instances, companies may integrate because the opportunity to do so was available and timely. Companies that fail to separate the action itself from the rationale underpinning that action may unknowingly incur significant disadvantages.

6.3.4 *Level of integration*[5]

The final dimension concerns the level of integration which a firm chooses to undertake. At the extreme, firms may decide on fully integrated responses where all their requirements for a given material, product or service are bought internally. In these instances, the supplying units are usually fully-owned subsidiaries and this alternative works best where:

1. the level of price competition is so great that being able to access the lowest cost alternatives is essential to competing effectively in a market;
2. the advantages derived from accessibility to scarce resources outweigh other factors;
3. capacity increases are not stepped in nature thereby creating investment obstacles in terms of growth or reduction in demand, and associated volumes.

The more usual level of integration is referred to as a *taper-integrated strategy*.[6] This describes the alternative where firms rely on outsiders to provide a portion of their requirements and so enables the integrated facilities to use capacity to the full by alternating the make/buy decision to advantage. However, such strategies, especially where they are exercised to the full, incur a number of disadvantages including:

1. Alternating the make/buy decision to advantage militates against developing good customer/supplier relations. In the long run it may alienate suppliers as such strategies often do not provide them with adequate lead-times to enable resources to be switched, capacity to be reduced or alternative sales to be secured.

2. By definition a taper-integrated strategy implies splitting volumes and reduces those conditions which maximise low-cost opportunities.
3. Alert suppliers may charge a price premium where volumes are low and subject to fluctuations.

The forms of integration discussed in this section comprise at least some degree of internal provision. However, there are several alternatives to integrated strategies which are explained in Section 6.5.

6.4   The Hollow Corporation

There is an increasing recognition of and growing concern about a phenomenon referred to as the 'hollow corporation'.[7] Where organisations have considered the question of how manufacturing should best be organised to meet the dynamics of their markets, many have simply shied away from addressing and incorporating the manufacturing dimension within the debate concerning the appropriate short- and long-term strategy for a business. The attraction of low-cost manufacturing opportunities in the Far East, Eastern Europe and Mexico have lured many manufacturers to subcontract substantial parts of their existing processes without due regard for, adequate understanding of, and sufficient in-depth debate about, the long-term implications of these critical and often irreversible decisions. The simplistic rationale of problem avoidance has such siren-like qualities as to make the decision difficult to argue against.

However, as mentioned in the previous section, the basic nature of these decisions and their long-term consequences not only to companies but also to the welfare of nations has neither been fully recognised nor adequately assessed. The attraction of short-term gains similar to those mentioned above is increased by the fact that such decisions bring the instant rewards of solution as well as profit. Moving offshore becomes a last resort to offset what are now for many organisations sizeable, inherent, structural disadvantages. The alternative is to become competitive in terms of the relevant dimensions of those markets in which a company decides to compete such as design, price, quality and delivery performance. But usually the impact of this short-term thinking has not been fully assessed. To the nation as a whole there is increasing dependency on imports, compounded by a loss of technology know-how and ownership which will invariably lead to being driven out of business altogether.

Companies pursuing this rationale rarely do so as a way of buying time to enable them to regroup strategically. For most it is a comprehensive solution in its own right with an apparent disregard for the long-term implications and inherent constraints imposed on future strategic options.

Furthermore, the ripple effect of imports means that for every £1 of imports there is a further substantial loss to a nation's economy as a whole.* In addition, as time goes on these offshore plants will draw the service jobs that surround manufacturing. And, at a company level, the effects are similar. Once skills have been transferred out then that know-how will eventually be lost within that company.

At the extreme, the post-industrial company could be vertically disaggregated, relying on other companies for manufacturing and many essential business functions.[8] They become industrial, corporate shells. And, there are strong forces pushing companies this way. In the short-term, these decisions offer fixed asset freedom and dynamic networking both arguably suited to meeting the characteristics of today's markets. Such arrangements allow companies to respond quickly to exploit new markets and new technologies. The organisations become more agile, flexible and responsive. Typically, firms need less capital, carry lower overhead costs and can better tap into outside technology. In essence, they are more entrepreneurial.

The outcome of this initiative is that 'manufacturing' companies of a new kind are evolving – those that do little manufacturing. They import components and assemble them or import the products themselves and sell them. The result is a hollowing of once-powerful manufacturing companies who, following a strategy of this kind, find themselves trapped in a position where their ability to compete is increasingly undermined by their own as well as

* The ripple effect concerns the real cost to an economy of imports. For each $1 billion of foreign-made consumables it was estimated that the total cost to the US economy was $1.43 billion on top of $1 billion imports themselves.[9]

competitors' actions. Unchecked, this will invariably lead to the abandonment of their status as strong industrial companies, and the retardation of their capacity for innovation and productivity improvement. The erosion of a nation's wealth-creating activity is the aggregate effect of these policies leading, in the end, to an undermining of the standard of living enjoyed by its people.

However, the full impact of the disaggregation philosophy on the welfare of corporations and nations is only now being realised. Many firms are finding themselves hamstrung. They are increasingly exposed to competition from suppliers yet have less security of supply and control of production with the inherent loss of design and manufacturing expertise which forms the essential springboard from which to launch their strategic response. Furthermore, the difficulty is that having once taken this strategic option, the problem of altering course becomes more difficult. The result is that strategic options become increasingly restricted and future positions reinforce original rationale, subsequent logic and chosen outcomes. To rebuild alternatives has infrastructure and timescale dimensions which are unappreciated and consequently, unaddressed.

6.5 Alternatives to Widening Internal Span of Process

The discussion, so far, has implied that the choices to be made also presented an ownership or non-ownership option. Either a company invests in the process through ownership or it buys out its requirements from suppliers. Many companies, faced with what they perceive to be as only two viable options, would consider that, in many situations, they had, in fact, Hobson's choice.* Being reliant on suppliers was not considered a feasible alternative.

Given this background and where greater control is considered necessary, alternatives to widening the internal span of process need to receive serious consideration by manufacturing companies. To help in the assessment of whether the preferred decision should be by investment or not, it is essential to separate

---

* Thomas Hobson, a Cambridge carrier, had a policy of letting out his horses in rotation, without allowing his customers to choose among them. Hence, they had to take or leave the one on offer.

strategic from tactical issues, and also to trace the strategic arguments to their functional source. Only in this way, will a business be able to establish clearly whether or not a decision has to be through investment ownership.

The two principal alternatives are based upon an appropriately high degree of liaison between those involved. The first of these is based upon a legal agreement or arrangement of some kind. The second springs from the recognition that it is in the best interests of all concerned to generate mutually beneficial links in order to exploit the combined opportunity.

6.5.1 *Joint ventures*

Companies can often find themselves needing to exploit opportunities, particularly in areas such as applied technology and research. Where a similar need exists in another company, and mutual benefits from joining together exist, then joint ventures suit both parties' needs.

Joint ventures are separate entities with two or more actively involved firms as sponsors. Because joint ventures draw on the strengths of their owners, they have the potential to tap the synergy inherent in such a relationship and the improved competitive abilities which should accrue. Since the late 1970s, the case of joint ventures has increased substantially. In 1983 alone, the number of cooperative strategies announced in some industries, such as communications systems and services, exceeded the sum of all previously announced US ventures in those sectors.[10]

This trend has continued so much that by now domestic joint ventures have become an important way of improving the strengths and reducing the weaknesses of cooperating businesses. The willingness of businesses to contemplate and undertake strategies involving a high degree of commitment and cooperation brought with it a new portfolio of opportunities from which they previously would have been debarred, by investment or lead-time barriers. Joint ventures should not, however, be seen as a convenient means of hiding weaknesses. If used prudently, such ventures can create internal strengths. They can be resource-aggregating and resource-sharing mechanisms, allowing sponsoring firms to concentrate resources where they possess the greatest strengths.[11] Box 6.1 provides a comprehensive list of reasons for

BOX 6.1
Motivations for forming a joint venture

A. *Internal uses*
  1. Share costs and risks (reduce uncertainty)
  2. Obtain resources where there is no market
  3. Obtain financing to supplement firm's debt capacity
  4. Share outputs of large, underutilised plants
     (a) Avoid wasteful duplication of facilities
     (b) Utilise by-products, processes
     (c) Share brands, distribution channels, widen product lines, and so forth
  5. Intelligence: Obtain a window on new technologies and customers
     (a) Improve information exchange
     (b) Improve technological and personnel interactions
  6. Create innovative managerial practices
     (a) Strive for superior management systems
     (b) Improve communications among small business units
  7. Retain entrepreneurial employees

B. *Competitive uses: Strengthen current strategic positions*
  1. Influence industry structure's evolution
     (a) Pioneer development of new industries
     (b) Reduce competitive volatility
     (c) Rationalise mature industries
  2. Preempt competitors ('first-mover' advantages)
     (a) Gain rapid access to better customers
     (b) Expand capacity, or vertical integration
     (c) Acquire advantageous terms, resources
     (d) Form coalition with best partners
  3. Respond defensively to the blurring of industry boundaries and globalisation
     (a) Ease political tensions (overcome trade barriers)
     (b) Gain access to global networks
  4. Create more effective competitors
     (a) Develop hybrids possessing owners' strengths
     (b) Have fewer, more efficient firms
     (c) Buffer dissimilar partners

C. *Strategic uses: Augment strategic position*
  1. Create and exploit synergies
  2. Perform technology or skills transfer
  3. Diversify
     (a) Rationalise (or divest) investment
     (b) Leverage owners' skills for new uses

forming joint ventures and is classified into internal, competitive, and strategic uses.

Joint ventures, therefore, not only share investment but, often more importantly, provide direction and make possible fresh opportunities.

Identifying the areas in which to focus attention, with the knowledge that the developments will have a commercial outlet, can give substance to this decision. Reducing risk, in this way, while also limiting the investments required to bring the activity to fruition, is an ideal solution. Joint venture arrangements provide this mix and, hence, provide a sensible alternative to the owner/non-owner options.

6.5.2   *Non-equity-based collaboration*

Where companies are unwilling or unable to cope with joint venture arrangements they can resort to an appropriate form of non-equity-based collaboration to meet their needs. These mechanisms provide the means of establishing working arrangements in areas of cooperation, which need a long-term base if the collaboration is to yield meaningful and useful results. Such arrangements include:

- Research and development consortia to enhance innovation and the exploitation of results.
- Cross-marketing agreements to provide opportunities, such as utilising by-products, widening product lines, and sharing distribution channels.
- Cross-production agreements to avoid facilities duplication,

offer vertical integration opportunities, and the transfer of technology know-how.
- Joint purchasing activities to enhance buying power in terms of
price gains and increased supplier allegiance.

6.5.3   *Long-term contracts*

Where technologies have already been established, many companies prefer to arrange long-term contracts with suppliers. For
both parties, such an agreement provides added predictability and
increased assurance, which helps when establishing long-term
plans. The key trade-offs here are between flexibility (in terms of
volume commitment and sourcing) and the classical set of gains,
which have to do with price and delivery. In this way, a customer
can enhance the commitment of suppliers to meeting its needs and
requirements, while providing increased stability for the supplier
itself.

6.5.4   *Customer-vendor relations*

Traditionally, many companies have restricted themselves to an
owner or non-owner position. Furthermore, the prevailing attitude toward suppliers has been to exercise the more extreme
positions within the two alternatives. At the non-owner end, companies choose to exercise the arms-length, free market philosophy
toward their suppliers. The consequence is that customer/supplier
relationships are based upon short-term agreements, which are
invariably multisourced. In this way, added leverage is gained by
playing one supplier against another as part of the drive to achieve
better terms, especially concerning price.
  This perceived need, especially by larger companies, to control
their own destiny by ownership or retaining the power over supplies through multiple sourcing, characterises the current view of
how best to manage these relationships. The 'you need us more
than we need you' syndrome is employed by many companies as a
way to threaten their suppliers. Typical of this approach is that
displayed by the motor manufacturers toward the automotive
component industry. Ford's review of the Japanese threat, referred to in Chapter 1, illustrates the classic position. Faced with the
realities of tough foreign competition. Ford's message to its sup-

TABLE 6.1
The role of customer-supplier relations in a company's competitive stance

The company's country of origin	The perceived base used for competitive analysis		
Western Europe/ North America	Car maker	*versus*	Car-maker
Japan	Car maker and its suppliers	*versus*	Car-maker and its suppliers

pliers, through a series of presentations, was to show them what they had to achieve in order to make Ford, and hence their own businesses, viable. The one aspect that was not mentioned is a most critical ingredient to Japanese companies' success: the customer/supplier relationships engendered by the Japanese motor manufacturer.[12]

How to assess which alternative is the better needs to be based on the view of what constitutes the business. The apparent misconception that separates the two approaches is that the American and West European truck and automobile companies consider that the competition is between car-makers, while the Japanese realise that it is a car-maker and its suppliers *versus* another car-maker and its suppliers (see Table 6.1).

Significantly outperformed, many companies are highlighting areas where comparative supplier performance is low. But it appears that they often fail to differentiate between symptoms and causes, or to appreciate that these results emanate from a comprehensive approach in which all parts are needed to make a successful whole.

These approaches, however, are in many ways much more difficult to manage than those based on the relatively simple premise of power or legal agreement. Ownership, open-market strategies, or contractual arrangements all provide a power base for the customer. Losing their power–base presents a much more demanding task. However, Japanese companies tend to look upon their key suppliers as partners in a joint venture. While this is not based upon a legal agreement, it is constituted on the shared understanding that it is a long-term relationship, to the benefit of both parties. Furthermore, it is not limited to a prescribed set of issues, as is often the case in joint ventures, and invariably so in long-term contractual arrangements. For this to work, it requires three important conditions to be made:

1. It is necessary that both organisations have a shared understanding of the long-term nature of what constitutes a mutually beneficial relationship. This does not, however, imply that the customer/supplier relationships are not rigorous. The essential characteristic which underlies this liaison is that their fortunes are interlinked. The Japanese capture the essence of this by using the term 'co-destiny'. But to make this happen requires two other important conditions.

2. As customers and suppliers are interlinked, and as such form part of the same business, they must each achieve the level and nature of the commitments involved. At the operational end of the business the elements of quality, delivery, and price must be met by the supplier in line with the customer's agreed needs. Similarly, the customer must fulfil the scheduling, payment, and volume agreements on which the suppliers have based their commitment.

3. Finally, it is essential for a company to recognise that not only is the quality of purchased materials and components rooted in the processes of its suppliers, but also, so is the basis for cost-reduction. To design components without an understanding of the process capabilities of its suppliers is a common approach in many Western manufacturing industries. To trade with a supplier, yet not systematically discuss how best to make changes for the common business good of both parties is difficult to explain away. An example comparing two approaches serves to highlight the differences involved. The procedure by which Western truck and automobile companies will typically incorporate changes to components or assemblies is time-consuming (normally several years), and provides little incentive to suppliers. However, the Boston Consulting Group's report on the British motor-cycle industry exemplified a basic difference when it summarised the approach adopted by a Japanese producer:

In 1974, Honda informed some parts suppliers that it did not want a parts' price increase for the next five years. Honda is now currently working closely with the suppliers to help them to rationalise and modify parts design. Honda is also suggesting new production methods and technology to the suppliers.[13]

Therefore the essential difference springs from the approach used by these organisations in encouraging and facilitating its suppliers to help to satisfy its own requirements and strengthen its own competitive position. Typically, the gains passed on to a supplier as a result of the latter taking the initiative to reduce overall costs are – due to the leverage exercised by the customer – disproportionately small to the effort involved. In this way, the contributions to the necessary drive on costs are isolated to those basically provided by the supplier. Honda, on the other hand, widened the contributions toward keeping prices low from a supplier-only position to one that included not only its own contributions, but also the joint contributions rising from the customer–supplier relationship it had forged. And this was in 1974!

6.5.5 Just-in-time production

Although dealt with more extensively in the next chapter, the just-in-time (JIT) production concept is an essential facet of some Japanese managements' drive for manufacturing and productivity improvement. JIT is based on a simple principle. The idea is for all materials to be active in the process at all times, thereby avoiding situations of cost without appropriate benefit. The concept is neatly summarised by Schonberger as the aim to 'produce and deliver finished goods just in time to be sold, subassemblies just in time to be assembled into finished goods, fabricated parts just in time to go into subassemblies, and purchased materials just in time to be transformed into fabricated parts.'[14] However, for this to work efficiently requires effective cooperation and coordination between the various parts of the process. Where these are not owned, then only sound supplier–customer relations will enable this to work. But the gains are considerable. Toyota can point to an inventory turnover of 70 times on purchased parts and work-in-process and 16 times if finished goods inventory is included.[15]

6.6 Conclusion

The different factors that motivate companies to change their span of process need to be carefully assessed. In the past, and carried on the winds of growth, many companies repositioned their point on the process span as a matter of course. Often born out of the belief that the company could manufacture anything, decisions to widen process span were taken without an adequate understanding of their strategic fit and the tactical consequences involved. In times where decisions to narrow process span need to be addressed, a similar strategic and tactical analysis needs to be completed.

With this to provide the basis for assessing the true extent of the process and infrastructure investments to be made, a company is now able to establish the key points on which to make its decision. In this way, it will be able to consider the benefits to be gained from the proposed repositioning, while clearly taking into account the trade-offs involved between the alternatives. Besides the strategic issues involved, span of process repositioning will enmesh a firm in a series of organisational issues that will require a careful reappraisal of its infrastructure. The extent of the change will itself establish the level of change involved. Increasingly, however, companies are becoming aware of the fact that single systems are inadequate to meet the varying needs of manufacturing functions. In the same way, span of process changes will make a significant impact on manufacturing.

Therefore, the key manufacturing issues are related to the size and nature of the manufacturing activity. Many Western industrial firms are faced with increased problems in terms of manufacturing control. For most, the response is to spend money on solving the control problem. Few start with the appropriate step of deciding what should or should not be retained as an integral part of an appropriate manufacturing strategy. Determining the size of the manufacturing task, therefore, is the necessary first step. This needs to be completed before investing in the manufacturing infrastructure, to ensure that the time and money spent is necessary and appropriate to the key manufacturing aspects involved.

Notes and References

1. R. H. Hayes and J. Abernathy, 'Managing Our Way to Economic Decline', *Harvard Business Review*, July–August 1980, pp. 67–77.
2. From T. J. Hill and R. M. G. Duke-Woolley, 'Progression or Regression in Facilities Focus', *Strategic Management Journal* (1983) vol. 7, pp. 109–21.
3. 'Why They're Integrating into Integrated Circuits', *Business Week*, 28 September 1974, p. 55.
4. For example, refer to C. Batchelor's review of the gains secured through subcontracting and reported in his article 'Lower Overheads and Increased Productivity', *Financial Times*, 23 April 1991, p. 14.
5. Refer to K. R. Harrigan, *Strategies for Vertical Integration* (Lexington Books, 1983) where these issues are also addressed.
6. Harrigan (1983), chap. 2 discusses these alternatives and offers frameworks to help in their selection.
7. See, for example, Special Report entitled 'The Hollow Corporation', *Business Week*, 3 March 1986, pp. 56–76.
8. *Business Week*, March 1986, pp. 63–6 introduces the notion of post-industrial corporations which could subcontract everything from manufacturing to invoicing customers.
9. *Source*: Data Resources Inc, reported in *Business Week* (March 1988) p. 61 and made up as follows:

Area of cost of the economy	$ million
● Imported automobiles	1000
● Other vehicles engaged in hauling raw materials and finished products	200
● Steel and fabricated metal parts	184
● Machine tools	98
● Rubber and plastics	67
● Non-ferrous metals	46
● Chemicals	40
● Other manufacturing	343
● Wholesale and retail margins, transportation, warehousing and utilities	348
● Mining	47
● Finances and insurance	39
● Plant construction	16
Total	$ 2428m

10. K. R. Harrington, 'Managing Joint Ventures – Part I', *Management Review*, February 1987, p. 24.
11. Ibid., p. 28.
12. An extensive review of this approach is provided in the NEDC Report, *The Experience of Nissan Suppliers: Lessons for the United*

Kingdom Engineering Industry, May 1991. This approach not only characterises the Japanese motor industry (also refer to J. Griffiths, 'How Toyota Filters its Component Suppliers' *Financial Times*, 10 April 1991, p. 11) but also other Japanese industries as well. Also refer to C. Batchelor, 'Supplying the Japanese – Painstaking Assessment of Product Quality – A Close but Informal Relationship', *Financial Times*, 21 May 1991, p. 12.

13. 'Strategic Alternatives for the British Motor Cycle Industry', a report prepared for the Secretary of State for Industry by the Boston Consulting Group (HMSO, July 1977) p. 34.
14. R. J. Schonberger, *Japanese Manufacturing Techniques: Nine Hidden Lessons in Simplicity* (New York: Free Press, 1982) p. 16.
15. Taken from G. O'Donnell, 'How Australian Industry Points the Way on Kanban', *Production Engineering*, July–August 1984, pp. 19–20.

Further Reading

Armour, T. J. and D. J. Teece, 'Vertical Integration and Technological Innovation', *The Review of Economics and Statistics*. vol. 62 (August 1982) pp. 470–4.

Arrow, K. J. 'Vertical Integration and Communications', *Bell Journal of Economics*. vol. 6 (Spring 1975), pp. 173–82.

Bailey, P. and D. Farmer, *Purchasing – Principles and Management* (Pitman, 1986) 5th edn.

Blois, K. J., 'Vertical Quasi-integration', *Journal of Industrial Economics* (July 1972) pp. 253–72.

Buzzell, R. D., 'Is Vertical Integration Profitable?' *Harvard Business Review* (January–February 1983) pp. 92–102. Offers an analysis based on the profit impact of market strategies (PIMS) data to assess a number of relationships including vertical integration and profitability; vertical integration, investment intensity, and return on investments; and vertical integration, relative market share, and profitability.

Cavinato, J. L., *Purchasing and Materials Management* (West Publishing Company, 1984).

Cherry, J. V., 'Vendor's Viewpoint: Quality, Response, Delivery', *Quality Progress*, vol. XVII, no 11 (November 1988) pp. 40–2.

Dempsey, W. A., 'Vendor Selection and the Buying Process', *Industrial Marketing Management* (1978) vol. 17, pp. 257–67.

Ford, H., *To-day and Tomorrow* (Productivity Press, 1988).

Gale, B. T., 'Can More Capital Buy Higher Productivity?' *Harvard Business Review* (July–August 1980) pp. 78–90.

Harrigan, K. R. *Managing for Joint Venture Success* (Lexington, Mass.: Lexington Books) 1986.

Kraljic, P., 'Purchasing Must Become Supply Management', *Harvard Business Review* (September–October 1983) pp. 109–17.

Petit, R. E., 'Vendor Evaluation Made Simple', *Quality Progress*, vol. XVII, no 3 (March 1984) pp. 19–22.

Porter, M. E., *Competitive Analysis* (New York: Free Press, 1980). Chapter 14 provides an extensive discussion of the potential benefits and limitations of vertical integration.

Schonberger, R. J., *Building a Chain of Customers* (Hutchinson Business Books, 1990).

Schmalensee, R., 'A Note on the Theory of Vertical Integration', *Journal of Political Economy* (March–April 1973) pp. 442–9.

Williamson, O. E., 'The Vertical Integration of Production: Market Failure Considerations', *American Economic Review*. vol. 61 (May 1971) pp. 112–23.

Manufacturing Infrastructure Development

7

The need for a business to resolve the issues of process choice in line with the manufacturing strategy requirement has been paramount in the book so far. This emphasis is necessary to understand clearly which manufacturing processes can best meet the needs of the market-place or how well existing processes provide the order-winners for products in different segments. However, the task facing manufacturing is not simply one based upon the choice and workings of the hardware dimension. When this has been analysed and the trade-offs reconciled the emphasis shifts. It now becomes equally important to ensure that the structure and composition of the functions which provide the necessary systems and communications within a manufacturing company are also developed in line with the manufacturing strategy requirement. Process choice concerns the features of hardware, the tangible ways in which the products are manufactured. But the task is more than this. The supporting structures, controls, procedures, communications and other systems within manufacturing are equally necessary to successful, competitive manufacturing performance.

These structures, controls, procedures, communications and other systems are collectively known as the *manufacturing infrastructure* which necessarily includes the attitudes, experience and skills of the people who form the basis of the manufacturing organisation charged with the task of providing the necessary support functions to the areas of responsibility involved.

212

As illustrated in Table 2.1 manufacturing strategy comprises both processes and infrastructure. Getting one in line with market needs and not the other will lead to inconsistencies similar to the levels of mismatch illustrated in the section on Product Profiling (pp. 146–51 and particularly Table 4.2). Thus, aligning process characteristics with market needs is insufficient in itself. The impact of infrastructure investments on sound manufacturing strategy provision is as critical as process choice and, in some companies, more so.

Furthermore, it is equally important to recognise that infrastructure developments are also characterised by their high level of investment and their fixed nature. These decisions, therefore, are as binding as their hardware counterparts and require to be made with the same clear link to the needs of a company's markets. If not, sets of problems will arise identical to those already highlighted when discussing process decisions. Requesting additional investment and time to undertake the redevelopment or reorientation of systems or other facets of infrastructure will be met by genuine concern about the need for additional investment and the lost time and opportunity involved.

Furthermore, as markets continue to be increasingly dynamic companies need to parallel these changes with appropriate development in manufacturing. The inherently fixed nature of manufacturing infrastructure is often coupled with an inertia for change which stems, in part, from the reviewing procedures adopted by executives. These are typically built on functional goals and perspectives which lead to situations where those responsible for the realignment of the essential components of manufacturing infrastructure are unaware of, or unable to respond to, the growing need to make the necessary and appropriate changes. One underlying message in Peters and Waterman's *In Search of Excellence* was that the essence of success depended much on the awareness factor.[1] Building the infrastructure on a manufacturing strategy base does just this. It gives appropriate direction and allows a choice between alternative sets of trade-offs to be made. The company then has a shared awareness of what is required in manufacturing if it is to support the current and future needs of the business in the best way. A commonly held recognition of the necessity of linking manufacturing through its process hardware and organisational software to the market-place is thus established.

FIGURE 7.1
The inexorable link between the components of manufacturing strategy with each other and with the business needs

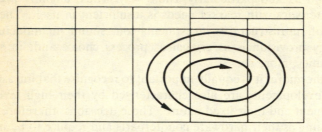

Showing them together and inexorably linking them together (see Figure 7.1) binds the prerequisites of manufacturing strategy to give them both coherence and synergistic purpose.

The infrastructure, therefore, represents part of the complexity inherent in manufacturing. If it is effectively to support manufacturing then it is necessary to get into the complexity within this part of the infrastructure of a business in order to understand and then develop it appropriately. This involves two important dimensions. The first is the way that the company is structured internally and why it has evolved that way. The second is recognition of the key perspectives to be taken into account when developing the important areas which comprise infrastructure.

By themselves, most elements of infrastructure do not require the same level of investment nor do they have the same impact on manufacturing's strategic role as does process choice, but taken collectively they do. Together their importance in providing the strategic support for the business cannot be overstressed. Similarly, the difficulties experienced through the interaction of inappropriate systems and the costs involved in effecting major changes can be of the same order of magnitude as those decisions involving manufacturing hardware. Transforming over time the support for the market-place into an appropriate collection of facilities, structures, controls, procedures, and people comprises the manufacturing strategy task. Hayes and Wheelwright conclude that:

it is this pattern of structural [*process*] and infrastructural decisions that constitutes the 'manufacturing strategy' of a business unit. More formally, a manufacturing strategy consists of a sequence of decisions that, over time, enables a business unit to achieve a desired manufacturing structure [*process choice*], infrastructure, and set of specific capabilities[2]

In relation to corporate strategy they recognise that 'the primary function of a manufacturing strategy is to guide the business in putting together the set of manufacturing capabilities that will enable it to pursue its chosen competive strategy over the long term.'[3]

7.1 Manufacturing Infrastructure Issues

Manufacturing infrastructure is composed of a complex set of interacting factors. Companies in Western economies have traditionally coped with this by breaking the infrastructure into appropriate sets of responsibilities or functions and deploying people to provide the necessary support. For this to work effectively requires a high degree of coordination and a link to manufacturing's strategic tasks. However, the reality does not bear out the theory. The way it tends to work is that these parts or functions are managed separately and come together primarily at the tactical or operational interface. Typically, developments within infrastructure are given the level of detailed attention they require at the points of application. It is at these levels where meaningful, in-depth discussion takes place, no doubt stimulated by the absolute need to make the particular area of infrastructure development work effectively. However, the merits of the individual parts and the way that they fit together are rarely encompassed by any strategic overview. For this reason, piecemeal developments, propounded in the main by specialists, lead to an uncoordinated approach to infrastructure design.

The essential requirement is for the basic parts of the organisational framework to reinforce and support the manufacturing task. This enables the company to get away from functionally based arguments and perspectives in terms of what is appropriate and important. The only way to achieve this is to orientate discussion on the requirements of the business. In this way it can replace functional argument by the corporate resolution between alternatives, and unilaterally stimulated argument of what is best for the business, by corporate-based argument of what is best for the business. This then provides a base on which to develop a comprehensive, coordinated and directed infrastructure to meet the firm's current and future needs. It not only enables a company to get its orientation right but will also enable it to avoid being saddled, in organisational terms, with the existence of functions which are no longer required or are inappropriately weighted when related to the business needs. Changing the *status quo* is difficult unless the firm knows why and how it wants or has to change. Only then is it able to move from subjectively based to objectively based analyses and decisions. In business terms this requires a very clear statement of what constitutes the manufacturing task – the manufacturing strategy appropriate to the company. Once this is understood and appreciated by the functional managers, a company can take the *status quo* and reshuffle it. It is then in a position to avoid situations where vested interests argue for the retention or growth in capabilities/capacities for their own sake rather than for their relative contribution to the current and future success of the business of which they are part.

Questions which stem from these views concern the reasons why functions hold on to their current level of size and why they argue for their own retention and growth. In many instances they do so because it is the best perspective they have. Only when a business orientates functions towards the outside (i.e. what the market requires) can it provide the opportunity for alternatives to be measured against corporate-related criteria. It is the provision of a common, relevant base which enables functional arguments to be put into perspective. It shifts the evaluation of proposals from the use of subjective to objective criteria. It gives appropriate direction to which all infrastructure development must aspire, whilst also providing the detailed checklists against which developments can be evaluated. In this way it ensures that it is the manufacturing strategy requirement rather than a functional or specialist perspective which will be met by these costly developments. Furthermore, by looking outward and forward, developments will be made with a knowing eye on future competition and thus become more likely to incorporate the manufacturing needs of tomorrow.

In this way, the functions which are charged with making effective infrastructure provision are given strategic direction. Without this, there is the real possibility that specialist support functions will pursue their own point of view, an underlying problem which many businesses experience today. Firms need the functional and specialist capabilities to make sense of the complexity. Without these inputs firms cannot reach the level of effectiveness necessary to meet today's competitive pressures. However, the difference between providing an infrastructure based upon a number of specialist views and one which is coordinated to meet the needs of a business by an appropriate strategy is significant for most firms and critical for many.

The review and incremental development of infrastructures within the strategic context of manufacturing is equally important – it concerns altering the balance or changing the focus of development so that it is in line with the manufacturing task and hence forms an integral part of manufacturing strategy. A firm's ability to backtrack on its decisions is also at times important. This activity, however, is often thwarted by the difficulties presented by specialists, highly analytical people capable of arguing their case with great clarity and strength protecting their own views and areas of responsibility, but doing so in a vacuum. Only the existence of a manufacturing strategy provides the parameters for analysis and debate either to reconcile arguments or views or redirect development work.

7.2 Infrastructure Development

Strategy is composed of the development and declaration of a shared view of business direction. Therefore, unless a business regularly and frequently updates its strategy not only will change go unnoticed, but the individual interpretations of strategy, rather than the strategy statement itself, will become fact. In both instances, fragmentation will occur and the necessary cohesion will diminish.

Approaching the successful development of infrastructure must also be done with care. Many companies have adopted a piecemeal approach by resolving one facet at a time, as often stimulated by the apparent need of the moment as by a carefully

FIGURE 7.2
Companies need to determine the level of manufacturing complexity before developing appropriate infrastructure

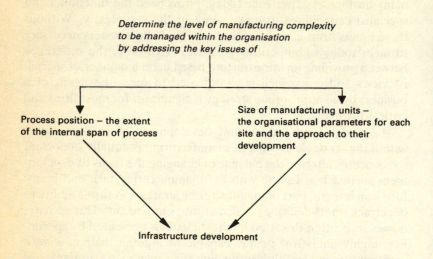

Determine the level of manufacturing complexity to be managed within the organisation by addressing the key issues of

Process position – the extent of the internal span of process

Size of manufacturing units – the organisational parameters for each site and the approach to their development

Infrastructure development

selected priority. Picking off one area makes sense as a way of coping with the complexity involved. However, many organisations even in these situations do not undertake the essential analyses which must precede and then determine the area for development. This preliminary analysis need not become a complex debate; Figure 7.2 points to the essential issues – the need to determine the process position and to define the size of the manufacturing units. Thus, rather than investing money, time and effort in resolving the current complexity, a company should define the level of complexity it wishes to handle. Only then is it able to decide how best to manage the chosen level, and only then is it able to resolve the infrastructure appropriate to its needs. Once a company understands both its manufacturing task and organisationally what it needs to be (its *organisational profile*), the direction and content of any infrastructure development will then be clear and comprehensible.

However, what many companies have done in the past is to

pursue the economies of large scale without fully evaluating the net gains involved (see Chapter 5 on focus). A classic approach to achieving these apparent gains has sometimes been to centralise both at corporate and plant levels. This has often led to centralised functions being created throughout the organisation. Uppermost among the counter-arguments is the increased complexity involved in large organisations and the difficulties of reshaping them in times of change. In many instances, the anticipated gains of centralised functions have proved to be an organisational El Dorado.

The theme of the chapter so far has been to emphasise the importance of the appropriate development of manufacturing infrastructure and stressing its significant contribution to providing the necessary manufacturing support to the market-place. However, before discussing some key areas of infrastructure design, it will be worthwhile to highlight four practical, but general considerations.

1. It is most important to determine and agree the important areas of infrastructure within manufacturing. The need to adopt a discretionary approach to change is essential in order to utilise scarce developmental resources in line with those areas which will yield the best returns. Emanating from the concept of the 80/20 rule,* this point emphasises the fact that the approach to change must reflect those areas which will have the most strategic impact.
2. As with process choice, it is necessary to establish and then choose between the sets of trade-offs which go hand-in-hand with each decision. The criteria, however, against which to measure the trade-offs must be concerned with manufacturing's strategic role.
3. The essence of sound infrastructure design is that it must respond to the dynamics of reality. To do this requires recognition that there are areas of incremental and major change, but that much of the necessary change can be achieved incrementally.

---

* The 80/20 rule reflects the implied relationship between two sets of data or consequences. In this instance, it illustrates the fact that 80 per cent of the total strategic benefit to be gained from infrastructure development will arise from 20 per cent of the areas of application. The use of the figures 80 and 20, however, are illustrative of the relationship implied in the selected phenomenon and not intended to be definitive.

Once this distinction has been drawn, it is essential that areas of manufacturing infrastructure are reviewed on a regular basis in order to effect the necessary developments including the simplification and even withdrawal of controls, systems and procedures. It is most important, on the other hand, to avoid wherever possible the need for major change. In many cases where major change is required it reflects the degree of mismatch between need and provision which has developed incrementally over time within the relevant area of infrastructure, and indicates the size and length of disruption which it will take place to put things right.

4. Linked to the issue of avoiding situations of stepped change is the decision of what constitutes the job of work and what is the role of specialists within an organisation. Although addressed later in the chapter it is important to emphasise early on that continuous development is easier to bring about where the responsibility for identifying and implementing improvements is locally based. Employee involvement creates conditions where incremental changes are met by incremental developments. On the other hand, control through specialisms tends to lead to situations where the need for changes goes undetected or unattended. In these circumstances, the requirements for change will often be set aside. This leads to situations where developments, when eventually addressed, tend to be large in nature and task priorities reflect this factor of size.

7.3   Important Infrastructure Issues

A company which fails to develop its infrastructure as part of its response to meeting the needs of its market-place is likely to experience two separate but linked consequences:

1. A worsening business position, because amongst other things, the systems and controls will fail to give executives the accurate and timely indicators necessary to help them to manage the business and initiate the necessary developments as required.
2. The key components of infrastructure necessary to help reshape or rebuild the business may not be in place at the time when they are most necessary and most urgently required.

The approach to developing the separate parts of a manufacturing company's infrastructure involves two integrated steps. The first is determining the market-place or competitive requirements; that is, the way in which products win orders needs to be the factor around which each aspect of infrastructure is built. The controls, systems, procedures, attitudes and skills involved will then be orientated towards those manufacturing tasks which are pertinent to the different products in terms of their relevant order-winning criteria. The second is the need to ensure that the necessary level of coherence and coordination exists in the various but related parts of manufacturing infrastructure. In this way, not only does the software pull in the same, appropriate, corporate direction but the company releases the synergy inherent in this substantial investment.

Those involved also recognise the symptoms of coherent direction and feel the facilitating and motivating benefits which occur as a consequence.

Selecting for specific discussion those infrastructure issues from the many which could warrant attention has not been easy. Although the factors of relevance and importance have been paramount in this procedure, there is embodied in that evaluation more than a small slice of subjective opinion. However, in many ways that factor is not so important here, because relevance will change between businesses, and the examples themselves are being provided primarily to explain the principles of infrastructure design and development, rather than as a comprehensive statement on manufacturing infrastructure.

The areas discussed in the rest of the chapter concern a number of organisational issues and some of the key areas of operational control. The other important aspects of infrastructure not covered here will need to be similarly developed using the same elements and procedures described in the following sections.

7.4 Some Organisational Issues

The development investment and the running costs required to maintain the support functions within a manufacturing business are high. The rationale for this high-cost provision is based, in part, on providing adequate and appropriate support for manufacturing in order to make this activity both more effective and more efficient. It is essential, therefore, to ensure that this is achieved. However, for the most part, the approach to developing relevant support for manufacturing has been treated by most organisations as an operational and not as a strategic issue. The consequence of this has been that in many businesses the approach to critical aspects of organisational design has not been based on the necessity to support manufacturing's strategic role. Some of the consequences of this are now discussed.

7.5   The Role of Specialists

Most Western manufacturing firms make an extensive use of specialists in running a business. The approach adopted by companies in the past has been to create functions comprising specialist staff to supply expert advice, guidance and activity in various relevant areas. The intention has been to provide the major line functions with the necessary help in terms of infrastructure provision within the organisation. In the past three or four decades this trend towards the employment of specialists has been a growing feature of manufacturing and other sectors of the economy.

It is important especially in terms of increasing world competition, that companies reassess this development both in terms of its extent and the appropriateness of its direction. Before discussing alternatives to the typical pattern of specialist provision currently used in most firms, it will be helpful to review some of the ways in which this concept of control has tended to evolve as a method of examining the current position whilst providing some possible insights into the ways forward. The emphasis throughout will be towards the manufacturing function although the points raised and suggestions made may well prove pertinent in other line areas.

7.5.1   *Concept of specialists is built on the principle of economies of scale*

The rationale underpinning the concept of control by specialists is to bring together staff to provide a level of capability, support and development which is deemed necessary to help line functions to meet the needs of a business. This is underpinned by the principle of economies of scale, an aspect addressed in Chapter 5 on focus. Furthermore, the placement of these groups has traditionally been on a functional basis and eventually, though not always initially, they have been positioned in a reporting structure which has been outside the main line functions.

The consequence of this is that several major difficulties are experienced by many of the companies adopting this concept of control. One of the principal outcomes is that it is not highly effective, for a number of reasons, including:

- *The question of ownership*   The lack of detailed understanding – shared by both line and staff functions – of the important perspectives of each other is legendary. To redress this in the past few years, words such as 'user-orientated', 'user-sensitive' and 'user-friendly' have become part of the standard approach in an attempt to overcome the inherent difficulties created by this organisational arrangement. However, attitudes and detailed insights take time to change.
- *Role clarity*   The roles and relationships shared by line and staff functions within the common decision procedures in which they are involved has led, in certain instances, to a large measure of misunderstanding and criticism leading even to periods of acrimony and derision. This is due, in part, to the people themselves, the different salary, reporting and working structures involved, the implied criticism of the specialist's activity, the high level of failures, apparent lack of interest or time allocation by specialists in the post-implementation period and the relative inexperience of specialists both in organisational and personal terms, which leads to a failure to appreciate that the only hard task in management is managing. However, the perceived roles of the line and support functions within the whole of these areas of development or day-to-day support procedures are too often not clarified either at the organisation or operational levels.

Line managers invariably see the specialist function as a means of improving an area of operational weakness. As busy executives, and not owning, in organisational terms, the time or control of the specialists involved, there is too often a tendency for line managers to take a reactive role in the key periods of the development programme, but given the fact that it is they who have to make the final decisions or to implement the decisions;

all that happens is that the time involvement is delayed until later on when the problems invariably arise. The results are far from effective.

- *Organisational relevance* The principle of control through specialisms and economies of scale is appropriate where markets are of high volume, and stable in nature. The 1980s saw markets increasingly moving away from those characteristics and the 1990s continues this trend. Companies, therefore, need to reconsider this basic tenet. It does not, however, mean that companies should swing to the opposite end of the continuum. They need to avoid the 0–100 management* response which has characterised many changes in the past. There are many points on the continuum besides 0 and 100 (i.e. where a company is now and the point which represents the very opposite set of characteristics). It does mean though that companies need to reconsider appropriate organisational responses to meet the changing and different needs of current and future markets. In most simply identifying those tasks which are clearly specialist in nature from those that are operational will start the process of reconsidering what tasks should go where.

7.5.2 *Functional silos*

In many organisations, the role and area of responsibility attributed to specialists has grown. However, this growth has been determined more on the basis of perceived organisational neatness than to make best use of the specialists' contribution and to meet the needs of the business. Typically, as illustrated in Figure 7.3, areas of responsibility, once within the province of the line functions, have been drawn into the authority sphere of specialists (Phase 1). Classically, what then happens is that an independent reporting structure evolves (Phase 2). The result is that key sets of responsibilities which need to be integrated into the line activities have now been separated and the inherent difficulties associated with this structure when trying to redress the lack of necessary

---

* 0–100 management is an expression developed to highlight the pendulum-like response to problems/disadvantages which typifies organisational action. On the other hand, companies need to reposition themselves on a gradual and continuous basis whilst clearly recognising that the diverse nature of markets will require diverse responses.

FIGURE 7.3
Typical phases in the evolution of specialist functions in an organisation

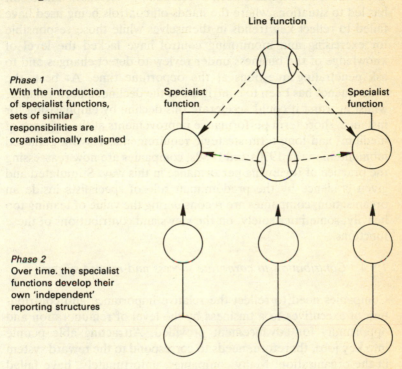

Line function

Phase 1
With the introduction of specialist functions, sets of similar responsibilities are organisationally realigned

Specialist function

Specialist function

Phase 2
Over time. the specialist functions develop their own 'independent' reporting structures

integration are now apparent in many companies. Functional silos have evolved in which individual goals and objectives tend to have higher priority in terms of resource allocation than does the support of line activities.

7.5.3 *Control from a distance*

Invariably, one consequence of this approach is that companies evolve into organisations with too many people and too many layers of control over manufacturing companies by financial analyses and reporting systems which have been developed without adequately reflecting the business itself. This increasing tendency has been brought about, in part, by the belief that effective management can be maintained at a distance, using controls, systems and feedback which have been developed by specialists. The result has led to situations where the hands-off controls being used have failed to reflect key trends in themselves while those responsible for exercising and monitoring control have lacked the level of knowledge of the business under review to detect changes and to ask penetrating questions at the opportune time. At best, the consequence has been to contribute to the decline in performance, whilst at worst it could accelerate this decline by emphasising for instance, short-term performance improvements at the expense of medium- and long-term strategic requirements. Having gathered momentum in the 1970s and 1980s, companies are now reassessing the practice of reviewing performance in this way. Stimulated and given credence by the predominant role of specialists inside an organisation, companies are reconsidering the value of leaning too heavily, sometimes solely, on the views and contributions of these functions.

7.5.4   *Contribution to corporate success and reward systems*

Companies need to reflect the relative importance and contribution of executives to a business by the level of remuneration and opportunity for advancement provided. Attracting able people into key jobs, therefore, needs to correspond to the reward system in the organisation. Many companies, unfortunately, have failed to differentiate between executives' roles and the direct impact they will have on the success of the business. What has unduly influenced salary structures and the opportunity for promotion are factors such as apparent scarcity, assumed contribution and market rates for salaries. The consequence has all too often been that higher salaries have been offered to those whose influence falls in the 20 per cent of the 80/20 rule. The result has been that the more-able people have been attracted away from those line functions whose performance affects the 80 per cent of what constitutes business success.[4]

7.5.5 *Too many layers*

Invariably, one consequence of this approach is that companies evolve into organisations with too many people and too many layers of management. At head office, corporate staff turn into expensive bureaucracies. At plant level, divisional staffs, built up by middle management as they get promoted, have been retained by their successors. Steward (McKinsey & Co) claims that 'ever since the 1960s, when we started to believe that a professional manager can manage everything, we've been on the wrong track'. The random rotation of managers, based upon this belief, led to 'the new managers, unfamiliar with the businesses they were expected to run, [hiring] staff to advise them. When they moved on, a new manager repeated the cycle . . . The problem was compounded when companies started going international'.[5] The economies of large-scale organisation have made their own unique input into this problem. 'Along with bigness comes complexity . . . And, most big companies respond to complexity in kind, by designing complex systems and structures. They then hire more staff to keep track of all this complexity . . .'[6]

The results are reviewed in Figure 7.4 which also illustrates the changes which have taken place in the 1980s and the further anticipated reduction in organisational levels by the year 2000.

The way forward has been to reduce the layers and cut out the fat. A typical response is that at the DuPont's Maitland plant (Ontario, Canada) which, during the 1980s, reduced the number of layers in organisational hierarchy from eleven to six (see Figure 7.5) and shed 700 employees, many of them highly paid middle managers. As in most organisations it was not that these employees were not doing a good job, it is that the roles they undertake slow down procedures and constitute tasks which do not add value. Whereas before, a production manager at the Maitland plant supervised 90 workers through 6 foremen, today he has a staff of 40 and no foreman. Similarly, if workers needed a new tool the decision to purchase came from higher up. Today they call the supplier and order it direct. Similarly, customers telephone the plant directly about orders so speeding up the procedure which previously would have gone through DuPont's Toronto head office and four layers of bureaucracy. The result is that everyone benefits from this kind of flexibility.[7]

FIGURE 7.4
The number of levels within a typical organisation at different times

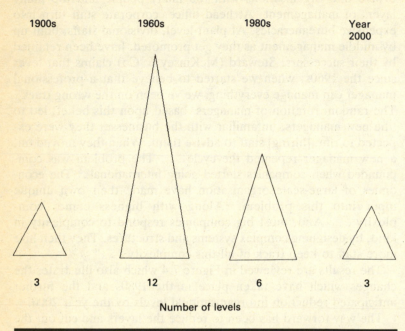

Number of levels

The way forward for many companies is increasingly clear. The question to be answered is 'Which is the best approach to take?' For many companies, the classic response has been to implement across-the-board reductions. Having cut the workforce and dispensed with the 'frills', managers would then be requested to reduce all round by an appropriate percentage. But these haphazard cuts left most corporate or central staff intact, the divisional ratios between managers and workforce rising, and organisations which became more sluggish and less profitable.

But this approach smacks of the specialist's view of an organisation. To make the bottom line come right, just change the figures around! However, this assumes that the structure which exists will be appropriate in a reduced form. Many businesses are realising that the one thing they must not do is to take an axe to the job. Reshaping an organisation requires careful surgery with reduc-

FIGURE 7.5
Shedding layers – DuPont's Maltland Plant reduced eleven levels to six between 1984 and 1988

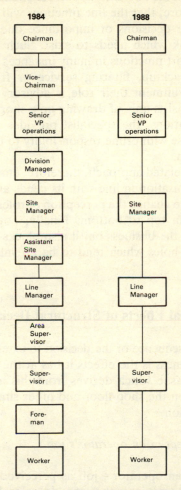

1984	1988
Chairman	Chairman
Vice-Chairman	
Senior VP operations	Senior VP operations
Division Manager	
Site Manager	Site Manager
Assistant Site Manager	
Line Manager	Line Manager
Area Supervisor	
Supervisor	Supervisor
Foreman	
Worker	Worker

tions in line with the business. It needs to start, therefore, with the business and build up from the bottom as well as down from the top. Many organisations in the past have only built top-down without an assessment of the contribution of each part to the business as a whole. This has merely added to the layers. However, reshaping an organisation needs to take into account the role of functions, establish the responsibility for decisions and boundaries of authority and agree the appropriate level and reporting structure between the line and support functions involved. It helps to clarify, therefore, that the line functions will in many instances always make the decisions of importance due to the authority/ responsibility link which needs to exist. Such a review will also reveal that support functions in many instances provide a clerical/ administrative back-up, filtering service or front position. For example, in recruitment their role is advisory and usually, and quite rightly, consists only of drawing up a short-list. In industrial relations negotiations, the specialist provides a first negotiating line to allow those with prime responsibility to take any necessary fall-back position.

The business-related approach, therefore, enables a company to develop its organisation in line with its needs and it also provides the opportunity to change the perception of roles at all levels in the organisation from top to bottom. Finally, not only is this procedure based on the business but it also blocks-off any functional or personal bolt-holes which tend to be prevalent in many companies.

7.6   Operational Effects of Structural Decisions

A significant consequence of the decision to extensively use specialists within a business is the effects it has at the operational level. One important issue which derives from this approach concerns role definitions on the shop-floor and other similar jobs throughout an organisation.

7.6.1   *The concept of an operator's job*

The concept of an operator's job as perceived in most Western manufacturing companies is that of a 'doing' task (e.g. operating a machine or assembling a product). For this reason, when there are no appropriate doing tasks to be completed, the dilemma facing the shop-floor supervisor is between recording a labour excess and completing work which is not required in the current period (i.e. creating inventory). This problem is made even worse by process

FIGURE 7.6
The separation of the three facets of work and the gap between them created by the organisational structure

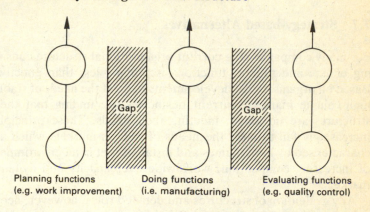

Planning functions
(e.g. work improvement)

Doing functions
(i.e. manufacturing)

Evaluating functions
(e.g. quality control)

investment. In their efforts to reduce the skill and input requirements of the doing tasks within manufacturing, management also reduce the job skills and the work involved when they invest in plant and equipment. In order, therefore, to redress the reducing job interest and to capitalise on the opportunity to use the time released in an effective way, it is first necessary to change the concept of work.

The premise on which this change should be built revolves around the fact that work, in effect, consists of not only the doing task, but also the tasks of planning, and evaluating.[8] In many companies, however, work has been separated into these three components, with each part completed by a different function. The rationale for this is a by-product of the use of specialists and the development of support functions within an organisation. Figure 7.6, therefore, is an extension of Phase 2 in Figure 7.3. It illustrates a typical structure, the separation of important activities at the operator level and the inherent gap created by the structure between these three intrinsic parts of work. This has resulted from the development of organisational structures which have emanated from the use of specialists and the growth of functional reporting procedures. It has led to a situation where the inherent contribution of operators to work-improvement activities has been lost and the essential link between the responsibility for manufacturing and quality has been severed.

7.7   Strategy-based Alternatives

For many companies, the current organisational structure consisting of line and support functions is proving less than effective. Based on organisational developments to meet the needs of stable, high-volume markets, current businesses are finding that these structures are no longer meeting their needs. These principles increasingly fail to meet the needs of today's markets which are characterised by low volumes and instability set in an environment of increasing competition, worldwide overcapacity and dynamic markets.

Any evaluation of structures and detailed roles, however, needs to be based on the premise: will it meet the requirements of the business? The suggested areas of change which follow are intended to reflect more accurately existing responsibility structures or are designed to facilitate an appropriate and relevant contribution being made by people throughout the organisation. If firms are to compete effectively in world markets then their structures need to be both dynamic and designed to tap the relative potential of all their employees.

7.7.1   *Functional teamwork concept*

One important change which Western companies need to consider is the breakdown of the currently held view of line and support functions. The alternative is to consider a move to build specialist functions back into the line and for them to report within that authority/responsibility structure. The principal consequences of this would be:

- Changing the reporting structures would remove the problem of the line management/specialist interface not working.
- Clarification of the current role of specialists into those areas which (a) are primarily within the scope of the specialism – for example, quality assurance, the development of robotics within

productivity improvement and production planning; (b) should be under the auspices of the line-management function – for example, quality control, internal efficiency activities and production control, respectively.

This, therefore, would enable an organisation to build its structure around sets of coherent, interrelated activities rather than, as at present, around activities which have similar names. It would not *per se* lead to reductions in people – although invariably it does – and, in fact, would sometimes lead to increases of staff in certain functions. Although pushing decision-making activity from the centre to the plant and from specialists into the line may not change staffing levels, it would dramatically change the relevance of activities undertaken and assignment priorities established. The benefit, for instance, for manufacturing managers to have the opportunity to generate cost analyses in line with their own perspectives and requirements and in line with their contribution to corporate decisions has to be seen to be believed.

The process, therefore, is one of reshaping overheads. To be successful it will need to challenge fundamentally current structures, attitudes and expectations. Organisations which are functionally driven and controlled through specialisms are top-heavy and unresponsive, and fail to capitalise fully on the abilities of its people and the opportunities which investment have created in terms of time-availability. Built into this re-look is the rationale of continuous improvement. The result is that not only do organisations become more cost-efficient they also become more effective. The sections which follow address the other issues which need to be introduced.

7.7.2 *The structure of work*

As implied by the comments on what constitutes work, organisations need to build back into the 'doing' task aspects of planning and evaluating. Enhanced by the *functional-teamwork* concept described above, and as part of the rationalisation of work and relative contributions by different employees, Figure 7.7 suggests how parts of those planning and evaluating activities, at present completed by support functions, should be reassigned to those currently responsible for the doing tasks. In this way, not only

FIGURE 7.7

The 'doing' task which now incorporates appropriate planning and evaluating steps, so much an intrinsic part of work

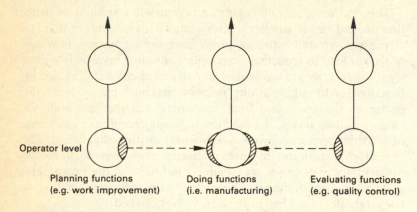

Operator level

Planning functions   Doing functions   Evaluating functions
(e.g. work improvement)   (i.e. manufacturing)   (e.g. quality control)

does such an action lend support to the arguments put forward in the last section but it also provides a tangible commonsense illustration of the effect this can have. These actions facilitate the materialisation of productivity-bearing improvements and at the same time create greater job interest for all concerned.

It releases specialists from 'non-specialist' work and gives operators work which involves the three important dimensions which make up meaningful tasks by broadening their responsibilities and allowing them both to plan and to evaluate the work they carry out.[9] Although these changes bring small returns in themselves, the cumulative effect can be enormous and the contribution made to providing manufacturing's strategic contribution, significant.

Examples from DuPont's Maitland Plant illustrate this. Under the previous system a customer's quality complaint was handled by head office. Now the operator who made the product goes to see the customer and decides how to correct the problem. Problems are cleared up more quickly and customers are happier. At the other end of the spectrum, 'staring at a bank of computers is not a stimulating way to spend a 12-hour shift. To make [an operator's] job more interesting and more useful to the company, [operators] are trained – in their off hours and at overtime rates – in computer technology. [They then become] responsible for maintaining computers in the plant's control room and for helping to develop expert systems'.[10]

7.7.3   Cascading overheads

Linked to both the structure of work and the role of specialists within an organisation, companies should seek to push work as far down the organisation as possible. Coupled (as is the concept of work structuring dealt with in the last section) to an investment by the firm in the training of the individuals involved, the systematic cascading of overheads will help to increase the level of flexibility required, allow any spare time created as a by-product of process investments to be usefully absorbed whilst also providing those involved with a more meaningful task.

This involves changing the levels at which decisions are made and allowing people to decide on how best to complete tasks once they have been given the relevant parameters and information involved.

7.7.4   Quality circles or productivity improvement groups

As part of the organisational changes advocated here, the introduction of quality circles or productivity improvement groups needs careful consideration. The necessary care in evaluating their role and contribution, however, has not always been exercised by those Western companies which have adopted them. In many instances they have been perceived as panaceas and as such have been evaluated and implemented at an operational level and not as part of a strategic organisational change to draw out the continuous improvement potential of the shopfloor.

This essential difference in the way that quality circles are perceived goes some way to explaining the overall rating attributed to this activity and reported in the 1990 *Manufacturing Futures Survey*,[11] – see Table 7.1. This assesses the level of pay-off over the two-year period, 1988–9, compared with the other twenty-six activities listed in the survey.

The concept of quality circles (their name derives from the fact that quality was Japan's initial, major, manufacturing problem after the Second World War, hence the change in name by some

TABLE 7.1
Relative pay-off from quality circles activity reported by region

Region	Relative pay-off from quality circles activity (1988–9)
Europe	23
Japan	3
USA	12

organisations to productivity improvement groups) emanates from Japanese business practice. It illustrates the impact of participation on the productivity increases which can be achieved in all aspects of performance by systematically involving workers in the improvement of quality, productivity and similar operations activities. This form of worker involvement in Japan has been growing rapidly. A review of the period from 1965 to 1991 shows a steady increase in the number of circles and their membership during these years – see Figure 7.8 below.[12]

By the late 1970s, many other countries in the world were adopting this approach. It was recognised as a way of providing the systematic involvement of the workforce and the returns on the investment of training given and time spent were impressive and numerous. Many reviews of the adoption of quality circles are available.[13] However, the distinction has not been drawn in many firms between a major organisational change adopted as an operational response, and one adopted as part of a strategy-led response to improving the effectiveness of manufacturing. This has led some reviewers to conclude that their observations suggest that 'in many US organisations . . . quality circles are already in the adoption–disappointment–discontinuation cycle that has been characteristic of many other managerial fads'.[14]

The failure of UK manufacturing companies to recognise the value of the shop-floor's contribution is widespread. The use of quality circles or productivity improvement groups, however, is an aid to redressing this imbalance and 'tapping what is probably our most underdeveloped asset – the gold in the mind of our workers'.[15] For this to be effective, however, the company needs to be genuinely committed to the principle of continuous improve-

FIGURE 7.8
The growth in Japan of quality circle members and membership between 1965 and 1991

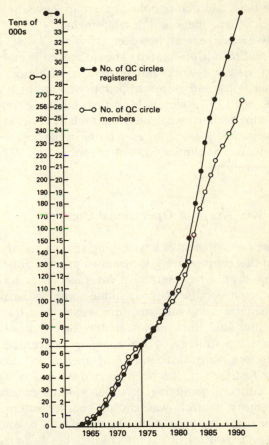

Source: Japan Union of Scientists and Engineers (May 1992), Personal Communication

ment and to accept seriously that this can only be achieved by participative management. The structures then need to be developed to make the *principle* work in *practice* and then to support its development throughout whilst not interfering with the nature of that development. In this way, companies are able to start tapping into their collective wisdom. The change, however, is a strategic one. It accepts that there are significant benefits to be derived from detailed, operational improvements, that implementing improvements quickly and effectively must be on a participative basis and that people, as a group, have the ability to evaluate each others' ideas and develop them.

Participative management, however, is not a soft style. It is both demanding and results-orientated. The difference is embodied in the changed views of work and relative contribution of those involved. Functions, and groups of people who are high potential contributors, need to be clearly identified. Similarly, other functions and groups need to be placed in their relative positions on the continuum depicting these features in terms of the business needs. Fulfilling potential or eliminating low contributors will bring noticeable improvements.

7.8   Some Key Areas of Operational Control

Infrastructure development is a wide-ranging area and the aspects addressed in this chapter are not meant to provide either a comprehensive or even a representative coverage. They have, however, been chosen because they constitute some of the important aspects of manufacturing infrastructure. Also, their treatment is intended to offer guidelines on how to develop other areas within the manufacturing strategy of the company concerned. In this section, therefore, only three facets of operational control are covered. The first, quality, has been selected because of its important role as either a qualifying or order-winning criterion. The second, inventory control, was chosen because often it is the biggest single asset in a manufacturing company's balance sheet. The final aspect, control of manufacturing, has been addressed because of its role in delivery performance, which concerns other important qualifying or order-winning criteria. In addition, the conclusion of the chapter discusses a payment-systems development chosen because of its inherent role in the motivation of people to achieve the relevant performance criteria to be provided by manufacturing and as an example of how all facets within infrastructure need to develop within a strategic overview.

7.9   Control of Quality*

Although in many instances, quality is a qualifying criterion in manufacturing strategy terms, its impact on market share has proved more dramatic than probably any other single factor.

In many sectors, Japanese companies have systematically increased the level of product quality to such an extent that they have fundamentally changed customer's expectations not only in these markets but as a general rule. Initially challenging existing norms where quality was working as a qualifier, they made and sold products where the level of defects was markedly lower. The results were dramatic. Suddenly, unable to meet the distinctive higher-quality levels, companies found that they were no longer qualifying to compete in their traditional markets. Loss of market-share followed. Forced to reassess the quality dimension just to regain a place on customer's short-lists, companies were required to reconsider their basic approach to quality provision and to take on board the markedly higher expectations of their customers. Today, quality is now a qualifier in many markets. Thus, failure to meet existing quality expectations or to track future improvements will lead to an order-losing scenario and attendant consequences.

In the past operational decisions to separate the total responsibility for quality from the person responsible for completing the task were not recognised at the time in terms of the strategic consequences that might arise. In project and jobbing, however, this division has rarely, if ever, been introduced. In continuous processing, quality checks have been built into the process thus retaining the link between the doing and evaluating task within the process itself. However, in batch and line, the responsibility for completing the task and achieving the required levels of quality whilst argued to be one and the same, are really two separate responsibilities (see Table 7.2).

Obviously, the most appropriate time to check conformance to the specification is when the item is made. However, under the systems still often used in batch and line processes, work is checked in a time-period following its production. Depending either upon

---

* The dimension of quality referred to here is conformance – see pp. 77–81 and particularly Table 3.4.

TABLE 7.2
Responsibility for quality control and the type of process

Type of process	The task	Responsibility for quality
Project and jobbing	The task and quality are normally integrated in the skills of the person	Usually vested largely in the performance of the task or provision of the service. Primarily the person responsible for this part of the process plus supervisory support
Batch and line	Work has been deskilled to reduce amongst other things, labour costs. Inspection and later quality control introduced	Theoretically the responsibility is still vested in the person providing the task with supervisory, quality control and inspection support. In reality, the quality control and inspection functions are seen as being primarily responsible for quality
Continuous processing	Quality is determined by the process and, therefore, reintegrates quality into the task	Usually built into the process as an integral part of the design. The facilities to monitor the quality are usually controlled by the same person who is responsible for other aspects of the task

Source: Terry Hill, *Production/Operations Management: Text and Cases*, p. 370

the length of time between production taking place and quality being checked or at what stages quality checks are taken will have a direct bearing on a company's ability to minimise the repercussions of work which is below specification.

This, therefore, raises two important issues concerning quality which need to be agreed by manufacturing at the corporate level and then form part of manufacturing's response to the business need.

7.9.1 *A reactive or proactive approach to quality*

The first issue is to determine whether to adopt a reactive or proactive approach to quality. In the former, the emphasis is towards detection with the objective of preventing faulty work being passed on to subsequent processes. In this way, the costs involved in rectification, scrap, returned products and non-repeat business will be minimised.

A proactive approach, on the other hand, emphasises prevention rather than detection. It requires the allocation of resources to make products right first time, more of the time. This is achieved by reviewing the quality of both design and conformance in order to identify the factors affecting these two features. Quality control is then designed around this analysis.

7.9.2 *The responsibility for quality*

The responsibility for quality concerns two separate issues. The first concerns defining the departmental responsibilities throughout the process; the second, the responsibility for measurement.

In recent years the distinction between quality assurance and quality control has become more marked. Quality assurance is the function charged with the task of developing the quality structure and the responsibilities and activities within that structure, together with establishing procedures to ensure that the organisation meets the agreed quality levels for its products. Quality control is that aspect of quality assurance which concerns the practical means of securing product quality as set out in the specification.[16] The separation of roles between the people completing the work and those given specific responsibility for checking the quality achieved, albeit as a back-up activity, has been in force for a

TABLE 7.3
Baldrige Award – points allocation by category

Category	Points
Information and analysis	60
Strategic–quality analysis	90
Leadership	100
Human-resource utilisation	150
Quality assurance of products and services	150
Quality results	150
Customer satisfaction	300
Total	1000

number of decades. This separation in many organisations has been further emphasised by the reporting systems which have developed (see Figures 7.3 and 7.6).

In order to facilitate manufacturing's task an infrastructure change has to be implemented. Quality control needs to revert to the set of activities for which manufacturing is responsible whilst the quality checks need to form part of the operators' role.

The importance of this essential change is gaining widespread recognition. One illustration of this is embodied in the points weighting allocated to this orientation within the Baldrige Award* (see Table 7.3). However, the extent to which Western companies have incorporated these fundamental changes in their pursuit of quality improvements is not as extensive as is generally assumed. Although commitment to quality improvement from top management is high, Baldrige examiners have found that applicants 'have been surprised to find they come up short at the other end of the organisational chart. Many companies with high-profile reputations for quality have been told to do more to empower their employees as well as their upper ranks.'[17]

---

* The Malcolm Baldrige National Quality Award is a US Government/Industry venture but supported solely by the industry-funded Baldrige Award Foundation. The first programme was in 1988 and entails assessment against the criteria given in Table 7.3.

However, the importance of achieving high product quality is being clearly recognised. Respondents in Europe and the USA placed product quality as their number one competitive priority over the following five years clearly signalling an overall recognition of this issue.* At the corporate level, companies clearly illustrate the importance they attach to achieving major improvements in quality. IBM, for instance, admitted at the beginning of 1990 that its overall defect rate was around three sigma or 66 810 defects per million operations. By 1994, IBM wants to reach six sigma, or 3.4 defects per million operations.[18]

The gains are considerable not only in terms of costs but also in customer relations and job interest. However, it will not happen overnight. Traditions die hard and the investment in training needs to be clearly recognised. However, with the responsibility for good quality work now back where it belongs, companies can also move from the reactive approach which they invariably adopt and one which is almost dictated by the existing departmental and on-line responsibilities for quality, to the proactive approach necessary to ensure that manufacturing will be able to provide the quality requirements which current and future markets demand.[19]

7.10 Control of Inventory

In most manufacturing companies, inventory is substantial, whereas the methods used to control it are casual. They lack the level of sophistication and insight appropriate to an item which stands at some 30–40 per cent of most companies' total assets. Whilst decisions to use funds for plant and equipment, for instance, are normally carefully monitored, the relative effort and attention given to the control of inventory is generally too little and too late. Increases in inventory happen and concern to exercise due control over this sizeable asset comes after the event. This is because inventory control is based on a number of operational activities without the strategic overview of control warranted by an investment of this size.

---

* Interestingly, Japanese respondents in the same Manufacturing Features Survey placed product quality as their number four competitive priority. They are now looking to other priorities to give them a competitive edge.

There are two general characteristics about inventory which illustrate, above all, the level of business disinterest in its control and the underlying perspectives on which existing controls are built. First, many companies take complete physical counts of stock on as few occasions as possible, often as little as twice a year to coincide with the financial accounting periods. Furthermore, when the date for stocktaking approaches it is common practice to create an unrepresentative picture of inventory inside the business by holding-off purchases at the front end and moving existing inventory inside the business itself. The rationale for this is to reduce the inventory holding *per se* and so record a more favourable position in relevant financial statements whilst also reducing the size of the clerical task involved. Manufacturing companies, therefore, look on these tasks as a chore rather than an opportunity to collect valuable data essential to the control of what is often the biggest single asset on their balance sheets.

Second, inventory breakdowns are normally expressed in terms of the stage the material has reached in the process: namely, raw materials/components, work-in-progress and finished goods. This choice, however, is made solely to facilitate the evaluation of inventory as an input into the profit-and-loss account and balance sheet. Thus, the outcome of this data-collection exercise is viewed primarily as a provision of information to the accounts function and not as an important opportunity to create the basis for controlling this large asset.

The purpose of having inventory in a business is to provide a set of advantages which reflect its needs. Depending on what constitutes the needs in the market-place and the agreed manufacturing requirements within the business, the size and spread of inventory will differ. Effective control, therefore, is based upon an understanding of why inventory is held where it is and what functions it provides. Currently, however, many companies attempt to control inventory by global, across-the-board mandates over short time-periods. This approach neither reflects the control nor time-dimensions of reality.

7.10.1   *Functions of inventory as a basis for control*

There are two broad categories of inventory: corporate and mainstream. Corporate inventory (normally accounting for some 20 to

25 per cent of the total holding) is the name attributed to those categories of inventory which do not provide a manufacturing function.[20]

The types of corporate inventory are numerous and will reflect the nature of the manufacturing company involved. Typical, however, of their types are:

- sales inventory to support customer agreements;
- sales inventory owing to actual sales being lower than forecast;
- marketing inventory to meet a product launch;
- purchasing inventory incurred to achieve quantity discounts;
- corporate safety stocks caused by uncertainty of supply (e.g. possible national or international strikes);
- slow-moving category under various related subheadings.

In order to control corporate inventory, information on the stockholding by category is required. Thus, the recognition and separation of this category into its appropriate types have to be completed. Once known, targets can be set in line with the business needs (and this may not always be a reduction), responsibility for its control can be charged to the appropriate function and inventory can be monitored. A company is then able to understand the return it receives for its investment, decide on the value for money associated with that holding and also use this information as part of its overall review of functions, customers, policies and the like.

The function of mainstream inventory is to facilitate the manufacturing process at all its stages. However, in order to exercise meaningful and effective control, the types of inventory within this category need to be understood and the relevant holding recorded against the various types involved. To do this three important aspects need to be recognised:

1. *The dependent/independent demand principle*   Where the rate of issue for an item does not directly relate to the use of any other item, then it should be treated as an item with an independent pattern of demand. Examples include finished goods and factored items. Conversely, items where the demand is linked to the use of other items are said to have a dependent demand pattern. For example, components and subassemblies. This distinction is drawn to ensure that companies recognise

that whereas the demand for independent items will have to be arrived at through forecasting or similar techniques, the demand for dependent items can be calculated.

2. *The functions provided by mainstream inventory* Holding mainstream inventory provides a number of distinct functions within manufacturing. These need to be distinguished and inventory data collected accordingly. The functions are:

- *Decoupling inventory* separates one process from the next, allowing them to work independently and separating otherwise dependent parts of the total operation. The emphasis is, therefore, on materials waiting for processes so that each process can be most 'efficiently' used. It is not found in jobbing or line because the person and process respectively move the inventory from one operation to the next on a continuous basis. It is, however, at the very essence of batch manufacturing.
- *Cycle inventory* relates to the decision to manufacture a quantity of products (sometimes referred to as a lot or batch size) which reflects criteria such as set-up to production-run length, customer-order size and call-off patterns. The rationale for cycle inventory is to reduce set-up costs and to help to maximise the use of process capacity by increasing production-run lengths.
- *Pipeline inventory* concerns the inventory support where companies decide to subcontract one process to an outside supplier at some time during the total process lead-time. All the inventory associated with this decision is classed as pipeline.
- *Capacity-related inventory* One way to cope with anticipated sales is to plan production in line with sales forecasts. This, however, often leads to a situation of peak-capacity requirements involving overtime, recruitment of additional labour and the holding of spare process capacity. Another way is to plan some sort of level production programme, stockpiling inventories in the low-sales periods for selling in the high-sales periods. This is known as capacity-related inventory and concerns transferring work from one time-period to the next in the form of inventory, and provides one way of stabilising production capacity in an environment of fluctuating sales levels.

- *Buffer inventory* concerns the problem that average demand, by definition, varies around the average. In order to cope with this, companies hold higher levels of inventory to reflect this variation. Buffer inventory's function, therefore, is to help to protect the process core against the unpredictable variations in demand levels or supply availability. The higher the service level or the lower the level of stockout risk set by a business, then the greater the quantities of buffer inventory required. A decision to hold inventory in excess of this requirement, however, should be classed as 'safety stock' and fall within a corporate inventory provision.

In undertaking this control task, an agreed area of the business is selected for analysis – it is not necessary to review the whole business. The purpose of the analysis concerns identifying where large blocks of inventory occur and not with assessing the whole of the inventory holding and the level of exactness called for in an annual stocktake, the results of which go into published accounts. Inventory is then identified by position in the process and by its function. If a parcel of inventory provides more than one function (e.g. those of cycle and decoupling) then an arbitrary split is made and the dual function recorded. As before, the data outcomes concern magnitude not exactness. Any large amounts of inventory are then further analysed and systematically reduced.

The key to inventory reduction, therefore, concerns removing that inventory which is not adding value. It eliminates the unnecessary and arrives at a level which is necessary to support current systems, and corporate commitments and decisions. To do this, companies need to identify the reasons why excess inventory has been generated, change the rules and procedures to stop this recurring and then use up existing inventory whilst preventing inflows of inventory except those which are necessary.

Many companies, however, compare current inventory levels with those proposed using alternative manufacturing planning and control systems. By doing this they compare current inadequate control with best-practice control of proposed alternatives. What companies should do is to reduce inventory levels to necessary norms and then decide whether or not the inventory reduction benefits accruing from alternative proposals are sufficient to justify the investments and changes involved. In this way decisions are made on a like-for-like basis thus enabling companies to identify the real sources of improvement.[21]

3. *The 80/20 rule* A review of inventory based upon a Pareto analysis* will almost certainly reveal that some 20 per cent of the items will account for about 80 per cent of the value. Using this as the basis for an ABC classification allows a company to exercise tight control over the relatively few items which are high in value. However, on the low-value items, excess buffer inventory holdings allow the controls to be simple and the records to be minimal.

Based on these three perspectives of inventory, the control exercised can now reflect the important, the large and the relevant. Once a business knows why and how much inventory is being held it can divert attention, effort and the level of control accordingly. Two examples to illustrate this approach will help to amplify the issues involved.

1. A company involved in manufacturing low-volume, standard products had 24 per cent of its total assets tied up in work-in-progress despite using a sophisticated scheduling system. The products involved represented hundreds of standard labour hours over many processes, including assembly, and were subject to schedule changes by customers. An analysis of its work-in-progress revealed levels of decoupling inventory which were a distinct over-provision of this function. The 80/20 rule typically prevailed. As response to customers' schedule changes was considered to be part of manufacturing's task, the company took several decisions concerning its high inventory holding. An ABC analysis on work-in-progress by product enabled it to cut back on cycle inventory and to shorten the process lead-time for high-value components and subassemblies deliberately. In future, high-value parts were made strictly in line with a customer's orders and were accelerated through the various processes by giving them priority. Low-value components and subassemblies were made in excess of requirements and sched-

---

* A Pareto analysis orders the data from highest down to lowest. The list provided then helps to show the 80/20 relationship which exists between the data being reviewed.

uled into the process well in advance of delivery needs. In this way, the advantages of cycle inventory were achieved for many items but at least-inventory investment. Similarly, they were now scheduled to 'meander' through the processes in a controlled way but offering efficiency opportunities without incurring correspondingly high inventory investment.

2. A plant which was part of a large group of companies received an across-the-board corporate directive to reduce inventory by 15 to 20 per cent in a given time-period. The plant involved manufactured optional features for vehicles. However, to make a sale, the customer required short delivery response to minimise the off-the-road time for any vehicle. In order to provide this distinctly order-winning criterion, the products had been designed to have a high proportion of standard parts and sub-assemblies to gain some economies of scale and to maximise coverage of the wide range of products involved, whilst minimising inventory holdings. Manufacturing, to meet this short lead-time, needed to hold all parts in stock so as to reduce the overall process lead-time and to allow itself the time to respond to the market. Only when inventory's role within the manufacturing strategy was explained was the corporate directive rescinded.

Finally, when reviewing inventory holdings it is important to look at Table 4.1. This table illustrates how the implications for inventory holdings in terms of raw materials/components, work-in progress and finished goods would differ with each choice of process. Therefore, as a starting-point the trade-offs involved between inventory investment, plant utilisation, efficiency and other operational factors need also to be taken into account when reviewing the fundamental decisions addressed in Chapter 4. However, this in no way precludes a company from changing the mix in trade-offs which surround inventory investment. The description of just-in-time production systems given later provides an alternative approach to managing processes. However, in so doing it picks up a fresh set of trade-offs for manufacturing and the business which, on the plus side, include a sharp reduction in inventory levels. It is essential, therefore, that the manufacturing strategy debate concerning process choice and the role of inventory in this configuration (see Table 4.1), explains and amplifies the implications for the business and the critical nature of the trade-offs involved.

7.11 Manufacturing, Planning and Control Systems[22]

Many firms see manufacturing investment and agreements on markets to be independent sets of decisions. Few appreciate the need for the link to be made. The result, which has been a theme throughout the book, is that firms have made and continue to make large investments in process and manufacturing infrastructure without setting them within a strategic context. However, the high cost and fixed nature of manufacturing investments and their key role in helping to secure the short- and long-term prosperity of a business makes this doubly risky.

7.11.1 *No strategy, poor systems*

One such area that illustrates the general problem outlined above is that of manufacturing planning and control (MPC) systems. As a large infrastructure investment and as a critical function in the management of manufacturing this provides a classic example of the panacea-driven approach which has characterised past decisions in the manufacturing function. Material Requirements Planning (MRP), Just-in-Time (JIT) and Optimised Production Technology (OPT) are recent illustrations. Bought more for their apparent benefits than business fit, it is not surprising that previous research reported that 63 per cent of the MRP applications studied,[23] cost as much as $5 million, yet failed to realise their full benefits.

*   *   *

A medium-sized US furniture company made high-volume standard products using simple process technologies, with few operations and little work-in-progress inventory. However, to support short customer lead-times there were high levels of finished goods inventory. The company controlled manufacturing using central scheduling and manual shop-floor controls supported by visual checking and verbal communications between departments. To improve equipment utilisation, productivity and order-tracking on the shop-floor the company installed a computer-based shop-floor control system with automated order-tracking, queue-control and capacity-planning features costing about $0.75 million. However, in business terms the principal area for improvement was an increased level of sales support by fulfilling customer orders more quickly while keeping the finished-goods inventory under control. The key to achieving this in manufacturing planning and control terms would have been to improve the master production-scheduling function to better reflect actual sales in plant schedules and so avoiding imbalances in finished-goods inventory character-ised by shortages and excess stockholdings. The investment in the shop-floor control system was not only unnecessary but resulted in added paperwork with a corresponding increase in overheads whilst diverting key supervisory effort from other areas.

*　　　　　*　　　　　*

Responding to the technology developments in the telecom-munications field, a European company moved from electromech-anical to electronic-based products. Whilst components for the old products were made in-house, using a range of batch processes and final assembly lines, the company purchased the new product technology in the form of components.

Beset with several dimensions of manufacturing change, the company retained its previous MRP system as a tested and proven device. However, in doing so it overlooked the critical shift in manufacturing. Whereas the old products required the emphasis to be placed on the control of a broad range of complex, internal processes and the inherent work-in-progress inventory, the key control issues for the new products were vendor-scheduling and component-inventory management. Retaining the previous MRP system led to a failure to switch resources to vendor-scheduling and to highlight component as opposed to work-in-progress hold-ing as the key area of inventory control. As a result, pressure was placed in the wrong areas, shortages increased and the control system was unable to cope with the new demands.

*　　　　　*　　　　　*

A UK aerospace company manufacturing a wide range of products at all stages in their life-cycles invested in a comprehensive, stan-dard computer-based MRP system to meet all its requirements. The complexity of the data, training needs and system running and support requirements were reflected in the costs involved – £5 million over a two-and-a-half-year period plus high running costs. A post-installation review highlighted the fact that although the system met the needs of original equipment products, it did not meet the needs of the spares business. It was estimated that 60 per cent of the original database investment was not necessary. Instead, the planning and control needs of the spares business could have been better provided, at significantly less cost, by simplified master-scheduling, materials planning and shop-floor controls whilst there was no need for the order-tracking, queue-control and priority despatching features essential to the OEM part of the business.

          *   *   *

7.11.2 *From panaceas to policy*

The examples given in the last section show how firms may invest in planning and control systems which, though sound in themselves, do not fit the needs of the business. The outcome not only results in unnecessary expenditure but also leads firms to assume that this aspect of manufacturing has been resolved.

The way for companies to improve the fit of these investments to the needs of the business is to link markets to processes and to MPC systems. This not only requires clear understanding of markets and the subsequent link to manufacturing but also of the way that MPC systems differ in themselves and the key characteristics they embody.

The market debate has been a consistent theme and the steps involved have been highlighted earlier. With this complete, companies next have to link markets through manufacturing strategy to the design of the master production schedule (MPS). The conceptual base for explaining differences and appropriate responses is given in Table 7.4. This shows how companies need to select the base type of MPS to reflect the characteristics of their markets whilst similarly matching other aspects of manufacturing on relevant dimensions. In this way, companies develop coordinated responses in line with market needs to improve the level of support within manufacturing.

In the same way, the other facets of planning and control systems need to be reviewed to enable firms to identify and develop

TABLE 7.4
Linking manufacturing strategy to the design of the MPS

	Strategic variables		Master scheduling approach		
			MTO	ATO	MTS
MARKETS	Product	Type	Special	→	Standard
		Range	Wide	→	Predetermined and narrow
	Individual product volume per period		Low	→	High
	Delivery	Speed	Difficult	→	Easy
		Reliability	Difficult	→	Easy
MANUFACTURING	Process choice		Jobbing/low volume batch	→	High-volume batch/line
	Managing changes in sales and mix		Through order backlog	Through WIP or FG inventory	Through FG inventory
	Meeting delivery speed requirements		Through rescheduling requirements	Reduces process lead time	Eliminates process lead time

Notes: MTO make-to-order MTS make-to-stock FG finished goods
ATO assemble-to-order WIP work-in-progress

relevant parts of the MPC system. Table 7.5 identifies the market and the manufacturing implications in terms of the design of materials planning approach. It helps to explain why time-phased or rate-based approaches are appropriate given the different market characteristics which manufacturing needs to support. In addition, it also shows appropriate processes whilst identifying the orientation of selected key tasks in manufacturing. Finally, Table 7.6 links these to the design of the shop floor control system and illustrates the rationale for alternative control approaches. Once again, it shows how alternative shop-floor control approaches line up with different market features and also provides a link to key manufacturing responses and tasks.

Thus, Tables 7.4–7.6 provide an overview of MPC systems and illustrate the way in which market differences require different MPC-system responses. They help to show how the elements of alternative systems are consistent within themselves and how the development of appropriate responses needs to be accomplished within all facets of this major aspect of manufacturing infrastructure provision. Equally, companies who fail to make these essential links will invest in systems which are inappropriate for the markets in which they compete and hinder manufacturing's ability to meet customer needs.

7.11.3   *Why don't panaceas work?*

Solutions presuppose that market requirements and hence corporate characteristics are the same. But today, nothing is further from the truth. Markets are not characterised by similarity but by difference. Therefore, linking elements of manufacturing strategy to markets is fundamental. Equally, a sound manufacturing strategy is one where decisions and investments in processes and infrastructure are consistent with a company's markets. Table 7.7 provides an illustration of two companies competing in different markets. It shows the link between their markets and relevant order-winners and qualifiers through to the corresponding manufacturing tasks, supported by processes and manufacturing planning and control systems.

It starts by showing the key differences in the markets served by the two companies. Tracing across from these market characteristics to the manufacturing responses shows clear differences in the

TABLE 7.5
Linking manufacturing strategy to the design of the material planning approach

	Strategic variables		Material planning approach	
			Time-phased	Rate-based
	Product	Type	Special	Standard
		Range	Wide	Narrow
	Individual product volume per period		Low	High
Markets	Ability to cope with changes in product-mix within a period		High Potential	Limited
	Delivery	Schedule changes	Difficult	Easy
		Speed	Through scheduling/ excess capacity	Through inventory
	Process choice*		Batch	Line
Manufacturing	Source of cost reduction	Overhead	No	Yes
		Inventory	No	Yes

* In jobbing, shop-floor control is handled by the operator

TABLE 7.6
Linking manufacturing strategy to the design of the shop-floor control system

	Strategic variables		Shop-floor control approach	
			Push type	Pull type
Markets	Product	Type	Special	Standard
		Range	Wide	Narrow
	Individual product volume per period	Total volume	Low	High
	Accommodating demand versatility		Easy / incremental	Difficult / stepped
		Product-mix	High	Low
	Delivery	Speed	Achieved by schedule change	Achieved through finished goods inventory
		Schedule changes	More difficult	Less difficult
	Process choice*		Jobbing / low-income batch	High-volume batch / line
Manufacturing	Source of cost reduction	Overheads	Low	High
		Inventory	Low	High
	Changeover cost		High	Low
	Control of manufacturing	Key feature	Order status	Flow of materials
		Basis	Person / system*	System
		Ease of task	Complex	Easy

* In jobbing, shop-floor control is handled by the operator

latter whilst illustrating how each set of responses is consistent with the market needs of each company.

This is how the task of manufacturing – in all facets of its support for the varied needs of markets – needs to be fulfilled. However, without the critical step of linking clear market definition to an understanding of the conceptual phase of manufacturing process and infrastructure options, the relevant and consistent choices will not be made, and the panacea-driven approaches will be perpetuated.

7.12   Conclusion

The JIT production system within Toyota has all the classic hallmarks of strategic infrastructure development. It works well because Toyota has demonstrated that it understands the need to reconcile the three major phases in its business – the before phase (its suppliers), the owned phase (its own processes), and the forward phase (the sale of cars through its networks). It works because Toyota has managed its forward phase in such a way that it freezes schedules, thus demanding or requiring little change in its own or its suppliers' processes. In this way, it has cushioned its manufacturing core from the instability of the marketplace, thus preventing it from being exposed. The stability so created means that Toyota is able to demand exact deliveries, so much a feature of the JIT production system. In this way, it has earned this favoured position and can, and does therefore, demand these benefits from suppliers, thus forcing the inventory forward and out of the system, rather than the other way round.

Many Western car companies do not appreciate these essential links. They show due sensitivity in the forward phase because they require to generate goodwill and motivate their distributors to sell more cars. In the before phase, however, the converse happens. They believe here that to threaten suppliers is the posture that will bring best results. And this is a very telling difference.

Providing a clear manufacturing strategy for the business enables those responsible for infrastructure development to work from a common base, in a common direction, to meet a common requirement. Historical or personal, in some instances almost

TABLE 7.7
Companies which serve different markets need to identify relevant manufacturing tasks and responses and to make MPC system investments which provide appropriate support for customers

Company	Market characteristics	Order winners and qualifiers	Manufacturing Strategy				
			Manufacturing		Manufacturing planning and control system		
			Task	Features	Master production scheduling	Material planning	Shop-floor control
COMPANY A	• Customised products • Wide product range • Low volume per product • Make-to-order • Initial v repeat orders • Future order call-offs	• Design capability • Delivery speed • Delivery reliability – Q, Q • Quality – Q • Price – Q	• Reducing process lead-time • To manufacture to engineering specifications and quality standards • Delivery reliability is critical	• Batch manufacturing • Long process routings • High precision work • Accommodate delivery and design changes with reliable deliveries • Labour cost equals 60% • Control of actual costs against budget • Scrap and rework order priorities + first orders + normal scrap allowance • First order processing uncertainties (process unknown, time estimates) • Process and product uncertainties	• Make-to-order/ assemble-to-order + Customer orders + Anticipated Forecast orders • Used for rough cut capacity planning due to long lead-time impact on delivery • Customer order promising	• Time phased material planning • Material is particular to customer orders • High obsolescence risk • Extra materials needed for scrapped items • Trade-off: shorter lead time vs raw material inventory	• Push system • Priority scheduling of shop orders • System supported by dispatching and production control personnel • Capacity requirements planning by work centre • Order tracking and status information

COMPANY B				
• Narrow product range • Standard products • High-volume per product • Seasonal demand • Sales from finished goods inventory at distributors • Introduction of new products • Changing product-mix	• Price • Delivery speed (through finished goods inventory in distribution divisions) • Quality – Q • Delivery reliability – Q • Basic design – Q and peripheral design changes	• To provide a low-cost manufacturing support capability • To support the marketing activity with high delivery speed through finished goods inventory	• High-volume batch and line production process • Short set-up times • Small batch sizes • Low cost manufacturing • Low labour cost • High material cost • Inventory reduction (raw material, components and WIP) • Overhead reduction (low MPC costs)	• Make-to-stock • Manufacture to forecast • Level production • Three month frozen planning horizon • Manufacture to replenish distribution inventories • Rate-based material planning • Pull system • Kanban containers • JIT flow of material • Low raw material, component, and WIP inventory

Q denotes a qualifier, a capability required in order for the company to enter and remain in its market

QQ denotes an order-losing sensitive qualifier, i.e. a capability which if not supported leads to a rapid loss of business.

esoteric views, fall by the wayside to be replaced by a strategic underpinning of infrastructure. The consequence will not only be to provide relevance by meeting the needs of the business, but also to provide continuity by ensuring that the long-term requirements are an integral part of current thinking and decisions. What militates against this is that, without a strategy-based approach, these wide multi-functional areas are more open to personal judgments, more prone to fixed ideas, and swayed by the argument of what is more readily available from the point of view of specialist provision, than what needs to be provided to meet the dimensions of manufacturing. Thus, the interactive nature of the dynamics within manufacturing, not being the responsibility of any one specialist or support function, is not at the forefront of the argument or application. The responsibility for this is clearly and wholly manufacturing's. Thus, by underpinning these with a clear and well-argued manufacturing strategy, the direction and mechanism for common evaluation will be provided.

On an entirely practical basis, the development and introduction of a payment system illustrates how any facet of infrastructure can and needs to be designed to support a company's competitive strategy, and not in keeping with the efficiency oriented perception of manufacturing's strategic role.

A medium-sized manufacturing company wished to replace its existing payment scheme for hourly-paid employees which had fallen into disrepute. The initial proposals centred on a classic productivity-based scheme, involving individual bonus-related earnings. When it recognised the need to develop this in the context of a manufacturing strategy, the company postponed work on the scheme until the necessary, earlier work was completed. Three order-winning qualifying criteria were highlighted – delivery speed, delivery reliability and price. With these now forming the basis of the manufacturing task, the scheme that was eventually developed reflected these criteria. Delivery performance now accounts for half the potential performance earnings, whilst the other half is for improvements in productivity. Furthermore, in order to encourage a broader view of work, the payments were made twice a year, and on factory-wide achievement related to attendance time.

The shape and emphasis, therefore, now more accurately reflected the needs of the business and in this way encouraged an important part of manufacturing's contribution by the way it was designed.

The Last Word: 'Why the West Will Lose'

On the need to challenge the way in which US and Western European companies organise themselves and to consider the definitions of role, responsibility, authority, specialists, and all the other facets of organisations, the last word belongs to Mr Konosuke Matsushita. The difference in views is stark, and the challenge to rethink existing approaches is clearly stated. One thing is certain – to be successful in the future, companies will need to be adaptive and effectively use all the resources within the business.

We are going to win and the industrial West is going to lose: there is nothing much you can do about it, because the reasons for your failure are within yourselves.

Your firms are built on the Taylor model; even worse, so are your heads. With your bosses doing the thinking, while the workers wield the screwdrivers, you are convinced deep down that this is the right way to run a business.

For you, the essence of management is getting the ideas out of the heads of the bosses into the hands of labour.

We are beyond the Taylor model: business, we know, is now so complex and difficult, the survival of firms so hazardous in an environment increasingly unpredictable, competitive, and fraught with danger, that their continued existence depends on the day-to-day mobilization of every ounce of intelligence.

For us, the core of management is precisely this art of mobilizing and pulling together the intellectual resources of all employees in the service of the firm. Because we have measured better than you the scope of the new technological and economic challenges, we know that the intelligence of a handful of technocrats, however brilliant and smart they may be, is no longer enough for a real chance of success.

Only by drawing on the combined brain power of all its employees can a firm face up to the turbulence and constraints of today's environment.

This is why our large companies give their employees three to four times more training than yours, this is why they foster within the firm such intensive exchange and communication;

> this is why they seek constantly everybody's suggestions and
> why they demand from the educational system increasing
> numbers of graduates as well as bright and well-educated
> generalists, because these people are the lifeblood of industry.
>   Your "socially-minded bosses," often full of good inten-
> tions, believe their duty is to protect the people in their firms.
> We, on the other hand, are realists and consider it our duty to
> get our own people to defend their firms, which will pay them
> back a hundredfold for their dedication. By doing this, we end
> up by being more "social" than you.
>
> Source: K. Matsushita, 'Why the West Will Lose: Extracts from
> Remarks Made by Mr Konosuke Matsushita of the Matsushita
> Electric Industrial Company, Japan to a Group of Western Man-
> agers', *Industrial Participation*, Spring 1985, p. 8.

Notes and References

1. T. J. Peters and R. H. Waterman, Jr., *In Search of Excellence: Lessons from America's Best-run Companies* (Harper & Row, 1982).
2. R. H. Hayes and S. C. Wheelwright, *Restoring Our Competitive Edge: Competing through Manufacturing* (Wiley, 1984) p. 32.
3. Ibid, p. 33.
4. A survey undertaken for the British Institute of Management covered 24 651 middle- and upper-ranked staff in 385 widely varied UK companies which together account for over 10 per cent of the UK workforce. The survey gives the average total money awards (including bonuses) for different levels in key functions in the year to January 1991. The table below gives the rank position for each function on the four top levels. Highest rewards rank 1, next highest 2 and so on.

Function	Director	Senior manager	Manager	Department head
Financial Management	1	4	3	2
Services	2	7	5	5
Company Secretary	3	1	1	1
Engineering design, etc.	4	9	10	8
Marketing	5	2	4	3
Personnel	6	6	7	7

Distribution	7	8	11	10
Sales	8	3	6	6
Manufacturing	9	10	8	11
R&D	10	5	2	4
Purchasing	11	11	9	9

These findings clearly illustrate the issue. The low ranking of manufacturing jobs is consistent at all of these top four levels. The gap is further illustrated by the table below which compares the rank 1 salary and manufacturing equivalent for the four levels.

	Average total money award (£s)		*Gap*	
	year to Jan. 1991			
Staff level	*manufacturing*	*rank 1 function*	*£s*	*%*
Director	48 180	Financial	60 166 11 986	25
Senior Manager	38 999	Company Secretary	52 260 13 261	34
Manager	33 597	Company Secretary	42 435 8 838	26
Department head	26 743	Company Secretary	34 649 7 906	30

As the last column shows, the reward difference expressed as a percentage of the relevant average manufacturing reward was never less than 25. One obvious consequence is that young managers on reviewing this position will be attracted away from line functions by higher rewards and quicker promotion. To turn this round will take many years.

Source: The above data is based on *BIM National Management Salary Survey* (Remuneration Economics, London) (April 1991).

5. 'A New Target: Reducing Staff and Levels', *Business Week*, 21 December 1981, pp. 38–41.
6. Peters and Waterman, *In Search of Excellence*, p. 306.
7. A detailed review of the changes at Du Point's Maitland plant is given in D. Stoffman's article 'Less is More', *Report on Business Magazine*, June 1988, pp. 90–101.
8. This and some of the other concepts discussed here are taken from a set of well-developed work-structuring principles which have been presented in various unpublished papers, 1979–81, by P. C. Schumacher, Schumacher Projects, Godstone, Surrey, UK.
9. A key feature of quality circles (dealt with later in this chapter) is that those involved not only implement their ideas but also evaluate the gains they yield.
10. Stoffman, 'Less is More', pp. 97–8.
11. *Manufacturing Futures Survey* (1990), INSEAD, Fontainebleau, France.
12. These figures are also provided in a year-by-year review of the adoption of quality circles within Japanese business – Forman Quality Control.

13. Other references to the adoption and outcomes of quality circles include 'Why Does Britain Want Quality Circles?' *Production Engineer*, February 1980, pp. 45–6; three articles published in S. M. Lee and G. Schwendiman (eds) *Management by Japanese Systems* (Praeger Publishers, 1982) Part II, Quality Circles, pp. 65–118; Terry Hill, *Production/Operations Management* (Prentice-Hall, 1991) pp. 374–7; R. J. Schonberger, *Japanese Manufacturing Techniques: Nine Hidden Lessons in Simplicity*, ch. 8 'Quality Circles, Work Improvement and Specialisation', pp. 181–98; M. Robson, *Quality Circles in Action* (Gower, 1984); D. H. Hutchins, *Quality Circles Handbook* (Pitman, 1985); I. A. Temple and B. G. Dale, *White Collar Quality Circles in UK Manufacturing Industry: A Study*, Occasional Paper Series, no 8510, Department of Management Sciences (UMIST, 1985); E. E. Lawler and W. A. Mohrmann, 'Quality Circles: After the Fad', *Harvard Business Review*, January/February 1985, pp. 65–7, and B. G. Dale and J. Lees, *The Development of Quality Circle Programmes* (Manpower Services Commission, 1986). In addition, J. R. Arbose in his editorial 'Quality Control Circles: the West Adopts a Japanese Concept', *International Management*, December 1980, pp. 31–9, provides a wide-ranging list of savings achieved from applications in various countries, a checklist for starting-up, and Professor Kaoru Ishikawa's list of the eight tools of problem-analysis in which group leaders need to be trained.
14. R. Wood, F. Hull and K. Azumi, 'Evaluating Quality Circles: the American Application', *California Management Review*, vol. XXVI, no 1, Fall 1983, pp. 37–53.
15. Arbose, 'Quality Control Circles', p. 31.
16. British Standard Glossary of Terms used in BS 4778 'Quality Assurance' (1987), Part 1, 3.6–3.7.
17. P. Burrows, 'Five Lessons You Learn From (Baldrige) Award Entrants', *Electronic Business*, 15 October 1990, pp. 22–4.
18. B. C. P. Rayner, 'Market-driven Quality: IBM's Six Sigma Crusade', *Electronics Business*, 15 October 1990, pp. 26–30.
19. There are many references to the advantages to be gained and examples of the results of such decisions. These include J. M. Juran, 'Product Quality – a Prescription for the West', *Management Review*, June 1981, pp. 9–20; R. J. Schonberger, *Japanese Manufacturing Techniques: Nine Hidden Lessons* pp. 47–82 and pp. 181–98; D. A. Garvin, 'Quality on the Line', *Harvard Business Review*, September–October 1983, pp. 65–75; C. Lorenz, 'A Shocking Indictment of American Mediocrity', *Financial Times*, 17 October 1983; Toyohiro Kona, *Strategy and Structure of Japanese Enterprises* (Macmillan, 1984) ch. 7, 'Competition Strategy', pp. 194–6; M. Imai, *Kaizen: the Key to Japanese Competitive Success* (New York: Random House, 1986) ch. 3; T. G. Gunn, *Manufacturing for Competitive Advantage: Being a World Class Manufacturer* (Cambridge, Mass: Ballinger, 1987); J. P. Alston, *The American Sumurai* (Walter de Gruyter, 1989); B. G. Dale and J. J. Plunkett, *Managing Quality* (Hemel

Hempstead: Philip Allan, 1990; N. Slack, *The Manufacturing Advantage* (London: Mercury, 1991) and M. J. Stahl and G. M. Bounds (eds) *Competing Globally Through Customer Value* (New York: Quorum Books, 1991).

20. See Hill, *Production/Operations Management: Text and Cases*
21. Ibid, pp. 261–2 for further details on this point.
22. The ideas, arguments and examples in this section are based on an article by W. L. Berry and T. J. Hill entitled 'Linking Systems to Strategy' *IJOPM*, 12, 10 (1991) pp. 3–16.
23. R. G. Schroder *Material Requirements Planning: a Study of Implementation and Practice*, American Productivity and Inventory Control Society, Falls Church, VA 1981.

Accounting and Financial Perspectives and Manufacturing Strategy

8

Two common denominators are used in manufacturing businesses as the basis for control and performance measurement. The first is the time base on which manufacturing principally works. Product-mix and volumes, capacity calculations, performance measures in terms of efficiency, utilisation and productivity all normally use the basic measurement of time. The second common denominator is that of money. At the corporate level forecast sales, performance measures, levels of investment and similar activities use the money base. The importance, therefore, of getting the correct links between the time-based and money-based measures is self-evident. Correct not only in terms of being accurate but also in terms of reflecting the key perspectives and dimensions within the business itself.

The money-based denominator issues which are addressed in this chapter are controlled by what, in many companies, is frequently one of the least-developed functions, that of accounting and finance. Based on approaches established when business activities were very different, this area has not really faced up to resolving many of the important changes in business with appropriate developments. This chapter highlights a number of areas which need to be addressed from the point of view of both manufacturing and overall strategy. It will link the areas of manufacturing and corporate strategy with accounting and finance and illustrate some of the key issues which need to be developed and

266

the essential direction which these improvements need to take. In addition, it will show the ways in which manufacturing strategy will influence, and in some cases, facilitate, some of these changes whilst also drawing attention to the essential nature of manufacturing's needs and the accounting and financial information provision.

The purpose of this chapter is to make a number of critical observations about the impact on manufacturing of finance and accounting practices. The observations are made from a manufacturing executive's perspective and it is, therefore, acknowledged that they may well be provocative when examined by the professional accountant. But, if this causes debate between manufacturing and finance executives the purpose of this chapter has been achieved, because the solutions to the issues addressed must be worked out in the context of a particular company's corporate and manufacturing strategies. Having said that the financial systems in a business can, and do, have a major impact on manufacturing's ability to develop and maintain effective competitive strategies, then one essential objective of the finance function must be to give manufacturing the ability to measure and assess its performance accurately in relation to major competitors and the competitive value of investment proposals. The chapter deals, therefore, with these two broad areas of interaction between finance and manufacturing. First, the effect on manufacturing strategy of investment appraisal methods and second, how management accounting systems critically affect the control and performance measurement of manufacturing operations.

8.1 Investment Decisions

The approach to developing a manufacturing strategy was explained in some detail in the earlier chapters. One important consideration which was highlighted in those explanations was the level of alternative investments associated with different decisions (see Figure 8.1). Many organisations, bounded by cash limitations, need to commit their scarce resources wisely. However, the criteria for assessing the level or nature of this critical corporate decision have rarely been arrived at with the care and in-depth analysis which is warranted. In many companies, investment deci-

FIGURE 8.1
**When developing a manufacturing strategy for a business, the
restrictions imposed at both ends of the procedure by the
necessary financial considerations are rarely understood or their
interaction acknowledged**

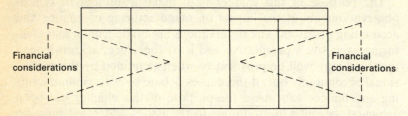

sions though initially chosen or stimulated by corporate competitive requirements are finally evaluated solely by accounting
measures and methods of appraisal. The interaction of these
financial measures on strategy and the consequent investment
decisions are illustrated by reference to the framework introduced
in Chapter 2.

Accounting methods of investment appraisal are generally
based upon one important premise – the relative return on capital
associated with each investment proposal under review. With
capital investment in limited supply and capital rationing a widespread consequence, the argument to invest predominantly on the
basis of return is not only built into the appraisal system itself but
is invariably reinforced by the discussion and argument which will
take place. In this way the figures will themselves unwittingly
support investment return as the predominant or even exclusive
measure on which to assess these key corporate strategy decisions.

The consequences of this undue weighting have been felt by
many companies and the ramifications within manufacturing industry have been widespread. The necessity to question this view
of investment decisions has stimulated a series of well-argued
articles and papers which illustrate the simplistic nature of the
accounting perspective and challenge its unevaluated application.
As early as 1974, Dean declared that 'because of our obsessive
concentration in short-term gains and profits, US technology is
stalemated'.[1] Hayes and Abernathy's 1980 article said it all in the

title 'Managing our way to economic decline',[2] and again with Garvin, Hayes captured the essence of the issues in the article 'Managing as if tomorrow mattered',[3] in which they make, amongst other things, a concerted challenge on current accounting approaches to investment appraisal. They provide a detailed argument to support their view that companies have increasingly turned to sophisticated, analytical techniques to evaluate investment proposals. The long-term result has been that many of the managers involved have 'unintentionally jeopardised their companies' future', and they summarise the consequences with the conclusion that 'investment decisions that discount the future may result in high present values but bleak tomorrows'.

Since then, the basic criticisms have been taken on by others particularly from the accounting profession. Of these, Kaplan well illustrates these growing concerns as clearly shown in the title of his book with Johnson, *Relevance Lost: the Rise and Fall of Management Accounting*[4] and again with Cooper in the two articles 'How Cost Accounting Distorts Product Costs'[5] and 'Measure Costs Right: Make the Right Decision'.[6]

8.2   The Need for a Strategic View of Investments

The key shift in emphasis which companies need to adopt when evaluating investments is to move increasingly towards a strategy-based review. What constitutes a sound investment needs to be measured by its contribution to the agreed corporate strategy and not by how well it meets the criteria laid down by a set of accounting rules and evaluations. Simmonds in one of several critiques of current management accounting observes that

> the emphasis . . . which accounting and finance have placed on return on investment over the years has subtly transmuted into a widely- and deeply-held belief that return comes from the investments themselves . . . The truth is much different. Sustained profit comes from the competitive market position. New production investment to expand sales must imply a change in competitive position and it is this change that should be the focus of the investment review. Without it, the calculations must be a nonsense.[7]

This sleight of hand has been detected by all too few companies. The consequence has been that increasingly the key factor by which investment proposals have been assessed has swung away from strategy considerations towards levels of investment return *per se*. Return must be defined in terms of improved long-term competitiveness rather than just short-term measures.

Changing the basis of investment appraisal is both complex and fraught with difficulties. It is one of those issues in which manufacturing executives have traditionally felt relatively weak and where those who control the cash are professionally very strong. The debate has therefore been one-sided, with manufacturing the casualty by default. The arguments that investments must provide a quick pay-back are financially (and emotionally) attractive. They tend, however, totally to over-simplify the investment issues at stake and fail to drive executives towards determining and analysing those fundamental criteria which constitute the components of competitive strategy.

A short section on investment can only begin to open up the debate from the manufacturing perspective by providing some guidelines which manufacturing can use to raise key questions. One hopes that finance executives will also use them to develop their own appreciation of the strategic issues involved in manufacturing investment decisions. Nine key contentions are made, each of which is expanded to give substance but none can be claimed to be comprehensively examined. They are:

1. Investment decisions must be based on order-winning criteria.
2. Financial control systems need to be developed to meet the needs of the investment evaluation process.
3. Investments are not separate decisions but need to be considered as part of a corporate whole.
4. There can be only one given reason to substantiate an investment proposal.
5. Excessive use of return on investment (ROI) distorts strategy-building.
6. Government grants are not necessarily golden handshakes.
7. Linking investment to product life-cycles reduces risks.
8. Manufacturing must test the process implications of product life cycle forecasts.
9. Investment decisions must quantify infrastructure requirements.

8.2.1   *Investment decisions must be based on order-winning criteria*

The impact of investment policy and appraisal methods on manufacturing strategy's contribution to the competitiveness of a business is clearly significant. If high hurdle rates are imposed then it will invariably lead to a decreasing capital investment. In times of capital-rationing the argument put forward in support of high return on investment thresholds is that they facilitate the process of creaming off the more attractive investment proposals and hence enable a company to equate the best opportunities with available funds. But this line of argument fails to assess the relevance of investment proposals in the context of an agreed corporate strategy. The result, at best, is a hit and miss affair when agreeing essential investments as part of manufacturing's strategic contribution and, at worst, is a failure to trigger off essential investments if manufacturing is to provide its important contribution to market-share objectives.

For instance, delays in appropriate investment would lead to a position where costs did not decline as expected. The result would be that achieved experience curve gains (see Chapter 3) would fall off and, if the delay itself and extent of the investment requirement were large, then loss of market share would eventually follow.[8]

Manufacturing strategy arguments for process investment to meet order-winning criteria other than price and the associated low-cost manufacturing task, come up against the difficulties of accounting and finance-based rationale. Proposals, for instance, to invest in processes which increase production flexibility when customer response and delivery speed are the key order-winning criteria will be difficult to prepare in an appraisal system where return on investment is paramount. Similar forces will also work against facilities focus, irrespective of the importance of its role within manufacturing's support of the business needs. As explained in Chapter 5, focus will invariably lead to process duplication (pp. 165–7). However, investment appraisal systems often fail to incorporate as part of the evaluation procedure the need to orientate facilities to meet the order-winning criteria of markets better. This, by implication, gives undue weight to return on investments/capacity utilisation perspectives, and will militate against these essential considerations.

Other accounting and financial perspectives will also work against the pursuit of focus in manufacturing. The desire and strength of argument by this function to manage earnings and cash flows by smoothing cyclical business swings carries substantial weight. However, focused manufacturing leads to greater interaction between manufacturing and sales/marketing and this leads to a higher level of shared dependence between these two prime parts of a business. One result is that it will increase the argument against smoothing with the dynamics of sustaining and improving market share becoming of greater significance and carrying more weight of argument than the smoothing preferences of accounting and finance.[9]

Investments such as computer-aided design (CAD) provide an example of the limitations in the accounting approach to investment appraisal. CAD is usually evaluated on the cost savings attributed to its introduction. However, a significant gain associated with this investment is the speed of response to customer changes, particularly in a make-to-order business. Often this increased competitiveness is not recognised by a company as part of its corporate strategy. So, the contribution that CAD can make in corporate strategy support will neither be evaluated as part of the investment appraisal nor will it usually be systematically developed and exploited at all stages in the business.

In a reflective mood, Drucker pinpoints a belief in its own accounting figures as one of the common mistakes made by companies, which always leads to trouble.

The conventions are very inadequate, inappropriate . . . It gives [companies] the wrong information. They don't know what the real savings are . . . Cost accounting gives you information on the cost of doing, but not on the cost of not doing – which is increasingly the bigger cost. Quality and downtime are neither of them in the model.[10]

Only where companies develop a sound understanding of their need to compete effectively in different market segments will they be able to recognise the importance of relevant order-winners. With these established and reflected in the evaluation of manufacturing performance, then their importance can be assessed and taken into account in judging appropriate investments. Until then, companies will continue to use apparently 'hard' data as the predominant, or even sole, arbitrator. The development of manufacturing strategy, therefore, needs to recognise the role of order-winners in this evaluation procedure and to ensure that these critical decisions reflect the business, and not accounting conventions.

Thus, an assessment of current and future markets in terms of order-winning criteria is an essential step in a company's investment proposal procedure. This is especially so where investments are based upon a forecast sales increase. This will be a review of the way that both the existing and proposed capacity support relevant order-winners and, in particular, should identify levels of match/mismatch in terms of the changes envisaged in the way a company will win current and future orders.

8.2.2   *Financial control systems need to be developed to meet the needs of the investment evaluation process*

Financial-control systems tend to be designed to meet the needs of accountants and, consequently, are usually structured around a network of expense codes/accounts numbers, clinically constructed to facilitate electronic processing and the extraction of final accounts and budget reports on a consolidated basis. From the accountant's viewpoint, this is a reasonable way of handling what is often complex analysis. The result, however, is that business transactions are then analysed on the basis of accounts codes available and are often squeezed through a straitjacket of top–down apportionment to provide accountants with a view of expenditure and its relationship to business activity.

The result of the approach outlined above is that in practice many financial systems seek to control expenditure by tracing actual expenditure to points of authorisation and comparing it with planned expenditure with the authorisation providing the link to establish explanation and the formulation of corrective action. As highlighted in the last section, these evaluation procedures do create major problems for a manufacturing company which is seeking to update its technology in response to the identification of order-winning criteria. In many instances the order-winning criteria may be:

(a) product-orientated, for example:
  • quality;
  • lowest cost supply;
  • modular construction;

or

(b) process-orientated, for example:
  • lead-time;
  • quantity ordered;
  • adaptability in terms of product range or customer order size.

Existing financial control systems, therefore, tend not to provide management with a realistic basis for analysis against these criteria. In fact, in some instances, existing systems are misleading.

Table 8.1 provides a summary of some of the key differences between traditional financial analysis (geared to a steady state, low-variety, high-volume and slow-change business environment) and the approaches to analysis required by the highly competitive nature of today's business environment.

8.2.3 *Investments are not separate decisions but need to be considered as part of the corporate whole*

Companies with multi-sites, and particularly multinationals, need to review investments within the context of total corporate markets and total manufacturing provision. In the past, investments have tended to be taken as a series of separate decisions. At best, process overlaps have been identified, but, usually, reviews of corporate marketing and manufacturing strategies which take into account the whole business have not been undertaken. The result is that the link between current and proposed investments has not been forged. The outcomes of this failure include excess capacity, uncoordinated strategic responses, conflict and a failure to capitalise on corporate size and worldwide presence. As one executive reflected on his company's failure adequately to embrace separate decisions as part of a corporate whole 'the outcome is that whereas the Group has companies everywhere (global reach) it does not compete on a global basis'. Part of the problem – and one of the

TABLE 8.1
Typical financial control system provision *v*. investment evaluation requirement

Dimension	Typical financial control system provision	Investment evaluation process requirement
Direction	Backwards • examination of the company's historical trading performance	Forwards • project future performance
Orientation	Internal • examine and report on current business performance	External • evaluate current and future markets and competitors
Timescale	Short-term • review performance monthly	Long-term • examine expected performance over a given period
Expenditure base	Revenue expenditure • trace performance on the evaluation of revenue	Capital expenditure • evaluate investment in facilities to incorporate risk
Control base	Return on investment • assess return in respect of the net capital employed	Cash flow control • relate expected cash flows to initial cash outlays

outcomes – for this company was that investments, being reviewed as separate decisions, did not require the corporate whole to be part of the essential context for these decisions. Overcapacity was rampant.

Given the increasingly competitive nature of global markets, companies need to move towards total reviews of their many businesses in order to assess within and between geographical regions. Only in this way can manufacturing's response be continuously reshaped. This will not only improve the fit between existing capacity, capabilities and chosen markets but will also provide an overall view of existing manufacturing capabilities in terms of current and future markets, the necessary investments which need to be made and the appropriate location of these within the total business.

8.2.4 *There can only be one given reason to substantiate an investment proposal*

Investment appraisals submitted for review will typically include an extensive list of arguments and reasons for supporting a particular proposal. What has happened in many companies is that the appraisal procedure has developed into an art form. Not only are the numbers massaged but also the rationale underpinning the investment typically encompasses a long list of arguments in the belief that the cumulative weight of these will win the day. The result is that the essential clarity which should pervade these critical proposals is neither recognised as being essential nor required by the evaluating decision procedure.

This results in two major disadvantages:

(A) *Stated reasons are not always reality*
In many instances, proposals reflect corporate norms and expectations which are recognised to be prerequisites for consideration let alone success. As Table 8.2 shows[11] the result is that key decisions are often taken for undisclosed reasons and essential control of investments and agreement on their underlying support for a business is obviated.

(B) *The essential argument needed to distil investment issues and insights is not considered necessary*
If investment proposals do not require a distinction to be drawn between prime and other reasons then the essential argument needed to distil the key issues is not an inherent part of these procedures. The result is that the essential rigour necessary for sound strategic argument is typically not undertaken. Furthermore,

TABLE 8.2

Documented and perceived[1] reasons for all investments from January 1987 to June 1989 – UK manufacturing company

Purchase reasons	Documented	Perceived
Cost reduction	50[2]	19[3]
Update/introduce new technology	37	55
Increase throughput/productivity	37	17
Increase capacity	37	27
Part of a reorganisation	28	34
Improve quality	25	16
Process dedication requirement	25	21
Reduce changeover times	21	–
Improve product flexibility	20	–
New process/existing technology	18	1
Reduce supervisory costs	16	12
Purchase of available machine	15	17
Improve material control	10	–
Reduce lead-times	6	–
Process modernisation	5	22
Automate process	4	–

Notes: [1] Perceived reasons were attained sometimes after investment had been made

[2] To be read: In 50% of the cases cost reduction was documented as a reason for investment

[3] To be read: In 19% of the cases, cost reduction was perceived to be a reason for investment

with the passage of time the real reasons for investments are lost and post-investment evaluations, if undertaken at all, are set against wrong strategic dimensions. The outcome is that 'before' and 'after' evaluations are typically not recognised as key steps in investment proposal procedures.

Companies, therefore, should adopt the maxim that there can be only one given reason to substantiate an investment proposal. The logic may appear at first to be simplistic but, on the contrary, the rationale is sound. If one reason alone cannot support an investment then the substance and focus of the arguments need to be questioned. Whilst such a procedure does not disallow listing secondary reasons it will force strategic debate and clarify the essential rationale underpining these key decisions.

8.2.5 *Excessive use of ROI distorts strategy building*

Western companies, highly sensitive to the reactions of the stock market and shareholders to short-term declines in profits, have become all the more prone to adopting a short pay-back posture. Furthermore, in times of low-profit performance, the pressure invariably increases to effect short-term recovery programmes as a way of demonstrating improvement and management action. In turn, the argument to set high thresholds can win the day where inadequate strategic direction and agreement have been reached, or where the real need for investment has not been identified. Like drowning men, clutching at straws seems at the time highly attractive to companies, a fact made even more so by the promise of higher returns. But investments in manufacturing processes and infrastructure taken out of their strategic context can commit a company for years ahead in an inappropriate direction. In practice, though procedures require detailed benefits to be clearly shown and explained, the level of benefits achieved is much less rigorously assessed after the fact in order to determine the extent to which reality measured up to the proposals and to identify why any significant disparities arise. A UK Survey in the early 1990s verified this practice. It found that while 96 per cent of respondents reported a requirement to demonstrate quantifiable future benefits from capital investment, only 58 per cent validated these after the fact.[12] Whilst not suggesting that hindsight is a substitute for foresight, such assessments provide a review of the effectiveness of these critical decisions. These analyses not only identify the actual level of return but also enable a company to measure the extent to which past investments have supported its corporate strategic requirements.

The approach to investment appraisal in Japan and West Germany has a different basis. When they invest they are often prepared to sacrifice the short-term for longer-term profits which accrue from market share and increased volumes. In this way they demonstrate two important differences in approach. The first is that they avoid the delusion that in an imprecise environment, numbers are precise and thereby reliable, and thus by using numbers, assume that the risk is reduced. The second is that to run a successful business, risks need to be taken.

Ohmae summarises the clear difference in approach between Western and Japanese businessmen by illustrating, with examples, the investments made by two Japanese companies and concluding that 'in neither case, however, is any attention given to return on investment (ROI) or payback period, let alone to discounted cash flow. In both, the dominant investment criterion is whether the new business is good for the corporation as a whole'.[13] He then continues to illustrate these differences by posing such questions as:

> **How many contemporary US corporations relying on ROI yardsticks would have embarked on the development of a business that required a twenty-year incubation period, as did Nippon Electric Company with its computer and semiconductor businesses? . . . Would Honda have so obstinately persisted in using its motorbike profits to bring its clean-engine vehicle to market if it were a corporation that measured the ROI of each product line and made its decisions accordingly? In fact, would any manufacturers be entering the four-wheel vehicle market in today's environment if ROI were the investment criterion?[14]**

In many companies a by-product of the emphasis on ROI in the corporate evaluation of investments has been an increasing tendency to view these proposals as a series of one-off, unrelated events, and not, as they invariably are, characterised by strategic sequence. Only when companies review investment decisions in the light of their corporate strategies, and, in turn their marketing and manufacturing strategies, will the essential cohesion be established. Until this happens, companies will be in danger of investing in ways which will not give them the necessary synergistic gains of strategic coherence. An example of what happens is provided by a company involved in the manufacture of office equipment and supplies which, over the years, had added on capacity in a piecemeal way. The result was a company with seven manufacturing units in the same road, only two of which were interconnected. Buying up premises as they were required made, on paper, a better return on investment than resiting the business. However,

the costs of handling and transport between units added complexity and overhead duplication. The position was only assessed
when a new chief executive called a halt to the proposal to add
another part to the 'rabbit warren'.

8.2.6   *Government grants are not necessarily golden handshakes*

With disproportionately high unemployment rates in certain parts
of the UK and the impact of declining primary as well as secondary
sectors of the economy, successive governments have, most understandably, pursued a policy of trying to attract manufacturing as
well as other activities to these areas in order to redress the
national imbalance. In a similar way, they have persuaded organisations to take on ailing companies or parts of companies to
avert significant instances of primary and secondary redundancy.
In addition, at plant level, governments have attempted to stimulate or support investment in manufacturing companies as a way of
helping to increase their competitiveness in world markets. In each
instance, the carrot has been a generous system of grants and other
awards. Many companies, attracted by the size of the hand-outs
and the cash and return on investment gains they represent, have
decided to take up the offer and relocate or establish all or parts of
their business in one of a number of distressed areas, take on a
relatively large piece of manufacturing capacity at one go, or
invest in numerical control equipment to improve their manufacturing process capability. Where clear strategic parameters have
not been established by these companies and the evaluation of
proposals has rested largely on the attractiveness of its return or
cash injection, then companies have all too often rued the day
when the decision was made. Bound by a minimum period of
residence, by the relative size of the investments involved or by the
desire to save face, at least in the short term or while the custodians of the decision still have responsibility for the business
concerned, companies find themselves hidebound. Examples are
numerous.

One carpet company integrated vertically into yarn production
instead of continuing its then current policy of buying from a
number of yarn suppliers. The mill selected was in a remote area
and some hundred miles distant from the carpet plants of the
parent company. Besides all the difficulties associated with

recruitment at all levels in the mill and the distances involved in what was a 'linked' process, it also incurred one additional and fundamental problem. The decision to split the processes into yarn and carpet manufacturing was made on the basis that it was a natural break in the processes involved. However, the manufacturing company had established its niche in the quality end of the markets. By separating the business at the natural break provided between the sets of processes involved, the manufacturer had facilitated the investment-orientated arguments. But, at the same time, the essential quality control link had been broken between yarn-spinning and carpet-manufacture, both of which were now a common, corporate responsibility. Thus, a manufacturing split based upon processes had ignored the essential qualifying criterion of producing high-quality carpets. The quick feedback and opportunity for close liaison were not easy to exploit. In the early months, justifying the investment from both parts of the total business became top management's preoccupation. Reality, however, proved more difficult to handle than the order-lines implied in the integration proposals.

A medium-sized company having decided to establish a subcontract machining facility was attracted to change its location decision from the industrial site of its first choosing to one some twenty-five miles away. The carrot offered was that the latter had a development classification attracting a high level of grant and expenditure exemptions. This alternative proved significantly more attractive to the executives, bank and other financial institutions who all developed a fixation on the impact it made on ROI, profit and cash flows. However, only when the order-winning criterion of delivery speed was clearly imposed into the debate did these accrued financial advantages pale into significance. Without the sales, the calculations had no foundation.

Finally, a large UK manufacturing company which had great difficulty in achieving adequate profit margins was persuaded to absorb part of another group of companies. The cash injection offered as part of the government proposal to avert job losses, swung the balance. The difficulties of absorbing such a large addition to manufacturing capacity, matching systems, controls and other parts of the infrastructure besides the production processes involved, added to the company's already difficult task. The rationalisation which ensued cast serious questions on the fit between the decision and the strategic needs and direction of the existing business.

But the policies of the 1980s are now being reviewed. In the UK for instance, the Department of Trade and Industry launched its Manufacturing Planning and Implementation Scheme in 1991. Offering financial support to small and medium-size companies who wished to invest in outside professional advice, the scheme was built round a new and distinctive feature. All assignments had to involve a strategic review of a company's markets as a prelude to the proposed developments, and external monitoring was built into the scheme at all stages including vetting of the advisor to ensure that the ability to undertake these tasks was a demonstrable part of an advisor's offering.

8.2.7   *Linking investment to product life-cycles reduces risk*

Many companies entering markets for existing, replacement, or new products make decisions on process investment which need to reflect the forecast demands for those items at the various stages in life-cycles. As explained earlier in Chapter 4 most products do not move from jobbing, to batch, to line levels of volume over the life-cycle. In fact for this to happen is rare. Companies assess the market or base their forecast volume requirements with customers and have to plan their investments in accordance with the relevant volume parameters established by these procedures. It does not make sense for them to invest at one level of volume and then reinvest in a higher volume process with subsequent market growth. However, the difficulty inherent in these decisions is the judgemental nature of predicting the future. Where a high level of certainty exists there is less difficulty in matching the process investment to eventual product volumes. However, in areas of uncertainty and given the characteristic ways of appraising investments and evaluating the various alternatives, companies invariably place themselves in a yes/no decision situation. With long delivery times for equipment, this position is further aggravated. Commitments have to be made months, sometimes years, in advance of the scheduled launch. However, an alternative to this can be considered in many situations. Figure 8.2 shows a projected life-cycle for a product. At 1, process investment decisions would have to be made and purchase orders raised in order for the plant

FIGURE 8.2
Alternative approaches to investment decisions

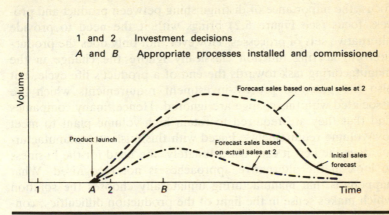

1 and 2   Investment decisions
A and *B*   Appropriate processes installed and commissioned

to be installed and commissioned to meet the intended product launch at *A*. The alternative approach is to delay the process investment decision until 2, hence allowing sales forecasts to be amended in line with the actual sales to date and revised projections. To illustrate, figure 8.2 gives two different levels of revised forecasts. The trade-off embodied by adopting this second approach is that the process choice would be more in line with the requirement. In this example, the new forecasts could be higher, lower or somewhat near the same as the original forecast. Hence, the eventual investments would be more in keeping with the actual sales levels. To do this and yet minimise investment would require that existing processes could cope with the manufacturing task to point *B*. The company would thereby not be able to meet the level of manufacturing costs necessary to yield adequate margins and, in this way, the trade-offs between loss of profits in the period between *A* and *B* and the risk of inappropriate investments being made, would have to be assessed.

8.2.8 *Manufacturing must test the process implications of product life-cycle forecasts*

A particular point to be made with regard to investments is that in many instances, investment proposals rarely cover each main phase of a product's life-cycle. Yet manufacturing's task is to produce the product over each phase of this cycle and respond to the consequent variations in volumes. Returning to Chapter 5 on focus, the importance of distinguishing between product and process focus (see Figure 5.2) brings with it the need to provide alternative sets of processes. However, not only does the production engineering function classically ignore the change in the manufacturing task towards the end of a product's life cycle, but also the potential process-investment requirements which are associated with this change are ignored. Hence, many companies find that they are required to retain high-volume plant to meet low-volume requirements. Faced with this mismatch manufacturing does the best it can. Unfortunately, the need for the business to look at the alternative approaches is not recognised. What happens is that manufacturing unilaterally chooses the solution which makes sense in the light of the production difficulties, constraints and performance measures, only to be changed in circumstances where the trade-offs involved in that choice have come under corporate scrutiny (for example, the inventory holding associated with making order quantities in excess of sales call-offs or requirements). Given that the order-winning criteria associated with the volumes involved at these stages in a product's life-cycle are invariably different (see Figure 8.3) then the process choice appropriate to these stages should be realigned, if manufacturing

FIGURE 8.3
Product life-cycles, order-winning criteria and process investment interact

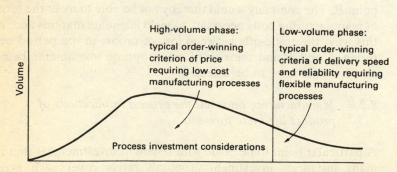

High-volume phase:

typical order-winning criterion of price requiring low cost manufacturing processes

Low-volume phase:

typical order-winning criteria of delivery speed and reliability requiring flexible manufacturing processes

Volume

Process investment considerations

is to be able to provide the essential criteria at each stage of a product's life-cycle. Thus, the investment proposal needs to include the processes necessary to manufacture effectively (in line with the varying needs of the market) throughout each stage.

The viability of a proposed product introduction should be over the whole of its life-cycle and so include the investments necessary to cope with the same time-period. This does not happen. It is assumed that the process installed for the high-volume phase is the only requirement. Where existing processes can cope effectively with the change in volumes, the costs involved with this transfer (often quite high) also need to be recognised in the initial stages and included as part of the corporate assessment.

8.2.9 *Investment decisions must quantify working capital and infrastructure requirements*

Many investment decisions are distorted in two ways. On the one hand, they ignore intangible, difficult-to-evaluate reductions or benefits which accrue from the investments.* Whilst on the other, they underestimate the working capital needs associated with each proposal and often ignore altogether the infrastructure costs which will be involved. The tangible nature of the investments associated with the equipment, plant and support services involved in a process have led to a clear identification of the costs involved. However, many areas of investment directly associated with the capital expenditure being proposed have been overlooked or ignored in the past and, in many instances, are understated or assumed to be unnecessary at present. Only in the last ten years have companies required a statement of the additional inventory necessitated by the process proposals under consideration. The drive by most companies to reduce inventory since the early 1980s has been one important stimulus for this change. Even so, many proposals understate inventory. This is because those involved in the preparation of a capital expenditure proposal are invariably not responsible for inventory levels within manufacturing. This

---

* A UK survey confirmed this point. Although 96 per cent of respondents were required to demonstrate quantifiable future benefits, only 55 per cent regarded intangible benefits as playing an important role in the justification process.[15]

leads to a significant underestimation of the levels which will actually be needed to sustain manufacturing.

The effect on the infrastructure requirements which will emanate from particular manufacturing process investments is often either underestimated or not evaluated when expenditure proposals are prepared. The failure is often that those responsible for either the control of manufacturing or the achievement of required levels of performance are not the same as those who prepare the proposals. Thus, an oversimplified review of infrastructure requirements is made. The consequence of this is that any increase in complexity goes unrecognised and the assumption is made that existing systems, controls and structures are not only appropriate but also adequate. The incremental nature of such assumptions leads to a deterioration in a company's ability to control and assess its manufacturing function and the eventual overhaul of one or more parts of its infrastructure. The costs associated with such developments can involve high expenditure. For example, one company estimated that to install a revised manufacturing control system in a typical plant cost upwards of £300 000.

Where a company is starting with a green-field site on which to make a single product, then its investment decisions will usually take full account of the need for services, systems and controls with regard to all the major aspects of infrastructure. However, most companies are more complex and are generally investing in existing plants or introducing products to be made in already up-and-running processes. Usually, investment considerations when introducing a product are more akin to the following examples:

1. The decision to enter a market will require an investment in all the processes necessary to manufacture the product in question. Whilst similar to the green-field site example referred to above, the product in this instance will be assumed to use existing site services, support systems and overheads. However, this assumption belies reality. It ignores the increase in complexity and corresponding demand placed upon the non-process aspects of manufacturing which go hand in hand with the decision and the resulting deterioration of the effectiveness of existing systems and structures.
2. Most product introductions also generally use parts of the existing

manufacturing processes. In these instances, therefore, the problem is compounded by the fact that there will be an increase in both inventory and in the complexity brought on by the shared use of existing processes and infrastructure and the interplay between them.

8.3   Operating Controls and Information

In order to assess its current performance a company needs control information which reflects the key areas of its manufacturing task. However, although there is a lot of information collected and recorded, many companies fail to separate the difference between records and control.[16] Furthermore, 'the development of the marketing orientation [in many companies] has led to an increase in the amount of market-based information available to management. In contrast the paucity and limited availability of relevant internal information is striking'.[17] One key problem area is that of management accounting. Although money is used as the common denominator to assess both current and future corporate performance this function is often lacking in relevance and sensitivity towards changing circumstances.

8.4   The Simplistic Nature of Accounting Information

The accounting information provided in most companies can be characterised in a number of ways (also refer to the previous section, including Table 8.1). In the first instance it is historically based. Although this is an inherent part of cost information, it seems to induce an attitude within accountants and an acceptance by the business that it is not of paramount importance to produce information which is relevant and as close to reality as can be achieved. The second characteristic is that invariably the information provided is primarily focused on management accounting relating to the business as a whole rather than the management control of manufacturing. This leads to the inadequate provision of information which is not only of a critical nature in itself but also is perceived by management as the basis for assessing performances and on which to make future decisions.

In broad terms, accountants primarily work on the basis of norms. They choose averages to simplify the measurement task. The procedure then is to compare each part of the business to a norm. However, the global nature of these comparisons hides the key to control. By failing to go back to the information from which the average has been drawn, the checks made obscure the level of performance achieved. As averages are a compilation of many parts, it is important to be able to assess the level of performance within each part. The argument put forward in defence of the approach adopted is that to collect and update data in this way would be very time-consuming and expensive. Therefore, it is necessary to simplify the procedures and tasks involved in order to make some sense of reality and to be able to report within an acceptable time-scale.

Reality, however, is complex. The controls need to reflect and measure reality. The accountants' approach is to simplify reality by simplifying the controls used. In this way they are able to account for all the parts, yet cope administratively with the task and also meet the audit obligation of 'accounting for everything in a systematic way'. However, the basis for control in companies needs to reflect the complex business issues and not the tasks required by company law. Hence, the controls need to reflect the size and importance of the area concerned – detailed controls for the significant areas and simple, broad-brush controls for the insignificant areas.

Several general examples will serve to illustrate these points:

- Most companies use total sales revenue as an indicator of successful performance. Invariably this leads to a situation where the contribution of individual products is not rigorously examined. In profit-and-loss account terms, the top line becomes the measure of sales performance, and the bottom line, the measure of manufacturing performance. What fails to be clearly distinguished is that the two performances are inextricably linked. The consequence of the lack of distinction between the two reinforces the argument by marketing of the need to retain all products. The simple measure of the marketing performance fails to distinguish the relative contribution of each product. Hence the conclusion that all sales are equally good business.
- It is usual for manufacturing's task to be based on a proposed or

forecast level of volumes. Invariably the volumes experienced differ from period to period, and over time. However, rarely are costings provided for the different volume levels involved. It is essential to establish costings for the varying levels of through-put. In this way, the costings appropriate to the volume levels experienced will be used. This will then allow a company to assess a period's performance in a more exact way and to establish the reasons for the level of achievement recorded.

- Accounting systems should reflect the type of processes being used. As shown in Table 8.3, the treatment of costs, pricing and the development of accounting procedures and controls will vary. The costing structure and performance reporting system needs to take account of these differences in order to distinguish between the provision of sensitive cost information and the measurement of performance.

- Plant decisions constitute a large business risk because of the size of the investment, the forecast sales basis for that decision, and the flexibility/process cost trade-offs involved and their relationship to the market. However, the accounting policy on depreciation reinforces this risk where it is classified in relation to the type of plant rather than the life of the product for which the plant is to be purchased. Typically, plant is depreciated by rule-of-thumb accounting classifications. For instance, one large manufacturing company used the rules in Table 8.4 which had been arrived at by historical usage and precedents.

The gains which accrued from having common accounting procedures belied the simplistic nature of this policy. As a consequence, this sizeable asset becomes detached from its essential business orientation in order to accommodate the administrative requirements of the accounting function and policies involved.

8.5   The Need for Accounting System Development

Demands for much-needed accounting system developments are not new. Criticisms levelled at existing approaches have become both increasingly vocal and broader-based in origin. However, so far these overtures have resulted in little progress other than some tinkering at the edges. Some argue that the concerted pressure for

TABLE 8.3
Some of the different accounting approaches depending upon the type of process

Aspect	Type of process	
	General-purpose	Dedicated
Overhead		
Recovery	Process- or product-orientated	Blanket rate per standard hour
Control	Complex control: needs to assess the impact of product mix and volume changes, alternative routings and other similar factors	Simple variance control derived from comparing actual to standard unit volumes
Costs		
Set-ups	Direct to product	Overhead rate based upon machine utilisation
Process scrap	Specific to the process or product	Blanket allowance
Quality	Direct to product	Overhead rate established
Tooling	Direct to product	Overhead rate established
Maintenance	Direct to process	Overhead rate established
Basis for pricing	Product cost basis	Contribution basis
Development of accounting procedures and controls	Bottom-up	Top–down

Source: Based on ideas developed by Clive Turner Associates, Redditch

TABLE 8.4
Rules-of-thumb accounting practices

Item of plant	Typical number of years over which plant was depreciated in all parts of the company
Tool-room equipment	25
Presses	20
Automatic lathes	15
Numerically controlled machines	10
Machining centres	5
Test	
dedicated	5
general-purpose	10

these improvements has increased because of growing competition and loss of market share.[18] In part this is so. But the real reason is not one of blame.[19] To be able to assess options and alternative strategies, companies need insights, and in the competitive climate of the 1990s, the pressure, both in terms of significance and speed to make strategic responses, has never been greater. However, accounting systems, even in their recording mode, do not provide information that helps the decision process. It is neither relevant nor timely. In addition and of a far more fundamental nature is the question-mark over accountants' perception of the role of accounting systems. Past history clearly marks them, at best, as being reactive. Hence, their bean-counter/record-keeper image. What is needed is an executive response, proactively developing systems which fulfil the needs of the decision-making processes necessary to meet the demands of today's markets and competitive threats.

Revisions are being made. A UK Survey in 1991 reported that in the previous five years 'significant revisions to cost-management systems were cited by 68 per cent of respondents'. However, the Survey also reported that many of these revisions 'were "traditional" rather than "new" accounting techniques and practices'.[20] The implication drawn by the authors of the report was that 'introducing advanced cost-techniques and practices may not be the best costing improvement for many businesses'. However, the concern is that developing basic systems will not give a company the insights it requires. For if traditional practices provided what was needed then the essential criticism levelled against these systems would not be widespread in nature and growing in volume.

In their attempts to improve the competitive nature of their performance, many Western European companies are paying greater attention to a whole range of improvements in quality, processes, inventory holdings and workforce policies. All are essential measures to effect this change. Not only is the level and urgency of response high but the approaches have challenged and are challenging the very basis of previous practice. However, the same cannot be said of accounting.

For example, in markets which are characterised by difference not similarity, and by a rapid rate of change 'most companies still use the same cost-accounting and management-control systems that were developed decades ago for a competitive environment drastically different from that of today'.[21] When trying to assess the level of contribution provided by each product as a prerequisite for judging what steps to take, many companies find that the accounting information provided fails to differentiate between them. Whilst everyone knows that higher volumes decrease costs and product proliferation increases them, rarely are these essential trade-offs differentiated within accounting procedures. Classically, the core activities generate the substantial parts of a business. However, in order to assess the trade-offs associated with product breadth and focus, companies need appropriate information to help them to arrive at sensible decisions. Non-core products are characteristically marginal in their contribution to a firm.

Far worse than this, they may create added cost which will be hidden by an average allocation to all products and customers. As a consequence, the essential core business may be de-emphasized or overpriced, while the marginal extensions of the product line and customers served may be underpriced or over-emphasized in their importance. This may be true even though a real competitive advantage exists in the core business while there is no comparable advantage in the extension coverage.[22]

The impact on business competitiveness can be significant.

8.5.1 *Working on the left-hand side of the decimal point*

Information used in companies is not accurate. Plus or minus 10 per cent is the rule of thumb used by many. Accounting information is no exception. That these 'analyses are rarely, if ever, exact (and) all they can do is give a "feel" for the financial dimensions of various activities and opportunities' is a realistic view.[23]

However, the typical presentation of accounting information is a give-away. Figures to one (often two) decimal points imply a level of data accuracy which is spurious. All that the system has provided is the refining of inaccurate data, and this problem is reinforced because typically the accounting function rarely reminds those using the data that it is not as accurate as it may appear.

Working only on the left-hand side of the decimal point brings significant advantages even using existing systems. The information is easier to use, its role as a help in the decision-making process is reinforced and the need to understand the issues and ensure that all relevant perspectives are considered is highlighted.

8.5.2 *Assessing current performance*

Companies control their businesses using different procedures working in different time-periods. At any moment in time, therefore, a company will have a strategic plan (usually agreed the previous year), budgets based on the strategic plan and revised budgets which reflect current events and levels of activity.

However, many companies then compare actual performance with the budget as the principal way of reviewing overall corporate performance.[24] But this comparison will not provide the insights into performance. Where companies revise plans or targets then it is the revised plan which needs to be set against actual performance. This will, therefore, enable actual performance to be set against the actual plan. Budget changes which result from adjustments to strategic plans need then to be reviewed separately in order to assess the planning procedure, the reasons for change and the impact of revisions on corporate expectations.

8.5.3 *Allocate, not absorb, overheads*

The accounting practice which leads to this situation is the application of the allocation and absorption approaches to overheads. In most manufacturing companies overheads are between 25 and 50 per cent of total costs,[25] and are usually increasing both in themselves and in terms of their relative size.[26] Yet all too often the bulk of these are absorbed. A review of one manufacturing company revealed that some 80 per cent of total overheads were absorbed. As these costs accounted for over 40 per cent of the total, the implications were alarming. The reason why overhead costs are predominantly absorbed is that it involves less administrative work and system maintenance than alternatives. Many accountants abuse this principle still further, by using one overhead absorption rate for several parts of the business involved, and often absorbing on a single basis rather than the number of bases necessary to reflect the business and improve the relevance of the information provided. One company within a group of manufacturing companies had seven sites with uses ranging from holding and distributing raw materials through spares, low-volume manufacturing and high-volume manufacturing to distribution of finished goods. Overheads for all seven sites were pooled and were then absorbed at one common rate for each site based upon the single factor of direct labour hours. Faced with declining profits, group executives turned to the basic performance evaluation of each site. The answers told them very little.[27]

A business needs more sensitive information at all times. The only meaningful way to account for this sizeable set of costs is to reflect reality. It not only needs to have each site accounted for separately but also to have the distinction drawn between products within a site. It is essential, therefore, for accounting functions to adopt the policy of allocating overheads wherever possible.* As a general rule, a minimum target of allocating 80 per cent of total overheads should be the initial aim. The consequences would be

---

* Overhead allocation involves the 'allocation', 'apportionment' or 'allotment' of overhead costs to the appropriate cost centre or cost unit. Overhead absorption is achieved by dividing the costs involved on a suitable basis (e.g. standard labour hours, direct clocked hours, direct labour costs, material costs or floor space) and then spreading them on a *pro rata* basis in line with the common factor which has been chosen.

that then only a relatively small portion of total costs would need to be spread on an absorption basis.

Information which provides more accurate insights is a prerequisite for making sound management decisions. This is particularly so regarding:

1. *products*   decisions concerning pricing and the impact on margins, sales and growth potential are at the very core of commercial activity and will significantly influence the financial performance of a company;
2. *opportunities for cost reduction*   where the sources and extent of costs are more clearly identified then the opportunity to reduce costs is improved. This opportunity is particularly enhanced by developments in activity-based costing addressed in the next section.

8.5.4   *Activity-based costing*

Activity-based costing (ABC) is developed on its premise of identifying costs on an activity rather than functional base. The latter is the approach currently used by many companies and one which directly leads to the need to disperse these groups of cost using some allocation/absorption procedure. The development of a system which identifies cost on the basis of activity eliminates the need for a two-stage procedure.

Thus in ABC, activities/transactions are the focus of the costing system, as it is they, not products, which cause costs to be incurred. It recognises that whilst products consume direct materials and direct labour, it is activities which consume overheard resources with products then consuming activities. Thus, ABC is particularly concerned with understanding the cost of activities and their relationship to products/services. The approach taken is as follows

- identify the major activities;
- determine the underlying factors which cause the activity to occur – known as *cost-drivers*;
- create cost-pools to collect activity costs which have the same cost-driver. The major activities (see above) must therefore constitute a homogeneous set of tasks and costs such that cost variations in any pool can be explained by a single cause;

- attribute the costs of the activities gathered with each cost-pool to the products/sources based on cost-drivers (i.e. how much of the activity has been used by the product/service in question)

In this way, therefore, ABC is a more sophisticated absorption/allocation system resulting in a more accurate identification of costs. As in Section 8.5.3, however, there are two important but distinct uses of the information provided by ABC – products and opportunities to reduce costs.

Product-related decisions

Analysis of the cost-structure of overhead activities enables full product/service, customer, market and profitability analyses to be completed. It is used, therefore, in support of key decisions such as

- product pricing;
- growth, decline, renegotiation or exiting from market segments, customers and/or products.

Reducing or reshaping non-value activities

Once a company's key activities have been agreed, ABC identifies non-value-added activities and questions whether they are necessary in part or at all and whether each activity is efficiently provided. It thus ensures that the cost of non-value-added activities is visible to management and so enables management to review the size and shape of overhead costs as part of its operational decision-making process.

However, whereas companies investing in ABC always use the new information in product-related decisions many do not use it to undertake the phase to review non-value-added activity.[28] In fact, any organisation which has not systematically reduced overhead costs as a direct result of ABC has failed to use this approach in the true sense of the word. Unfortunately, many businesses still fall into this category and thereby miss many of the real opportunities for overall improvement. A Survey in 1991, in fact, revealed that whereas 32 per cent of respondence have ABC in place, only 11 per cent were using cost-drivers as performance measures.[29]

8.5.5 *Focused manufacturing helps to identify overhead costs*

The concern that the accounting functions have failed to develop systems which would improve key insights into product costs and non-value-added activities has been expressed earlier. The last two sections have addressed key perspectives and reviewed recent developments to meet these criticisms.

However, a significant reason why the accounting functions have been unable to provide adequate costing-system developments has been the fact that the problem has become too complex to be handled by a single solution. However, unless companies find ways of being able to drive out costs and arrive at sound product decisions, they will have problems in competing effectively in today's tough market conditions.

Adopting the manufacturing-strategy principles of focus and plant-within-plant facilities (see Chapter 5) will also facilitate the provision of more accurate cost information. These approaches enable a company to identify more easily the overheads associated with each part of manufacturing and similarly help the company to assess the contribution provided by each part to the whole business. This change brings with it a shift from the principle of accounting for overheads on a functional basis to that of a dedicated overhead allocation. Thus, instead of the costs involved in providing a support function being summarised as a total for that function, it changes to a policy of accounting for those overheads which are dedicated to or are directly in association with a part of manufacturing. Not only does this now enable a company to assess more clearly the contribution of its different parts, but in times of change it will enable a company to take out or increase the vertical slice of overheads associated with that part of the process under review. Thus, it allows change to take place in a more orderly and sensible way. Accounting decisions are now more in line with manufacturing strategy needs. It avoids accentuating the already wide gap between the support needs of manufacturing activities and the perceived role of support functions. Thus, as overhead costs are now clearly identified with a particular sector of manufacturing, the level and nature of support can be agreed to meet the current needs of that sector and to reflect any changes identified in the future.

A further refinement to these changes involves making any

functional overhead into a business unit. This then enables a business to move away from the position where an accountant or accounting procedure spreads the unallocated overhead on some arbitrary basis in order to make the books balance, to a position where each part of the business declares a budget for the amount it intends to purchase from each overhead function. The gains are obvious.

Beware, however, of two possible developments

1. the counter-argument put forward by accountants that these changes are difficult to accomplish and lack a high degree of accuracy. These changes will, in fact, enhance the value of this information in the light of the business needs both in terms of relevance and accuracy
2. attaining accuracy as an end in itself. The corporate gain is providing information to help to prioritise product decisions and cost-reduction activities

8.5.6 *Create business-related financial information*

The key role of business-related financial information has been highlighted in the sections concerning cost-system developments. As an essential input into developing both a marketing and manufacturing strategy, accounting information is rarely designed specifically to provided analyses which would form an integral part of the formulation of either function's strategic statement. Examples of key marketing information in addition to those specifically mentioned earlier include:

- *customer sales and profitability* An assessment of both the sales and total costs associated with selling to and support for major customers would enable a company to establish the true worth of these relationships;
- *market share and profitability* Identifying the value of sales in each market, its relative size, associated costs to promote and support relevant activities and the level of profitability for each market segment would be an essential input into formulating a marketing plan.

For the manufacturing side of the business, information which is rarely provided by existing accounting systems but which would, in turn, offer invaluable insights in the strategy formulation includes:

- cost estimates of manufacturing at varying levels of throughput;
- capacity analyses identifying the contribution of each product in terms of any bottleneck or limiting factor in manufacturing's existing capacity, and known as analysis of contribution by limiting factor. This would enable companies to assess proposals to increase capacity and to decide how best to allocate existing capacity in the meantime;
- cost estimates for supplying items outside the normal product range.

Finally, the need to separate out those costs incurred by manufacturing but not induced by manufacturing decisions is seldom reflected in the control statements provided by the accounting system. Excess manufacturing costs incurred as a result of a change in schedule to meet a sales or customer request, for instance, are usually not shown under their own separate headings, e.g. 'manufacturing excess cost due to customer schedule change'.

8.5.7 *Provide performance related financial information*

The final area of development concerns the provision of accurate performance-related information. As the measurement of actual performance needs to be set against targets which reflect reality so levels of performance within a business will differ from one part to another. Not all products can be expected to be able to achieve the same performance standards during each and every year of their lives. Therefore, why should products in different stages of their life-cycles be forced to meet the same minimum standard each year? For this to be appropriate it would mean an unbalanced portfolio made up solely of products all in the same stage of their life-cycles.

Once performance expectations have been resolved the next issue concerns the level of expected activity. Budgets, by definition, are out of date by the time they are completed. It is necessary, therefore, to revise the budget figure by using the latest information. In this way, the basis for establishing and assessing levels of performance is changed from a budget to a latest-estimate basis. One clear example of this is the use of flexible budgeting which changes the cost base in line with actual volumes and alters the basis for related cost information (e.g. overhead absorption either by traditional or ABC systems).

The last illustration concerns the distortions which businesses experience as a result of the way in which inventory values are calculated. In many situations, inventory desensitises cost information by becoming a cost buffer. Most accounting systems assume that costs are held in the value of work-in-progress as calculated in the system. What often happens is that accumulated cost excesses are discovered when the inventory is physically counted at the end-of-period stocktaking and then recorded as an inventory or stocktaking loss. As inventory is physically counted in many firms but twice a year, control or responsibility is not easy to establish.

8.6   Conclusion

The growing criticism of existing accounting systems and investment appraisal procedures is more than justified. The accounting profession in many Western European countries has secured a role which is perceived to be, and for which responsibility and resource has been given as the key provider of financial information. Unfortunately, accountants have generally been reactive in responding to the changing needs of business and have spent too much of their time keeping records rather than providing information for, and partaking in, the control and development of the business. The description of 'bean-counter' sits well.

Two general misconceptions have contributed to this:

- management concerns developing not just maintaining existing procedures;
- like other functions, accountancy has failed to recognise that its role is subservient to that of the business. Its prime task is to respond to and meet the needs of a business. The *raison d'être* of a function exists through the business. Functions do not exist in their own right. Evaluating a function's contribution, therefore, needs to be set within this frame.

The potential contribution of accounting and finance functions is significant. The key insights and overall executive role it can bring to a business are considerable. However, for this level of effectiveness to be realised, changes in need and developments in response must be recognised and their provision both timely and appropriate. This chapter has posed several issues which need to be embraced and addressed. Of these, three dimensions need to be at the forefront of accounting provision.

8.6.1 *Markets are changing*

The traditional perspective of productivity and evaluation of investment decisions needs to be modified in line with the needs of the business and to reflect how these needs are secured. The principle which should drive today's businesses is based on keeping existing customers and winning new ones, not lowering labour costs. Cutting lead-times, boosting quality, improving delivery reliability, reducing inventories and supporting product range are factors which top the list in these endeavours. Accounting systems and financial reviews need to reflect this.

8.6.2 *Businesses are characterised by difference*

Difference not similarity characterises today's businesses. Rules and procedures need to embrace this. Levels of control, therefore, should be established to ensure that the more difficult and complex a proposal then the less formal and bureaucratic the approach. Investment proposals for relatively small sums are well-served by laid-out procedures and predetermined hurdles. Major investments on the other hand, are ill-served by such approaches. Yet usually one set of rules applies and is characterised by bureaucracy in the belief that the essence of control has its root in well-defined procedures.

However, major investments need approaches which are the very opposite of current developments and executive behaviour. The maxim should be that the larger the investment, the more informal the approach and the lack of definition within the procedures used. Thus, major investments should be strategy-led and subject to open debate, ideally involving non-executive contributions in order to enhance neutrality. Putting forward functional proposals in line with agreed and structured procedures discourages strategic debate, stifles discussion and encourages rationalisation – the very opposite of what is required to handle these complex and fundamental strategic decisions.

TABLE 8.5
The three phases in an investment programme showing the sequence involved, the nature of the investment and the tangible nature of each phase

Phase	Time-scale	Features of the investment	Tangible nature	Features of evaluation and control
1.	Pre-operating	Fixed assets in the form of plant, equipment and associated installation costs	High	Constitutes taking one investment in isolation. Traditional investment appraisal techniques used which are *cash-flow* orientated
2.	Operating	Supporting working capital in the form of inventory		The investment now becomes an integral part of the business summary. It reverts to revenue accounts which measure *profit* to investment as the basis of control or
3.	Operating	The service and support overheads necessary to provide an appropriate level of infrastructure	Low	assessment. Control of individual investments now relatively loose – rarely have post-audits

Source: Based on ideas developed by Clive Turner Associates.

8.6.3 *Linking process investment decisions and the evaluation of control systems*

In many companies the link between process investment decisions and the need to provide supporting infrastructure in the form of control systems is not appreciated. This distinction arises from the fact that decisions about processes are not only tangible but they are also taken at a different phase in the decision sequence (see Table 8.5). On the other hand, the sizeable investments associated with manufacturing-process decisions of working capital and infrastructure are often obscured for exactly the opposite reasons – they are less tangible and occur in the operating phase of the installation.

Furthermore, when a process investment is installed on the shop-floor a distinct accounting change takes place. At the pre-operating stage highlighted in Table 8.5 a process is singularly evaluated in great detail as part of the investment appraisal system and is cash-flow orientated. However, once installed this same process will no longer be treated as an individual item in accounting control terms. Instead, it will be controlled by a number of broad-brush accounting systems based on profit. It will become just part of a functionally based set of assets and costs comprising a range of investments, different in terms of usage, degree of dedication to the manufacture of specific products, age and support-system requirements. The change in accounting treatment highlights the contrasts involved and the necessary high level of control in the pre-operating phase compared with the lack of sensitivity in the global controls once the asset is being used.

8.6.4 *The ways forward*

What then are the ways forward? These involve changes at two levels in the organisation. At the top, many executives have perceived their role in accounting and finance in a different form. Often they become involved in, or even spearhead, activities designed to generate earnings by financial transactions. This has the major drawback of diverting management effort and interest away from the business core. They become more distant from the prime profit-generating activities of a manufacturing business. They start to control from a distance. Without the understanding of each firm's strategy, they feel unable to contribute to the essential developments which must be made in the tough competitive climate of manufacturing. They feel exposed and become less able to evaluate the necessary long-term alternatives. As a consequence, they increasingly exert pressure by short-term measures and assessments. Lower down the organisation, plant executives being measured by the success of the business in the short-term often respond by adopting similar opportunistic patterns of behaviour such as reducing expenditure or withholding investments in order to increase profits and improve cash flow in the short-term. Similarly, groups of companies often monitor investments centrally and against a common set of criteria. However, they leave the post-installation assessment to be taken at plant level. Seen as part of their role, the group executives' action reinforces the predominant role of financial measures when assessing investments and weakens the key responsibility link between the investment decision and its future evaluation. The need to decentralise these responsibilities could not be more strongly argued.

The way forward is through the emergence of strategy-based decisions and controls. Accounting and manufacturing need to determine together the investment criteria and day-to-day accounting-control provision which should be adopted. Not only will this reinforce the orientation of manufacturing towards its key tasks but it will also provide information which is both relevant and current. This growing awareness of the need for strategic management accounting needs to be accelerated if companies are to be able to make sound manufacturing and other strategy decisions based in part, on these essential details.[30] It is most necessary, therefore, that firms stem the apparent drift away from their manufacturing focus.

Perhaps a final lesson which West European companies may consider is that 'in Japan, perpetuation of the enterprise, not profit, is the driving force. As Toshiba's Okano puts it: The company is forever.'[31] Although in no way implying that this should be adopted as the corporate-value system, it highlights one essential difference. Strategy is the driving force; survival and success will only be achieved through a strategic orientation and this must become the pattern by which companies both give direction and assess current and future performance.

Notes and References

1. R. C. Dean, Jr., 'The Temporal Mismatch – Innovation's pace *v* Management's Time Horizon', *Research Management*, May 1974, pp. 12–15.
2. R. H. Hayes and J. Abernathy, 'Managing Our Way to Economic Decline', *Harvard Business Review*, July/August 1980, pp. 67–77.
3. R. H. Hayes and D. A. Garvin, 'Managing as if Tomorrow Mattered', *Harvard Business Review*, May–June 1982, pp. 71–9.
4. H. T. Johnson and R. S. Kaplan, *Relevance Lost: The Rise and Fall of Management Accounting* (Harvard Business School Press, 1987) includes important insights into accounting systems, for example, Chapter 8, 'The 1980s: The Obsolescence of Management Accounting Systems'.

5. R. Cooper and R. S. Kaplan, 'How Cost Accounting Distorts Product Costs', *Management Accounting*, April 1985, pp. 20–7.
6. R. Cooper and R. S. Kaplan, 'Measure Costs Right: Make the Right Decisions', *Harvard Business Review*, September/October 1988, pp. 96–103.
7. K. Simmonds, 'Strategic Management Accounting' in R. Crowe (ed.) *Handbook of Management Accounting* (Aldershot: Gower Publishing, 1988) 2nd edn, pp. 25–48.
8. Several authors highlight these types of consequences including Boston Consulting Group's Perspective, 'The Experience Curve – Reviewed: II History'; S. Rose, 'The Secrets of Japan's Export Prowess', *Fortune*, 30 January 1978, pp. 56–62 and Simmonds, 'Strategic Management Accounting' (see note 7).
9. This argument also forms part of S. C. Wheelwright's Research paper no 517, 'Facilities Focus: a Study of Concepts and Practices Related to its Definition, Evaluation, Significance and Application in Manufacturing Firms', Graduate School of Business, Stanford University, 12 December 1979, p. 55.
10. G. Foster, 'Drucker on the Record', *Management Today*, September 1987, pp. 58–9 and 110.
11. S. Parkinson, T. J. Hill and G. Walker, 'Diagnosing Customer and Competitor Influences on Manufacturing Strategy', in F. Bradley (ed.) *Marketing Thought Around the World*, Proceedings of the 20th Annual Conference of the European Marketing Academy, Dublin, May 1991, pp. 741–55.
12. R. Davies, C. Downes and R. Sweeting, *UK Survey of Cost Management Techniques and Practices, 1990/91* (Price Waterhouse, 1991) p. 11.
13. K. Ohmae, 'Japan: from Stereotypes to Specifics', *The McKinsey Quarterly*, Spring 1982, pp. 2–33.
14. Ibid, p. 3.
15. *UK Survey* (1991) p. 11.
16. T. J. Hill and D. J. Woodwock, 'Dimensions of Control', *Production Management and Control*, March/April 1982, vol. 10, no 2, pp. 16–20.
17. K. J. Blois, 'The Manufacturing/Marketing Orientation and its Information Needs', *European Journal of Marketing*, vol. 14, 15/6, pp. 354–64.
18. For instance, refer to W. L. Ferrara, 'More Questions than Answers: Is the Management Accounting System as Hopeless as the Critics Say?', *Management Accounting*, October 1990, pp. 48–52.
19. Ibid, p. 48.
20. *UK Survey of Cost Management Techniques and Practices 1990/91* (1991) p. 16.
21. R. S. Kaplan, 'Yesterday's Accounting Undermines Production', *Harvard Business Review*, July/August 1984, pp. 95–102.
22. Boston Consulting Group Perspective no 219, *Specialization or the Full Product Line* (1979).
23. Ferrara 'More Questions than Answers' (1990) p. 52.

24. *UK Survey (1991)* p. 11, reported that budget *v.* actual was employed by 98 per cent of respondents as a performance measure. However, only 35 per cent utilised flexible budgeting procedures.
25. A fact confirmed in the 1991 UK Survey which reported that for 51 per cent of all respondents, overheads represented 26 per cent or more of total costs.
26. The increasing size of overheads was clearly shown in the comparison of cost structures between 1960 and 1986 given below:

Element of costs	1960	1986
	percent of total	
Direct labour	22	15
Direct materials	56	53
Overheads	22	32
Total	100	100

Source: 'Management Accounting in Advanced Manufacturing Environments Survey', *Computer-Aided Manufacturing International* (CAM-I) January 1988. Also, C. Berlinger and J. Brimson, *Cost Management in Today's Advanced Manufacturing: The CAM-I Conceptual Design* (Harvard Business School Press, 1988) quoted an earlier survey in the USA by the National Association of Accountants showing similar cost trends.

27. Kaplan, 'Yesterday's Accounting' (1984) p. 96, provides another example of what, all too often, is a common situation.
28. However, the *1991 UK Survey* revealed that whereas 90 per cent of respondents used costs as an important factor in establishing prices (p. 12), only 30 per cent 'attempted to allocate indirect/non-manufacturing costs to products on a cause and effect basis' (p. 13).
29. *UK Survey (1991)* p. 15.
30. K. Simmonds, 'Strategic Management Accounting'. See Note 7 earlier.
31. Ohmae, 'Japan: from Stereotypes to Specifics', p. 7.

Index